ABOLISHING THE TABOO

DWIGHT D. EISENHOWER AND AMERICAN NUCLEAR DOCTRINE 1945-1961

Brian Madison Jones

Helion Studies in Military History Number 7

I0892901

Helion & Company Ltd

Dedication: for Shannon

Helion Studies in Military History
No 1 *Learning from Foreign Wars. Russian Military Thinking 1859-73* Gudrun Persson (ISBN 978-1-906033-61-3)
No 2 *A Military Government in Exile. The Polish Government-in-Exile 1939-45, a Study of Discontent* Evan McGilvray (ISBN 978-1-906033-58-3)
No 3 *From Landrecies to Cambrai. Case Studies of German Offensive and Defensive Operations on the Western Front 1914-17* Capt G.C. Wynne (ISBN 978-1-906033-76-7)
No 4 *Playing the Game. The British Junior Infantry Officer on the Western Front 1914-18* Christopher Moore-Bick (ISBN 978-1-906033-84-2)
No 5 *The History of the British Army Film & Photographic Unit in the Second World War* Dr Fred McGlade (ISBN 978-1-906033-94-1)
No 6 *Making Waves. Admiral Mountbatten's Radio SEAC 1945-49* Eric Hitchcock (ISBN 978-1-906033-95-8)

Helion & Company Limited
26 Willow Road
Solihull
West Midlands B91 1UE
England
Telephone 0121 705 3393
Fax 0121 711 4075
Email: info@helion.co.uk
Website: www.helion.co.uk

Published by Helion & Company 2011

Designed and typeset by Farr out Publications, Wokingham, Berkshire
Cover designed by Andrea Mages Photography, LLC
Printed by Lightning Source

Text © Brian Madison Jones
Photographs as individually credited

ISBN 978 1 907677 31 1

British Library Cataloguing-in-Publication Data.
A catalogue record for this book is available from the British Library.

All rights reserved. No part of this publication may be reproduced, stored in a retrieval system,or transmitted, in any form, or by any means, electronic, mechanical, photocopying, recording or otherwise, without the express written consent of Helion & Company Limited.

Front cover image - Operation Ivy Mike: The United States detonated the world's first hydrogen bomb in the Pacific Ocean on 1 November 1952, just three days before the election of Dwight Eisenhower as President of the United States (National Archives); Rear cover image - Marines participate in A-Bomb tests, 22 March 1955 (National Archives)

For details of other military history titles published by Helion & Company Limited contact the above address, or visit our website: http://www.helion.co.uk.

We always welcome receiving book proposals from prospective authors.

Contents

List of Illustrations

Acknowledgments

Though this has been a selfish project, it has not been a solitary effort. I owe the deepest gratitude to those who have given selflessly of themselves to support the completion of this book. I owe tremendous gratitude to Jack Holl who supervised the dissertation at Kansas State University which ultimately became the basis for this book. At Kansas State, my thanks also go to Donald Mrozek, Sue Zschoche, David Graff, John McCulloh, Joseph Unekis, Chad Litz, and Tracy Turner. This book would not have possible without the help of Jim Leyerzapf, Herbert Pankratz, and David Haight at the Dwight D. Eisenhower Presidential Library and Patricia Hand and Matthew Schaefer at the Herbert Hoover Presidential Library. My thanks also go to John Smail, George Warren, Daniel Butcher, and Deborah Quick for providing me opportunities to teach while completing this manuscript. Thanks also are due to Andrea Mages who designed the book's cover.

For their support and friendship during this process, I am grateful to Jason and Angela Buchanan, Chris and Sonya Vancil, Lisa and Mike Mundey, Dan and Sally Friedman, and Micah and Michelle Booth. My many thanks go to Tim and Nancy Mages, Tim and Andrea Mages, Becke and Tony Barlow, and my grandparents, Harry and Shirley Wood, for their support. I am monumentally grateful to my sister, Ashley Gragg, and her husband, Rick, for their genuine commitment to my academic endeavors. My deepest thanks go to my parents, James and Susan Jones, who have done so much for me that I can not hope to express it all in these short sentences.

Finally, I can only begin here to express my gratitude to Shannon, my wife and my best friend. Shannon carried the weight of this project on her shoulders just as I did, but never once did she question the soundness of my choices, complain about the sacrifices we made, or waver in her support of me. The completion of this book is as much a result of her dedication, her effort, her patience, and her wisdom as mine.

Introduction

Only three men were in the room that morning for the president's regular National Security Council briefing. James Lay, Executive Secretary of the NSC, took the meeting's minutes; the Special Assistant for National Security Affairs Robert Cutler gave the briefing and President of the United States Dwight D. Eisenhower considered the subject of Cutler's discussion: the role of nuclear weapons and nuclear technology in American life. The briefing notwithstanding, the president had been thinking on this subject for some time and had already decided on a course of action. The time had come for a serious revision to the Atomic Energy Act of 1946 "in order that atomic weapons be treated like other weapons," the president told Cutler. After all, he continued, "if there is to be peaceful usage of nuclear material, its handling and production needs to be considerably unshackled from restrictions which were originally appropriate." He suggested to Cutler "that the taboo on the use of atomic weapons be abolished."[1] That October morning President Eisenhower expressed his desire to take advantage both of those peaceful usages and the tremendous military value of nuclear weapons. In addition to necessary changes to existing legislation, he also sought to convince the American people that nuclear weapons were virtually the same as other weapons and that they could and should be used to maximum potential for the purposes of national security.

As president, Eisenhower believed that nuclear weapons, both fission and fusion, were acceptable and desirable assets to help protect U.S. national security against the threat of international communism. He championed the beneficent role played by nuclear weapons, including both civilian and military uses, and he lauded the simultaneous and multi-pronged use of the atom for peace and for war. In this, he desired to make nuclear weapons as available, useful, and ordinary for purposes of national security as other revolutionary military technology from the past, such as the tank or the airplane. The president also developed plans to exploit nuclear technology for a variety of peaceful, civilian applications that he believed could contribute to national strength. Through this effort, Eisenhower occasionally pursued seemingly conflicting initiatives, but nonetheless consistently advanced his view that strength through nuclear technology was a possible, necessary, and sustainable means to protect U.S. national security. In the end, Eisenhower's assessment of the role and value of nuclear technology was profound, sincere, and pragmatic, but also simplistic, uneven, and perilous.

After considering the variety of initiatives in the realm of nuclear policy that Eisenhower pursued, some scholars have characterized the president's policies as discrepant. This perceived contrast led at least one observer to suggest that the president suffered from "nuclear schizophrenia."[2] The evidence to support this view is striking. In his Atoms for Peace speech of December 1953, less than a year into his first term, Eisenhower pledged the full effort of the United States "to help solve the fearful atomic dilemma--to devote its entire heart and mind to find the way by which the miraculous inventiveness of man shall not be dedicated to his death, but consecrated to his life."[3] Still, during Eisenhower's terms in office, his administration conducted as central to national security over 160 tests of nuclear weapons. At the same time, the administration oversaw the construction and operation of only a handful of civilian nuclear power reactors.[4] The president simultaneously worried about the spread of nuclear weapons to irresponsible states, but successfully negotiated over three dozen bilateral treaties, agreeing to ship fissile material and nuclear reactor technology abroad if agreeable nations renounced any future pursuit of nuclear weapons. As the Cold War grew more intense through the 1950s, he feared for the fate of Americans in the event of a nuclear war, but summarily dismissed a recommendation in 1957 to spend $25 billion over five years to build fallout shelters which might have saved tens of millions of Americans in the event of nuclear war. The documentary record reveals both the great danger and fear of nuclear war fostered by Eisenhower's strategic nuclear initiatives as well as steps taken by the president to mitigate or end the threat of nuclear war such as Atoms for Peace and the implementation of a testing moratorium. For Eisenhower, the use of the atom for such a wide variety of objectives reflected his personal conviction that the use of nuclear technology in service of the republic involved cost and value, danger and safety, fear and hope, evil and good.

Because he believed nuclear technology so effectively served his goal to defend national security through strength, Eisenhower sought to reverse the perception that nuclear weapons were inherently dangerous and immoral. He advocated steadily and consistently for the proper and acceptable use of nuclear technology to contribute to the safety of the republic. His early commitment to nuclear weapons, his implementation of nuclear policies aimed at both peace and security, and his continued insistence that the nuclear weapon constituted simply another weapon in the nation's arsenal all sought to lessen the nation's fear about its nuclear future. Only when Americans understood the boost to national strength provided by nuclear weapons would they be comfortable enough with these weapons of mass destruction to accept them fully into national life, Eisenhower believed.

Eisenhower remained committed throughout his presidency to the building of strength to meet the communist threat and he also succeeded in making nuclear weapons and nuclear technology ordinary, abundant, and indispensable. At the time of Eisenhower's inauguration in January 1953, America possessed 841 nuclear weapons, both atomic and thermonuclear, which could unleash nearly 50 megatons of explosive power.[5] These weapons could be deployed in combat either by Strategic Air Command bombers or by any one of the twenty 280-millimeter atomic cannons stationed in parts of Europe and Asia. At the end of his second term in office in 1961, America's nuclear stockpile totaled 18,638 nuclear warheads with a massive 20,491 megatons of explosive power.[6] Eisenhower had increased the numbers of weapons 22 times and the total yield of those weapons 400 times. Beyond the addition of more and better nuclear weapons, military modernization efforts under Eisenhower included the B-52 intercontinental jet bomber, the Army's Jupiter and Air Force's Thor intermediate range ballistic missiles, the liquid-fueled Atlas intercontinental ballistic missile, as well as the Navy's Polaris missile which was deployed on nuclear-powered submarines such as the USS *George Washington*. The advanced, solid-fueled missile, the Minuteman, was also in development. As a result of Eisenhower's efforts, America's nuclear arsenal was advanced, mobile, deliverable, and fearsome. Beyond just the military, Eisenhower engendered efforts such as Project Plowshare and Atoms for Peace to demonstrate the peaceful applications of nuclear technology. Taken together, Eisenhower's efforts were aimed in part at convincing the American public and the international community of his genuine desire for peace at the same time that he helped to entrench atomic and thermonuclear weapons into the American national experience.

If he had the opportunity, Eisenhower would have preferred to eliminate nuclear weapons altogether. He often complained that, "if he knew any way to abolish atomic weapons which would ensure the certainty that they would be abolished, he would be the very first to endorse it." He remarked to his National Security Council in June 1954 that "he thought it unfortunate that nuclear weapons even existed." "But the clock could not be turned back and there was no way that any agreement could be worked out that would assure with certainty that these weapons could be abolished," he continued.[7] Absent that agreement, Eisenhower embraced nuclear weapons as a means of defending national security.

Eisenhower approached the question of how to defend national security through nuclear weapons with an array of disparate ideas and programs which worked simultaneously toward sometimes divergent objectives and were unified only by a simple conception of national strength. As both a military officer and a political figure, Eisenhower believed national strength was the product of the sum total of America's efforts. Biographer Robert Donovan explained that Eisenhower's working philosophy of national strength was "to take the many ingredients of national power – airplanes, ground forces, battleships, industry, the economy, the spirit of the people – and blend them in such a way as to insure essential security for the United States . . . it is the sum of American power that counts."[8] More precisely, Eisenhower believed that American national strength grew from four sources and those sources were financial, military, industrial, and moral in nature. Further, he believed that nuclear technology supported and sustained each of the four. His emphasis on building cumulative national strength for national security and his conclusion that the nuclear weapon contributed to that strength required him to compartmentalize intellectually from one another those four sources. Rather than a systematic view that was arrived at mechanistically and considered methodically, Eisenhower's view was improvised and segmented.[9]

First, Eisenhower thought that nuclear technology provided a great opportunity to build the economic strength of the nation through the fiscal discipline provided by the bomb's proper use. From his experience during the Truman administration between 1945 and 1952, Eisenhower came to understand how the Cold War strained the American economy. He worried that poor planning or fiscal irresponsibility over the long term might threaten America's national security as much as military weakness or internal subversion. He feared that the demands of national security would create a state-run economy which would stifle both free-market capitalism and liberal democracy resulting in a garrison state in the United States. In response, he came to emphasize the role of nuclear technology to provide a proper defense structure at a cost the United States could afford.

Second, Eisenhower believed in the value of the nuclear weapon to provide strategic military strength. Though he may have objected to the use of nuclear weapons on Japan at the end of World War II, he did so because he believed that an escalation of violence was not necessary to defeat Japan, not because he believed the atomic weapon would be ineffective. During his presidency, Eisenhower threatened the use of nuclear weapons to help bring an end to the Korean stalemate. Before 1954, Eisenhower considered tactical nuclear war with atomic weapons possible and winnable. After the advent of the thermonuclear weapon, Eisenhower adopted a grand strategy often called massive retaliation. The tremendous explosive yield of and surprising radioactive fallout created by early thermonuclear tests suggested to Eisenhower the great risk involved in using nuclear weapons for any tactical purpose. Because he wanted to retain the fission weapon as a military asset, he needed to integrate successfully fusion weapons into the U.S. arsenal. He employed the doctrine of massive retaliation as a strategy to take advantage of the awesome power of the new hydrogen bomb without sacrificing the tactical value of smaller-yield nuclear weapons. An increasing reliance on thermonuclear weapons and a strategy of massive retaliation allowed Eisenhower the flexibility first to avoid war if possible and second to achieve victory if necessary.

Third, Eisenhower pushed for the expansion of civilian nuclear power for domestic and international reasons and supported the advancement of basic nuclear science in hope of building American industry. Inside the United States, Eisenhower wanted the government to expand access to nuclear materials and nuclear technology for private development. At less cost to the government and with greater results, private companies could build nuclear power plants and provide for the electrical needs of the national industrial economy. In addition, world demand for cheap electrical power grew every year, particularly in Europe, which was struggling to rebuild its industrial capacity following the devastation of World War II, and in the third world, where new nations struggled to build satisfactory infrastructures and to balance national self-determination with superpower demands to choose sides in the Cold War. Eisenhower imagined that nuclear technology could meet the demand and promote good will between the United States and Europe as well as the desperate non-aligned nations of the world.

Last, as the primary steward of American nuclear technology, Eisenhower endeavored to showcase the virtue of nuclear technology and its proper moral use by the United States. The president had characterized the nuclear weapon, which was initially and principally a weapon of massive destruction, as a "hellish contrivance."[10] Despite his rhetoric, he also believed that humankind's proper management of the weapon could demonstrate the positive value of nuclear technology in support of freedom and peace against the evils of international communism and the Soviet Union. Freedom was a spiritual right that must be defended with arms, but the basic morality of the nation must not be sacrificed in defense of that freedom. Eisenhower carefully maneuvered through this dilemma as he employed the nuclear weapon to advance general and nuclear disarmament as a necessary first step toward a peaceful end to the Cold War. As that effort sputtered, he attempted to negotiate a nuclear test ban treaty and ultimately a moratorium, both of which, Eisenhower hoped, would demonstrate the United States' commitment to good will and peace. He also used nuclear technology for programs such as Atoms for Peace which the president thought would ease fear, provide hope, and contribute to peace in the world.

Because nuclear weapons so clearly and effectively served the national interest, Eisenhower concluded they were a force for good. He argued that, like any other weapon system, nuclear weapons could contribute to a variety of national political, strategic, and economic goals. Indeed, he understood the fission and fusion weapon in only the most rudimentary and practical way. His limited technical understanding came from the information provided to him in early scientific briefings, from reading the Smyth Report, and from the collection of documents on the atomic age edited by Bernard Brodie called *The Absolute Weapon*.[11] Later, Eisenhower also gathered information from the Atomic Energy Commission Chairman Lewis Strauss along with presidential advisors James Killian and George Kistiakowsky. Still, the president expressed only minimal interest in how and why the nuclear weapon worked. He remained focused instead on the practical, the attainable, the knowable aspects, rather than the theoretical, of how fission and fusion served his purposes. The president noted and appeared to understand that his plan for national strength based on nuclear weapons involved great danger, but accepted that risk as unavoidable, minimal, and ultimately tolerable. His desire to capitalize on what he saw as the many benefits of a fully developed and deployed nuclear arsenal led him to a grand strategy which often blurred the distinction between atomic and thermonuclear devices and effectively likened the explosive power of nuclear weapons with that of conventional bombs used in previous global conflicts. At the same time, his under appreciation for the difference between conventional explosions, explosions yielding kilotons, and those yielding megatons allowed him to move the world dangerously closer to global annihilation through a massive buildup of weapons. Although he was deeply concerned about waging war in the nuclear age, Eisenhower's trepidation about nuclear conflict did not discourage him from pursuing and implementing nuclear policies which ultimately and fully committed the United States to the use of nuclear weapons for national defense over the long term. He accepted that danger provided that he was also able to pursue peaceful objections with the same nuclear technology. For Eisenhower, the risk of nuclear war did not outweigh the immediate, tangible rewards of national strength, the containment of communism, and the pursuit of peace.

1

Eisenhower in History and Memory

Any study into Eisenhower's thinking about nuclear weapons must be rooted in the growing literature on this important historical actor. As the subject of historical investigation, Eisenhower has become increasingly popular in the years since his death in 1969. Following the opening of vast amounts of research materials at the Eisenhower Presidential Library in the late 1970s as well as the resurgence of conservative political strength and the increased attention on the presidency, scholars became more interested in the life and times of Dwight Eisenhower. As Eisenhower studies proliferated, Ike's reputation enjoyed a resurrection. "Eisenhower gave the nation eight years of peace and prosperity. No other President in the twentieth century could make that claim," one scholar reflected.[1]

At one time Eisenhower was considered as "do nothing" a president as some of the least remembered and least admired chief executives in American history, such as Warren Harding and James Buchanan. In 1962, Arthur Schlesinger's poll of scholars placed Eisenhower as twenty-second best of thirty-five presidents. Eisenhower rose to twelfth in David Porter's poll of 1981, and Robert and Tim Blessing's poll of 1982 bumped him to eleventh. In 1996, Eisenhower cracked the top ten among scholars when both a *Chicago Tribune* poll and another poll by Schlesinger's son, Arthur Schlesinger Jr., placed Eisenhower as ninth best, just behind the great and near-great presidents, Abraham Lincoln, George Washington, Franklin Roosevelt, Thomas Jefferson, and Andrew Jackson. Schlesinger attributed Eisenhower's meteoric rise to the failings of his successors. "The more his successors got into trouble," he wrote, "the better Eisenhower looked."[2] Schlesinger also noted that Eisenhower's growing prestige had much to do with the opening of his presidential papers. A wealth of information became available, and researchers increasingly found a great deal more to Eisenhower than earlier scholars had. Still, historian Stephen Rabe remarked, scholars "would never have joined the pilgrimage to Abilene unless they judged the Eisenhower years worthy of study."[3]

a. Ike's Friends and Critics

Eisenhower was the subject of many studies even before he became president. His role as Supreme Allied Commander in the European Theater of Operations propelled him to a position of global prominence. As early as 1944, even before the war ended, popular biographies of Eisenhower by his acquaintances hit book shelves in the United States and Europe.[4] The authors of these works explored Eisenhower's childhood, his adolescence, and his formative years at West Point and as a junior officer as well as his role in formulating major war plans for the conflict against the Axis Powers. These biographies provided little in the way of scholarly analysis, offering instead entertaining, anecdotal material to satisfy the public's demand for more detail about a national hero. Francis Trevelyan Miller claimed to write the first full biography of the general in *Eisenhower, Man and Soldier*. In this and similar works, Eisenhower emerged as an American folk hero. Whether on the gridiron, the baseball diamond, at work in a creamery in Abilene, at West Point or as a commissioned officer, Eisenhower realized his own American dream with hard work and commitment. "He is the typical American from the typical American home town," Miller explained, "who started at the bottom and has worked himself up on his own merits to become one of the most powerful figures in the world today."[5]

After the war, Eisenhower continued to attract the public's attention. Filled with exuberance after the great victory of World War II, Americans wanted to know as much as possible about prominent wartime leaders. To meet this demand, associates of Eisenhower began publishing first-hand narratives about their own personal relationship or experiences with him.[6] Further, according to at least one scholar, "Every war in American history has produced a national hero in its victorious military leader, and, usually, has sought to honor him with the presidency."[7] No sooner had the general returned from the war than talk of "Eisenhower for President" swirled in some political circles. In *Eisenhower, The Man and The Symbol*, popular columnist and nonfiction writer John Gunther outlined Eisenhower's vast military and diplomatic experience at Supreme Headquarters, Allied Powers in Europe (SHAPE), his unassailable leadership abilities, and his overall personal and professional capacity to serve as president of the United States. "To sum up, the General would be orderly, decent, and honorable in the White House," Gunther wrote.[8] Journalist Allan Taylor wrote that the trust the American public has in Eisenhower "reflects a spontaneous trust, amid confusion and peril, in the strength, integrity, common sense and ability of a man who believes in the American people and who has shown his capacity to deal with threats to his country's heritage."[9] Kevin McCann, Eisenhower's personal assistant from 1946 to 1951, agreed. In *Man From Abilene*, McCann wrote: "Eisenhower has emerged in ten short years as one of the great political catalysts of our time – a man whose mere presence seems to overcome national boundaries and the force of whose personality can dissolve the traditional conflicts that for centuries have held the European nations apart."[10] The nation agreed with the positive assessment of all three authors. When Eisenhower ultimately decided to run for the presidency, he defeated Democrat Adlai Stevenson solidly in the 1952 election.

At the height of Eisenhower's popularity during his first presidential term, favorable literature poured forth from journalists, scholars, and partisans alike. New York *Herald Tribune* journalist Robert J. Donovan sought to chronicle Eisenhower's first three years in office with first-hand accounts and personal observations.[11] Pulitzer Prize-winning biographer Merlo John Pusey argued that the Eisenhower years had been "a buoyant, forward-moving, and fruitful period." "His major concern with great problems, his simplicity of manner, his dedication, and his deep regard for the welfare of his fellow citizens," Pusey wrote, "are reminiscent of Lincoln."[12] Eisenhower's wartime mess sergeant and shameless booster Marty Snyder celebrated the president's first term in office and prepared for his second presidential campaign. "Dwight D. Eisenhower has been an excellent President; he has been an excellent friend," Snyder asserted, "I intend to go on working to have him remain both."[13]

The first generation of professional Eisenhower scholars took issue with some of the more uncritical accounts of this early period. They sought foremost to demystify, with scholarly detachment, the heroic Eisenhower who had emerged from these early accounts

President Dwight D. Eisenhower (National Archives)

of the 1940s and 1950s. According to Schlesinger Jr., this scholarship grew in part from the general disdain for Eisenhower among intellectuals in the 1950s. Some scholars, thinkers, and academicians of the period, including Schlesinger, resented Eisenhower's veiled contempt for intellectuals, his trouncing of Stevenson in 1952 and 1956, his rapid transformation from the friend of Soviet Marshal Georgi Zhukov into anti-communist, and his transition from apolitical American patriot into vehement critic of the New Deal. They wanted to believe that Eisenhower had been co-opted by more conservative elements within the Republican Party who then turned his popularity into a dam to hold back the tide of liberalism. Accordingly, these orthodox scholars saw the thirty-fourth president as an unintelligent and uninvolved chief executive who allowed his powerful subordinates to run the government while he fished, played bridge and golf, and collected contributions on behalf of the Republican Party. They fostered "the notion of a genial, indolent man of pied syntax and platitudinous conviction, fleeing from public policy to bridge, golf, and westerns."[14] Eisenhower's political inexperience, lack of intellectual power, and discomfort with the demands of the presidency contributed greatly to the dangerous state of national malaise during which the Soviet Union grew stronger and the United States grew weaker, some orthodox scholars argued. As the Soviets appeared to match the United States in military strength, Eisenhower became bored with the multitude of administrative tasks required of the president. His boredom soon turned to frustration after which he wavered, delegated, and then vacationed, some suggested.[15] Even in works by his political associates such as Emmet Hughes, Arthur Larson, and Sherman Adams, "Eisenhower emerges as a man of force, dignity, and restraint who did not always understand and control what was going on, was buffeted by events, and was capable of misjudgment and error."[16] Because the president was aloof and out of his league as chief executive of the United States, the Eisenhower era was, according to one scholar, "the time of great postponement."[17]

b. Revisionist Scholars and Beyond

Major revision of Eisenhower scholarship began in the 1970s for two reasons.[18] First, the struggles of his successors made Eisenhower and his administration look far better by comparison and thus more interesting for study.[19] The growth of the power of the presidency under Lyndon Johnson, the military quagmire in South Vietnam, and the excesses of the Nixon administration, including the Watergate fiasco, forced many to take another look at the Eisenhower years. Within that context, Eisenhower simply did not look so bad anymore. "Eight years of Eisenhower: seven and a half of peace," former Eisenhower critic Richard Rovere wrote in 1971, "ten years of Kennedy, Johnson, Nixon: almost ten solid years of war."[20] Scholars became more interested in discovering just why Eisenhower seemed to succeed and by extension why his successors seemed to fail. Second, as the Eisenhower Presidential Library and the National Archives and Records Administration began the systematic review and opening of Eisenhower's presidential papers, scholars got a better look at just how Eisenhower governed. "The opening of his papers," one-time Eisenhower critic Schlesinger was compelled to write, "showed that the mask of genial affability Ike wore in the White House concealed an astute, crafty, confident, and purposeful leader."[21] While they all did not agree on specifics, revisionists did agree that Eisenhower was a far more successful leader whose style was more subtle and sophisticated than previously thought. In sum, Eisenhower revisionists revealed a more active, engaged, and influential president.[22]

One of the most influential of the early Eisenhower revisionists was political scientist Fred Greenstein. He argued that Eisenhower guided his administration with a hidden hand, skillfully and effectively working his subordinates, the press, and other government leaders behind the scenes.[23] "Whatever the merit of Eisenhower's policies and actions," Greenstein wrote, "they were *his* policies and actions, not the result of drift or of aides who worked their will on a passive president."[24] Greenstein concluded that Eisenhower's style of leadership was both activist and "low-profile" and thus not always evident to every chronicler. Eisenhower "deliberately cultivated the impression that he was not involved even in the most successful of the maneuvers in which he directly participated," he argued. What orthodox scholars saw as Eisenhower's presidential inaction intended to protect his own personal popularity, Greenstein saw as a carefully calculated effort to maintain that personal prestige in order to achieve his larger political goals.[25] Greenstein offered as evidence a case study of Eisenhower's handling of the controversy stirred by Wisconsin Senator Joseph McCarthy. Through hidden-hand leadership and skillful use of language, Greenstein found Eisenhower actively and purposefully working to challenge McCarthy behind the scenes as McCarthy searched for communists in Eisenhower's government and in the Army. Eisenhower's strategy for neutralizing McCarthy, Greenstein maintained, was to engage him indirectly, to deny him direct executive attention, to refuse to dignify his accusations with a vigorous response, and to respond obliquely when McCarthy attacked.[26] He admitted that not all of Eisenhower's efforts were successful, but he emphasized that Eisenhower deserved more credit and less criticism for trying to neutralize McCarthy. Greenstein's *Hidden-Hand Presidency* became the inspiration and the baseline for many to revisit the Eisenhower presidency.

The flood gates of revisionism soon opened and a torrent of scholarship on Eisenhower poured forth as historians and political scientists found more examples of Eisenhower's leadership, diplomatic skill, good intentions, and terrific successes. Biographers such as Herbert Parmet and Robert Divine lauded Eisenhower's execution of political leadership at home and abroad.[27] Parmet's treatment of Eisenhower accentuated the president's "remarkable record," noting that Eisenhower was careful and conservative. He navigated a steady, middle-of-the-road course for the nation. He was not a political genius, but he possessed natural political instincts that allowed him to operate successfully within his party and his government.[28] In *Eisenhower and the Cold War*, Robert Divine concluded that Eisenhower, not John Foster Dulles, was the architect of the administration's Cold War foreign policy. The president exercised great skill, patience, and caution in negotiating the dangerous diplomatic world he inherited, Divine continued. He argued that Eisenhower's great foreign policy successes were inherently negative: "He ended the Korean War, he refused to intervene militarily in Indochina, he refrained from involving the United States in the Suez crisis, he avoided war with China over Quemoy and Matsu." While he recognized that Eisenhower experienced failures in Cuba and Vietnam, where problems lingered for later administrations, Divine praised the president as an advocate of peace and restraint amidst a throng of cold warriors.[29]

In the realm of nuclear issues, revisionists paint Eisenhower as an energetic, active president who occupied a central role in the formulation of nuclear policy and who pursued, above all else, peace in a world threatened by thermonuclear war. These authors conclude that, as he labored to achieve peaceful uses for atomic science, "Eisenhower dominated the formulation of nuclear policy in a way that no other President has before or since." In *Atoms for Peace and War*, historians Richard Hewlett and Jack Holl argued that Eisenhower presided over the origins of the nuclear world and they described Eisenhower's approach to nuclear policy as consistently proactive, committed, and energetic. The proposals contained in his Atoms for Peace speech, for example, defined the debate about the use of nuclear energy for several decades, while his steadfast commitment to minimizing the risk of and dangers inherent in nuclear war demonstrated a desire for peace in a world too familiar with war. [30] To his credit, Eisenhower kept the nuclear debate centered on great issues, of war and peace, of hope and fear, and of right and wrong and thus became the primary nuclear architect for the United States. Historian Richard Immerman concluded that Eisenhower was indeed the first post-World War II president to develop a "systematically articulated body of thought on war, peace, and security in the nuclear age."[31]

More recently, a post-revisionist trend has emerged. Orthodox Eisenhower scholars viewed Eisenhower as an inept president with few policies, and revisionists saw him as an exceptional president with successful policies. Post-revisionists evidenced a combination of the two. They argued "that the Eisenhower presidency was more complex than and not as successful as many revisionists have maintained" but they also accepted "the basic revisionist argument that Eisenhower was a thoughtful and skillful leader."[32] Revisionists had not been sufficiently critical of Eisenhower, according to these scholars, and the flaws in his character, his leadership, his vision, and his efforts needed greater exploration, consideration, and analysis.[33] Chester Pach and Elmo Richardson, for example, maintained that Eisenhower "used his power resourcefully – and often successfully – in domestic and foreign policy to accomplish his objectives" but that "his greatest failures were not from lethargy or ineptness but lack of vision."[34] In foreign policy, Robert MacMahon argued that Eisenhower mistook nationalism for communism and saw the Soviet Union as the prime mover of all discontented social movements throughout the globe. "This failure of perception … constituted a major setback for American diplomacy," MacMahon wrote, and "in this critical area, then, the Eisenhower record appears one of persistent failure."[35]

Post-revisionists have also objected to the glowing assessments of Eisenhower's foreign policy in Cold War battlegrounds, such as Vietnam and Korea. In South Vietnam, for example, revisionists such as Robert Divine had relished Eisenhower's restraint.[36] David Anderson saw Eisenhower's Vietnam policy as "an example of flawed containment" which was essentially "negative" and only "sought to hold off defeat and wait for a better day with little regard for the internal dynamics of Vietnamese society."[37] During the Korean War, Rosemary Foot believed that other factors played a greater role in bringing North Korea and China to the negotiating table than Eisenhower's strategy. The overall impact of Eisenhower's threats of nuclear attack upon both adversaries has been exaggerated by revisionists, she argued.[38] Gordon Chang contended that Eisenhower's failed leadership and ambiguous policies nearly brought America to war with China over Taiwan in 1955. Despite Eisenhower's blundering, the two nations avoided war only because Chinese Premier Zhou Enlai backed down before the critical moment of confrontation. Indeed, Chang continued, Eisenhower's nuclear blustering over Taiwan encouraged Mao Zedong to begin earnest pursuit of a Chinese nuclear weapon so as to be prepared for the next crisis.[39]

Post-revisionists also described Eisenhower's record as mixed on nuclear issues, including nuclear testing and disarmament. H. W. Brands has indicted Eisenhower for his simplicity and inability to get his foreign policy team to agree on an appropriate strategy. Brands argued that Eisenhower's grand nuclear strategy, the New Look, which emphasized a nuclear deterrent over large conventional forces, left the U.S. with "the worst of both worlds: the high risks of strategic warfare and the high costs of limited conflict."[40] Brands also argued that Eisenhower to a certain degree manufactured the crisis over Taiwan in 1954-55 out of a desire to validate the credibility of his nuclear deterrent. Eisenhower was disinclined to look for a peaceful solution to the crisis because he sought to prove that nuclear weapons were a usable part of America's military machine.[41] Focusing on the Surprise Attack Conference of 1958, Jeremi Suri concluded that Eisenhower doomed disarmament negotiations with the Soviets by stubbornly insisting on an agreement on inspection and verification of any disarmament treaty before a political discussion might even take place, by failing to secure agreement among key members of his cabinet regarding disarmament goals, and by employing tactics that would have eroded the obsessive secrecy that the Soviets so vigorously protected.[42] Martha Smith-Norris argued that the Geneva Test Ban Talks of 1958-60 failed because Eisenhower stubbornly refused to separate test ban talks from the larger disarmament issue. Despite that the other major parties including the British and the Soviets modified their position in pursuit of a deal, Eisenhower refused to deal because, she continued, the president never wanted an agreement, but instead only desired to appear to want one.[43] Other post-revisionists depict an Eisenhower who was engaged, concerned, and committed to peace, but also as a failure for reasons of his own doing. Benjamin Greene argued that Eisenhower began pursuit of a nuclear test ban treaty in his first term before Adlai Stevenson raised the issue in the 1956 presidential campaign. According to Greene, Eisenhower believed that Stevenson ruined any chance the president had to negotiate a deal in secret and the president unfortunately used deceit and outright lies to conceal his own desire for a test ban.[44]

c. The Intellectual Eisenhower

In the spirit of post-revisionism, some effort must be made to analyze Eisenhower the intellectual, that is, one who thinks deeply and critically about issues, in this case, nuclear issues. Early accounts of Eisenhower's intelligence were quite critical. Eisenhower's mind, Richard Rovere wrote in 1950, was "unschematic, distrustful of fine distinctions, given to overstatement, impatient with theory, eager to make translations into the realm of matter and things, concerned with the effect of ideas rather than their validity."[45] Not surprisingly, Eisenhower's political opponents thought very little of Eisenhower's perspicacity. After Harry Truman opined how he might have successfully handled Fidel Castro and his revolution, the man from Missouri quipped that, "Of course, that son of a bitch Eisenhower was too damn dumb to do anything like that. When Castro decided to go in the other direction for support, Eisenhower was probably still waiting for a goddamn *staff report* on what to think."[46]

Even Eisenhower's friends were not reassuring. From the beginning of his political campaign in 1952, Eisenhower recognized that his staff underestimated his intelligence. "All they talked about was how they would win on my popularity. Nobody said I had a brain in my head," Eisenhower later recalled.[47] John McCone, Chairman of the Atomic Energy Commission in the final years of Eisenhower's presidency, tried to argue that Eisenhower stacked up well against other recent presidents. According to McCone, the greatest intellectual capacity as a scholar belonged to John Kennedy; as a negotiator, Lyndon Johnson; as a decision-maker, Harry Truman. "On the other hand, if you [sic] talking intellectual capacity in terms of person who could see the breadth of his total responsibility and reach some decisions as to what is best for the country, given the conditions in which he found himself," McCone continued, "Eisenhower would be by far the best." McCone considered Eisenhower a "thoughtful man" who had an ability to select capable men and give them great responsibility.[48] Sherman Adams was typical of other colleagues who saw Eisenhower as intelligent, but certainly not as an intellectual. "Eisenhower was not much of a reader," Adams recalled, he was so "impatient with the endless paperwork of the presidency" that he asked his staff to distill long documents down to one page.[49]

Overall, confidants and assistants praised Eisenhower's leadership as the best example of the man's intelligence. Rather than offer a litany of examples to support their claims, most of the memoirs by Eisenhower's aides accepted that because of his previous and current positions his ability to lead was unassailable. Speech writer and presidential aide Emmet John Hughes was so impressed that he attributed the greatness of Eisenhower's leadership to some, unseen mystical or spiritual source. "So gray and distant and secret" was Eisenhower's ability to lead, Hughes wrote, that it has confused the politician, evaded the historian, and baffled the philosopher.[50] According to Attorney General Herbert Brownell, Eisenhower allowed for "maximum autonomy" among those he trusted, and, in the executive branch, his appointees were always those whom he could trust. "His brand of political leadership may have led others mistakenly to underrate him," Brownell wrote, "but Eisenhower's own sense of equanimity and his past accomplishments did not force him into a false posture of deliberately instrumental presidential activism." That is, Eisenhower did not need to act as if he was in control because he was and he knew it. Because he allowed his subordinates room to maneuver and because he accomplished the goals which prompted his run for office in 1952, Eisenhower was a successful leader and an intelligent man, according to Brownell.[51]

Eisenhower was also praised for his deep understanding and respect for the traditions and procedures of the American republic. Arthur Larson described Eisenhower's presidential style as a product of three principles: "a profound–almost exaggerated–respect for the dignity of the office;" a need for restraint on the tremendous power of the executive office within the context of the separation of powers; and a conviction that the president must not exploit his powers for any purpose beyond the scope of his constitutional duties.[52] Sherman Adams noted that Eisenhower "knew more about the intricacies of high government than many professional politicians" and that his "military experience had given him a considerable knowledge of government."[53] Brownell similarly noted that Eisenhower had an "intense feeling for and a developed understanding of the structure of the American government." His training at West Point and his commitment to separation of powers and the scope of presidential responsibility made Eisenhower an ideal candidate for the presidency. [54]

Accordingly, Eisenhower's associates defended his intelligence against attacks. The self-proclaimed Republican egghead and presidential speech writer Larson discounted those who considered Eisenhower unintellectual. He recalled one instance when the man who supposedly never read anything but Western stories corrected a comment by Larson on Greek history. When Larson noted he felt a bit like Alcibiades the Just, the fifth century Greek, Eisenhower interjected, "You mean Aristides the Just." Eisenhower knew American history as well, though the best example Larson offered was that Eisenhower could recite Lincoln's "house divided" speech. Larson countered the president's critics by suggesting that Eisenhower's unintellectual appearance was merely a facade carefully cultivated by his aides and by the president himself. Eisenhower did read newspapers even though the president himself had remarked that he did not; he did not read western novels, except when his aides told the press he did. Larson did not call Eisenhower an intellectual, but noted that "the unintellectual, easygoing image" was not congruent with the Eisenhower Larson knew.[55] The architect of containment, George Kennan, agreed. During some discussions about Cold War policy, Kennan remarked that Eisenhower displayed his own "intellectual ascendancy" over every other man in the room, Kennan included.[56] Eisenhower's was a unique sort of intelligence, according to some who knew him well. Attorney General Brownell wrote of the president's "genius to understand" how to pursue political goals and to maintain simultaneously the trust of the populace in his benevolent intentions.[57] James Killian described Eisenhower as a man always open to and supportive of innovative and creative endeavors in science and technology.[58] Sherman Adams wrote of his quiet respect for Eisenhower who in crucial meetings listened more than he spoke and asked questions of those who knew better the issues under consideration. Eisenhower's participation "brought the whole discussion into clearer focus."[59]

Scholars since have considered the idea of Eisenhower as an intellectual with caution. "The cant of the age had it that Eisenhower was too tired or lazy or dumb to take command of his job," Michael Beschloss wrote.[60] This refrain grew no doubt from comments like those of David Lilienthal who noted that Eisenhower was "one of the least profound men" in such a high position.[61] Eisenhower biographer Piers Brendon questioned "whether Ike had the requisite intelligence to do the top job." His "'statesmanlike' equivocations smacked at best of intellectual ineptitude and at worst of moral cowardice," Brendon continued. He was simple and lacking in sophistication and his "garbled verbiage appeared now to betoken not so much sincerity as stupidity."[62]

The view of Eisenhower as something less than intelligent was sometimes attributed to Ike's own writings. Vincent De Santis criticized Eisenhower's memoirs as they revealed only what he did and very rarely what he thought.[63] In his memoirs, Eisenhower rarely delved into the why of matters, but instead only reported on the who, what, where, and when of his life experiences. This may have been the product of his professional education. Military historian John Keegan compared Eisenhower's intellectual training to that of an Orthodox Jew who was drilled in a dead language and was expected to memorize large chunks of important works. For purposes of military exams at West Point and the Command and General Staff College, this type of training sufficed, but it stimulated little capacity for historical or analytical thought, Keegan argued.[64] Another historian commented that, at least at Fort Leavenworth, Eisenhower's training had been intended only to produce "disciplined staff officers." "Command school did not encourage independent thinking or the analysis of political affairs," Zachary Davis wrote. Students were given tactical battlefield problems and their answers were graded based on how closely they matched the "time-honored answers."[65] Soldiers, like Eisenhower, "are trained to defend the existing social order rather than to examine it critically," another observer wrote.[66] The product of this training would be a mind certainly capable of extensive memorization and factual recall to impress many, but might not result in a probing and inquisitive mind seeking precise answers to complex problems.

Historians and political scientists have been hesitant to characterize Eisenhower as an intellectual in part because Eisenhower never described himself that way. Though he certainly considered himself intelligent, Eisenhower never referred to himself as an intellectual and routinely expressed disdain for academics and other thinkers in the United States and elsewhere. He valued "solid common sense" over academic learning and was inherently distrustful of those who pursued and respected the latter. Allen Dulles, for example, knew that he had won his case for CIA intervention in Guatemala in 1954 when he saw his political opponent, who planned to argue against intervention, appear in the Oval Office carrying three hefty legal tomes to help make his case.[67] Commenting on Robert Oppenheimer and Harry Dexter White, two Ivy League graduates accused of being sympathetic to communism, Eisenhower opined they "were two miserable offenders – misled by the fact that they were probably overly educated for their own good and had a consequential feeling of arrogance."[68] In 1958, for example, when Eisenhower requested a study of likely human endurance during and after a future nuclear war, the president informed his National Security Council that he "did not want a lot of long-haired professors to undertake such a study, but rather some down-to-earth knowledgeable people."[69] Eisenhower reproached his friend and former advisor C. D. Jackson for an article Jackson published in *Life* magazine in 1958. "I must confess ignorance of even the existence of the pseudo-philosophical Frenchman who developed the doctrine of existentialism," Eisenhower remarked. The president lampooned Jackson for use of the word "lamaseries," as Jackson likely only did so "to remind the average reader that it would be wise to check his impressions against the dictionary." Of course, Eisenhower already knew the word, but doubted that Abraham Lincoln, "a master of expressive prose," would ever have used it.[70] In this case, Jackson neatly fit Eisenhower's borrowed definition of an intellectual: "one who uses more words than necessary to tell more than he knows."[71]

Even Eisenhower's closest friends and advisors sometimes were confused by his self-deprecating comments about his own intelligence. Sherman Adams recounted an instance in the midst of the Korean crisis when Eisenhower was trying to get South Korean President Syngman Rhee to follow America's advice. Eisenhower lamented that this was one of those times when he needed the help of "someone more intelligent than I am."[72] At one point in October 1957, after Sputnik, Eisenhower conceded to C.D. Jackson, "I often wish that I had someone around, like yourself, who is willing to tackle a large problem, eager to think it through, and to come up with a concrete suggestion for a coordinated plan of attack (and not merely another speech by me!)"[73] On other occasions, Eisenhower seemed either to be feigning or purposefully modest. In a letter to Swede Hazlett, Eisenhower wrote of a letter that he had received from Harold Whicker. "Some of his sentences are a little on the lengthy side for my simple mind, but even so he succeeds in expressing himself clearly and forcefully," Eisenhower wrote.[74]

Eisenhower has fared better recently even among the academics he ordinarily disdained. Scholar George Quester queried simply "Was Eisenhower a Genius?" and he answered in the affirmative. Arguing as would Werner Heisenberg, Quester postulated that to be able to observe directly or to evidence Eisenhower's genius would naturally serve to disprove its existence. Indeed, "genius in politics requires that one conceal one's genius." Eisenhower understood that the best way to achieve results in politics was to play dumb. Quester's view of the nature of genius fit nicely into revisionist claims that one need not like the ends to appreciate the genius of the means.[75] Or, as Richard Immerman noted, "the shortcomings of his strategy must not obscure the intellectual acuity and perspicacity that gave rise to it."[76]

The best treatment of Eisenhower as a thinker so far was Robert Griffith's examination of the president's economic world view. Griffith examined Eisenhower's conception of what the author termed the corporate commonwealth which was a coherent and consistent view of the American economy and the means needed to guarantee its successful and prosperous operation. According to Griffith, Eisenhower saw inherent contradictions within modern capitalism which could be overcome by a citizenry that avoided class conflicts, restrained greed, and discouraged wicked partisan debates. Class warfare ultimately resulted in statism, which stifled the American entrepreneurial spirit under the false notion that the government should guarantee and provide economic prosperity for all Americans regardless of circumstance. Through cooperation, self-restraint, discipline, and disinterested public service, these pitfalls could be avoided.

Griffith was quite careful not to describe Eisenhower as an intellectual. "Eisenhower was not, of course, a profound or original thinker," Griffith casually remarked. But he did offer other insights into Eisenhower's thinking. Through his career in the military, "Eisenhower absorbed the principal elements of his education: a respect for the efficiencies of organization, a contempt for politics and politicians, a distrust of popular democracy and of the masses whose 'class fears and prejudices are easily aroused,' and, finally, a strong commitment to duty and to the ideal of disinterested public service."[77] Griffith's study of Eisenhower's conception of the corporate commonwealth integrated several elements of his thinking about a variety of matters and emphasized consistency and purpose rather than contradictory economic and political notions. But Eisenhower did not need to be an intellectual, as Griffith noted, to possess a certain consistent view of things, particularly the value and function of nuclear weapons in service of the American republic.

d. Eisenhower and Hiroshima

Any study of Eisenhower's view on the role of nuclear weapons in America must be based in part on how he understood those weapons. In turn, Eisenhower's understanding of nuclear weapons can not be fully explained without considering the circumstances in which he learned of them and their first use. Eisenhower first became aware of the American atomic bomb project in late 1942 when Major General Leslie Groves, military head of the Manhattan Project, instructed Major General G. V. Strong to brief General Eisenhower on the wartime need to destroy the nascent German atomic bomb project. Army Air Corps General "Hap" Arnold and Major General T. T. Handy authorized Strong's mission to suggest a bombing or sabotage mission against German heavy water plants in Norway.[78] Allied commando raids in October and November 1942 and again in February 1943 ultimately succeeded in destroying the plants, but they were quickly rebuilt.

His second encounter with the atomic bomb came on the eve of Operation Overlord in May 1944 when Major A. V. Peterson briefed Eisenhower on the possibility that radioactive materials might be used against allied troops during the upcoming invasion of France in 1944. No record of the briefing exists, but it very likely followed the parameters of a War Department memorandum of 22 March 1944. In that communication, General Groves wrote that "radioactive materials are extremely effective contaminating agents; are known to the Germans; can be produced by them and could be employed as a military weapon."[79] "I was told that American scientists were making progress in these two important types [bacteriological and atomic]," Eisenhower wrote in his war memoir, "and that as a result of their own experience they were to make shrewd guesses concerning some of the details of similar German activity." In the briefing, Eisenhower received what he later called "remarkably accurate estimates of the existence, characteristics, and capabilities of the new German weapons." These estimates allowed American and British high command, even higher than Eisenhower, to take action to impede or eliminate German scientific progress in these areas. "We sent intermittent raids against every spot in Europe," Eisenhower wrote, "where scientists believed that the Germans were attempting either to manufacture new types of weapons or where they were building launching facilities along the coast."[80] On May 11, Eisenhower wrote to Chief of Staff General Marshall to confirm that Eisenhower had indeed received the message. He made a "careful analysis" of the information provided by Peterson and passed it along to a limited number of persons with the proper precautions and in strict secrecy.[81]

Eisenhower also was instructed by General Groves and General Marshall to gather more intelligence on Nazi nuclear operations. "We had to learn as soon as we could what the Germans might be able to do if they exerted every possible effort to produce an atomic weapon," Groves remembered. The Alsos program sought this information and began as early as 1939 to uncover information on the heavy water plants in Norway and on other similar operations in Italy. After the Normandy landings, Alsos sponsored infiltration missions by small troop elements behind enemy lines and into Germany to collect data for the allies.[82] According to Groves, Eisenhower was provided a letter requesting that the Allied commander give the Alsos commander "every facility and assistance at your disposal which will be necessary and helpful in the successful operation of this mission."[83] Near the very end of the war, U.S. high command expressed concern about German atomic research falling into the hands of advancing French or Russian armies. At the request of General Marshall, Groves advised Eisenhower about the possibility of a small redeployment of troops to guard against that possibility. "According to this plan, American troops would have to get into and hold the area long enough for us to capture the people we wanted, question them, seize and remove their records, and obliterate all remaining facilities," Groves remembered.[84] Eisenhower did not describe in any detail any of the briefings he may have been given on the status of the American bomb project. Indeed, it was quite possible that Eisenhower knew more about the atomic bomb project in Germany than in the United States.

What Eisenhower knew and thought about the bombings of Hiroshima and Nagasaki is more certain and informative. Scholars including Gar Alperovitz and Barton Bernstein challenged the view that President Harry Truman had ordered the atomic bombings of Japan exclusively to save American lives and to bring a quick end to the Pacific War as had been argued in a good amount of postwar scholarship. They argued that Truman had other motivations to use the bomb, including to deter the Soviet Union from entering the Pacific war and to intimidate the Soviets into resolving upcoming postwar disputes about Eastern Europe and the Pacific along American terms. They further questioned Truman's assertion that the bombs saved millions of American lives and that Japan intended to fight on through the fall of 1945. To support their view, revisionist scholars such as Alperovitz argue that General Eisenhower saw the atomic bombings of Japan as militarily unnecessary, a point supported by Eisenhower's claim that he argued against using the bomb to his immediate superiors Secretary of War Henry Stimson and President Truman before the bomb's use on Japan. Alperovitz concluded that Dwight Eisenhower was the only major American commander who maintained his human morality and rightly opposed the atomic bombings of Japan.[85] Barton Bernstein, who also agreed that the bombings were not necessary, rejected Alperovitz's conclusion that Eisenhower opposed the use of nuclear weapons.[86]

The debate among historians relies upon only a few pieces of evidence. For his part, Alperovitz relied mostly upon Eisenhower's own claim that he opposed the bombings in July 1945 and that Eisenhower made this point known to Secretary of War Stimson, claims which came only after the war. In *Crusade in Europe* published in 1948, Eisenhower wrote:

Mushroom cloud from the Hiroshima atomic bomb, 6 August 1945 (National Archives)

> I had a long talk with Secretary Stimson, who told me that very shortly there would be a test in New Mexico of the atomic bomb, which American scientists had finally succeeded in developing … I expressed the hope that we would never have to use such a thing against any enemy because I disliked seeing the United State take the lead in introducing into war something as horrible and destructive as this new weapon was described to me. Moreover, I mistakenly had some faint hope that if we never used the weapon in war other nations might remain ignorant of the fact that the problem of nuclear fission had been solved … My views were merely personal and immediate reactions; they were not based on any analysis of the subject.[87]

Alperovitz buttressed this claim with evidence from an interview Eisenhower granted to historian Herbert Feis in 1960 in which Eisenhower repeated his claim that at the time he did not see any value in the use of the atomic bombs on Japan. Further corroborating evidence came from Eisenhower's 1963 memoir, *Mandate for Change*:

> The incident took place in 1945 when Secretary of War Stimson visiting my headquarters in Germany, informed me that our government was preparing to drop an atomic bomb on Japan. I was one of those who felt that there were a number of cogent reasons to question the wisdom of such an act … But the Secretary, upon giving me the news of the successful bomb test in New Mexico, and of the plan for

> using it, asked for my reaction, apparently expecting a vigorous assent. During his recitation of the relevant facts, I had been conscious of a feeling of depression and so I voiced to him my grave misgivings, first on the basis of my belief that Japan was already defeated and that dropping the bomb was completely unnecessary, and secondly because I thought that our country should avoid shocking world opinion by the use of a weapon whose employment was, I thought, no longer mandatory as a measure to save American lives. It was my belief that Japan was, at that very moment, seeking some way to surrender with a minimum loss of "face."[88]

Alperovitz also cited similar evidence from a magazine article of 1963 and from the recollections of Eisenhower's son John S. D. Eisenhower and his brother Milton Eisenhower, both of whom relied on Dwight Eisenhower's recollection to sustain their own.[89]

Bernstein looked upon Alperovitz's evidence with suspicion. He argued that no reliable documentary evidence supported Eisenhower's claim and thus the claim can not be accepted at face value.[90] In Bernstein's view, much can be inferred from the position of Chief of Staff General George Marshall, one of Eisenhower's mentors and a man for whom Eisenhower had great respect. Bernstein argued that "General Marshall was the dominant figure before the end of the war in thinking about tactical use" of nuclear weapons against Japan.[91] Marshall was hesitant about the strategic use of the atomic bomb against Japan, a sentiment he shared with Secretary of War Stimson. Though strategic bombing had been utilized so far in the war, some still objected to the indiscriminate bombing of noncombatants. However, Marshall believed the atomic bomb would be useful against military targets in preparation for the coming invasion of Japan in November 1945. According to Bernstein, the fact that Marshall was thinking about using atomic weapons as support for the coming Kyushu invasion suggests that Marshall did not believe Japan was near surrender. Further, if Marshall did not believe that Japan was finished, Bernstein concluded, why would Eisenhower conclude differently, especially considering Eisenhower knew less of the Pacific war than did Marshall? "The only one of the Joint Chiefs who actually had raised serious pre-Hiroshima doubts about the use of the A-bomb had been General Marshall," Bernstein maintained. "He had not objected to its use, but he had strongly urged – presumably for ethical reasons and the protection of America's moral reputation – that the weapon should be used on a truly military target," Bernstein argued.[92] Alperovitz and Robert Messer countered that "Marshall simply was not 'in the loop' when it came to many of the political-diplomatic issues surrounding the bomb."[93] Bernstein retorted that Marshall believed the invasion of Japan was still necessary, regardless of the Soviet invasion and regardless of the bomb, and that Eisenhower would more than likely have shared that belief.

Without dismissing Eisenhower's 1948 objections, his arguments certainly proved convenient politically as he was able to distance himself from the increasingly unpopular Truman and endear himself to some Republicans. Eisenhower's statement of opinion on the bombings carried little political risk for a man as popular as he. American war veterans widely respected, admired, and loved Dwight Eisenhower and they had no grounds to doubt his support of the American fighting man. At home, few Americans could question Eisenhower's patriotism and the general-turned-university president ran little risk of alienating himself from the body politic. His critique of the atomic bombings however did cement his status as a man of peace in a time of war. Also, Eisenhower's objections to the atomic bombings interjected him into the political debate and simultaneously raised him above the political bickering of the time through a display of his compassion, intelligence, and common sense. By the time Eisenhower decided to run for president, he had successfully established himself as a popular and capable leader who was distinct from both Democrats and some Republicans and quite knowledgeable about atomic affairs. These characteristics translated into a sizable electoral majority for Eisenhower in 1952 as American voters overwhelmingly selected the former General to lead the United States deeper into the nuclear era.

2
Restoring Economic Strength

As president, Dwight Eisenhower sought to use the atomic bomb to help restore strength to the American economy for the ongoing struggle against international communism. Though this necessity was juxtaposed with a desire to augment American military power, the buildup of conventional armies and atomic weapons since 1945 had already created military power unequaled in American history. But, at what cost, Eisenhower wondered. Eisenhower worried that the economic policies of the Truman administration had jeopardized American fiscal solvency with a rapid jump in defense spending and the consequent budget deficits. Beginning in 1953, Eisenhower insisted that his administration address this fiscal danger to national security even before considering others.

The new president concluded that a rapid and sizable increase in the number of atomic weapons would afford him the ability to maintain proper military power at a reduced monetary cost. In this effort, Eisenhower intended to make atomic weapons more powerful, more abundant, and more useful to the republic in ways beyond simply their function in war. This was a necessary first step toward fully integrating the atomic bomb into national life and exploiting fully the bomb's potential for financial benefit as well as its explosive power. For Eisenhower, the restoration of economic strength to the nation through the proper use of the atomic bomb would yield substantial positive results, most notably a cumulative increase in national strength and an augmented ability to wage the Cold War.

In 1953, Eisenhower did not fear the prospect of atomic war as much as he feared that the United States was already becoming a garrison state. Tactical atomic war in the days before the Soviet hydrogen bomb proved less than terrifying to Eisenhower than the impact of a command economy on American freedom. In his view, atomic war with fission weapons seemed less likely and less destructive to the United States than a lack of fiscal discipline and the inevitable economic downturn. He worried particularly about Truman's plan to meet Soviet military strength with American conventional and atomic forces. Eisenhower believed this type of military commitment required fiscal discipline to ensure economic prosperity over the long term. If government spending for national security continued to rise and larger deficits persisted, the government might be required to take direct action to reduce the risk of inflation, unemployment, recession, and depression. Any sort of reactionary governmental interference would unnaturally inhibit the free operation of market forces and create an American economy founded not on free trade but on government regulation. In the resulting garrison state, the economy would operate under the control of a powerful, centralized government which used taxation, wage and price controls, and tariffs to steer the economy. Under a garrison state, the free market upon which the American economy depended and in which Eisenhower placed great faith would suffer. In a garrison state, state power would also threaten an erosion of traditional American rights and liberties. Eisenhower "believes that free enterprise is the underpinning of all freedom," journalist Richard Rovere wrote in 1950, "he thinks we worry too much about security and too little about liberty."[1] For Eisenhower, deteriorating economic freedom threatened political freedom as well. If both were crushed under the weight of the garrison state, Americans would no longer need to defend the United States against communism; the communists would have already won.

To alleviate this terrible risk, Eisenhower implemented a new national security policy, dubbed the New Look, which aimed to build economic strength as well as military strength. In the midst of Cold War, the United States needed cumulative national strength, and military strength without comparable financial strength would leave the nation vulnerable. "The U.S. must wake up & prepare a position of strength from which it can speak serenely and confidently," Eisenhower wrote, and "we must hold our position of strength without bankrupting ourselves."[2] He anticipated that if he committed to a buildup of nuclear weapons early and a steady reliance upon those weapons over the long term he would not have to choose between fiscal restraint and discipline on one hand and military power on the other.

a. No More Than Adequacy

Between the end of World War II and 1953, Eisenhower learned a few lessons on the requirements of the Cold War economy and viewed the economy then as did many contemporary American conservatives. In short, he believed that individual and corporate taxes should be low, government spending should be limited and effective, and the government should do its best to keep the economy flowing according to demands of the free market. This general economic philosophy aimed primarily at avoiding deficit spending and the accumulation of a national debt.[3] Eisenhower believed strongly in the value of balanced budgets, and he opposed government price and wage controls. He sought to achieve real economic growth without inflation and believed that balanced budgets at best or budget surpluses at worst were ways to achieve those goals. Low taxes and limited government interference allowed the private sector to stimulate economic growth through the proper use of financial resources.[4]

Eisenhower was no laissez-faire capitalist however. He accepted Social Security as part of the American political landscape, and, at least according to goals of the Republican Party in 1950, he even favored an increase in Social Security benefits "with due regard to the tax burden on those who labor."[5] In addition, particularly during times of war, Eisenhower expected labor and management to work together to ensure high levels of production. If necessary, the government could help negotiate or even mandate cooperation between the two groups. He also supported a minimal amount of federal aid to education. Still, Eisenhower was regarded by Ann Mari May as "the most fiscally conservative president of the postwar period."[6]

In November 1945, Eisenhower became Army chief of staff and his primary job was to find the best way to carry out the Army's mission as set by the president. That mission involved organizing a proper military force structure within the context of the rapid demobilization of troops after World War II as well as providing for the modernization of the armed forces to meet postwar threats, including the introduction of atomic weapons technology. Other concerns for Eisenhower included developing plans for military unification and for Universal Military Training, as well as unofficially mediating disagreements between Army Generals Douglas MacArthur and Lucius Clay.

noted, "coupled with a decent program (arranged in priorities coordinated among services) for successively higher levels of preparations."[14]

He recommended that studies should be made for every price point between 10 and 16 billion, and emphasized the need to plan effectively. "No economy & efficiency can be produced in military preparations except on planned and steady basis," he insisted. If the government budgeted too much, unexpected cuts resulted. If too little was budgeted, new appropriations became necessary and even more costly. The result of Eisenhower's kind of intricate planning would be less redundancy, less waste, greater efficiency, and more effective spending.[15] The $14.3 billion and $11.7 billion allocated for the two fiscal years 1946/1947 and 1947/1948 were too low to provide for national security and to lower the national debt as well, according to Eisenhower. He estimated about $15 billion for all services per year would be sufficient.[16] "If we could use that sum *intelligently* & *logically* what a difference it could make," he remarked. Eisenhower wanted that $15 billion to be a high water mark at best or a plateau at worst for spending in this area.[17] In making his case, Eisenhower insisted that it was not necessary to "sacrifice security to worship a balanced budget." The United States "wanted adequate security – we wanted no more than adequacy," he later explained.[18]

The planning for fiscal year 1950 proved more difficult than Eisenhower imagined. The Joint Chiefs of Staff continued to argue amongst themselves and with Forrestal about each service's budget requirements. These personal and political battles played out in the press, and Eisenhower feared that they might appear soon in Congress which might undermine all future budget requests. For his part, Forrestal was unable to rein in the Joint Chiefs of Staff perhaps because he began to show the symptoms of the mental illness which later contributed to his suicide. Nonetheless, the chiefs ultimately agreed upon $14.4 billion, but Eisenhower expected Truman to cut the request to below $14 billion. If the Congress made additional changes to the budget upon which the military experts coordinated and agreed, "the resulting organization is bound to be out of balance so far as overall professional opinion is concerned." Eisenhower coached Forrestal not to accept any budget which served only to allay internal dissent. "You must believe in the soundness of the method by which the decision was reached and in the eventual accuracy of the result," Eisenhower instructed.[19]

In recent years, inflation had played havoc with military expenditures. "During 46, 47 and early 48 I pleaded for a 15 b. budget. We never got it & we're suffering because of it," Eisenhower believed, "now inflation has raised everything so much that even the 15 begins to look inadequate."[20] The need to get defense spending under control and balance the budget grew more urgent every fiscal year, and the deficits contributed to inflation which further hampered the ability to buy what the military required at a price the nation could afford. Eisenhower labored "to balance the budget over the business cycle, and thus keep the price of weapons, like the price of everything else, from multiplying."[21]

With budget problems and rivalries still causing havoc, Truman appointed Eisenhower as primary military advisor to the president and the secretary of defense and as temporary presiding officer of the Joint Chiefs of Staff on 11 February 1949. "Pres. & Mr. F. apparently assume that I have some miraculous power to make some of these warring elements lie down in peace together," Eisenhower remarked.[22] This was precisely the reason Truman and Forrestal continued to involve Eisenhower in these important developments. Eisenhower's task in this position was to manufacture agreement among the Joint Chiefs of Staff on "must tasks and, therefore must appropriations, around which a desirable peace time structure can be built." He continued to believe "that 15-16 billion per year is all that this country need spend for security forces – if it is done every year (with some additional amounts to cover past deficits)."[23] Getting these funds and using them efficiently to prepare for the long term was Eisenhower's central preoccupation both as advisor to Forrestal and as temporary chairman of the Joint Chiefs of Staff. Eisenhower advised the chiefs to prepare a basic war plan, the first step in his "red brick" plan, and to follow that by finding the minimum cost to procure these forces followed that.[24] This was Eisenhower's task, and absent an agreement, Eisenhower remarked, "I'll quit & begin criticizing."[25]

Eisenhower's record as interim chairman proved mixed. On the one hand, he persuaded the Joint Chiefs to accept a unified budget and set a precedent for all future chairmen. On the other hand, he became increasingly frustrated with Truman and the new Defense Secretary Louis Johnson, who filled the post after Forrestal. Eisenhower insisted that the defense budget be kept at a certain level consistent with national security, but the White House and the Pentagon continued to cut the budget over which Eisenhower had labored and for which he finally got the agreement of the Joint Chiefs. "General Alfred Gruenther, head of Joint Planning, and I wanted a $16 billion budget as minimum," Eisenhower remembered, "Secretary Johnson kept making it less and

President Truman and General Dwight D. Eisenhower, 31 January 1951 (Harry S Truman Presidential Library)

less and I asked to be relieved."[26] After suffering an acute attack of gastroenteritis on 21 March 1949 which kept him away from his duties until 11 May, a frustrated Eisenhower gave up his temporary duties at the Pentagon in July 1949 and concentrated exclusively on his job at Columbia.

Nineteen forty-nine proved a defining year for the Cold War and for Eisenhower. On 29 August, the Soviet Union detonated its first atomic bomb and ended the American atomic monopoly. To meet the new Soviet threat, Truman took action. On 28 September, the president and the Congress agreed upon funding to create a new anti-communist defense alliance, the North Atlantic Treaty Organization. In addition, Atomic Energy Commissioner Lewis Strauss wrote President Truman on 25 November to encourage immediate action to build the thermonuclear bomb. The following January, Truman announced America's intention to build the hydrogen bomb with all possible speed.[27]

In early 1950, the National Security Council began work on what eventually became NSC-68, a document which helped reposition the United States to fight the Cold War. The NSC agreed that the United States now existed in a perpetual state of war and the nation needed to respond accordingly. The Soviet Union and international communism constituted a hostile and immediate threat that demanded a massive military buildup in the United States as well as the mobilization of American society for this new conflict. "We must, by means of a rapid and sustained build-up of the political, economic, and military strength of the free world, and by means of an affirmative program intended to wrest the initiative from the Soviet Union," the document explained, "confront it with convincing evidence of the determination and ability of the free world to frustrate the Kremlin design of a world dominated by its will."[28]

Ever the professional American soldier, Eisenhower avoided getting too involved in the partisan political debates over these momentous issues. He spent much of this time fending off requests from friends, associates, and others for him to enter politics. Then, on 25 June 1950, North Korea invaded South Korea, and, like many others, Eisenhower became greatly concerned. "I have no business talking about the basic political decision (to support or not to support South Korea)," Eisenhower wrote in his diary, but "I believe we'll have a dozen Koreas soon if we don't take a firm stand." What the United States needed now was proper strength. "Remember, in a fight we (our side) can never be too strong," he continued, "we must study every angle to be prepared for whatever may happen even if it finally came to the use of an A-bomb (which God forbid)." On 6 July 1950, he traveled from New York to Washington to testify before a Senate subcommittee and to meet with various officials including General Marshall, who would soon become secretary of defense, and President Truman. He reminded the Senate that it was vitally important that nations of the world know something about our "latent strength" and later told the president of the need gather support quickly and to build strength for the intervention in Korea.[29] American, South Korean, and United Nations forces under General MacArthur seemed to take Eisenhower's advice to heart. A landing at Inchon in September 1950 turned back the North Korean advance, and MacArthur pushed the enemy back across the 38th parallel. With imminent defeat avoided and a stalemate emerging, Eisenhower grew increasingly concerned with the Truman administration's fiscal policies and the subsequent effect on America's ability to wage the Cold War.

b. In the Land of the Controlled Economy

To meet the threat in Korea as well as any future threats, Truman planned to augment U.S. military capabilities. He sent immediately to Congress a $4 billion supplemental spending request to support expansion of the Army, Navy, and Air Force as well as the Atomic Energy Commission. When he submitted the budget for fiscal year 1951, the president requested a total of $69.5 billion for a variety of national security requirements. The president forecasted he would request $56 billion for the following two years and $45 billion for 1955, assuming that the war in Korean ended in June 1951. He believed that an increase in expenditures for both conventional and atomic forces best prepared America for the long haul.[30] Eisenhower was disheartened. "Some of these officials think we can buy security," he commented, "solvency and security can scarcely be separated, yet I hear talk of $55 billion a year for several years. Tragic."[31] To meet these security needs, the nation would need to borrow money to produce military hardware and wage war which could cause inflation and result in supply shortages. Eisenhower worried that to relieve these economic pressures in the interest of war the government would likely raise taxes, fix prices and wages, and maintain tighter control over credit.[32] The free market economy soon would become a controlled economy.

Eisenhower believed that American political leadership had failed the republic. "Goddamit, is there no desire to know where we are going?," he exclaimed. James Forrestal did not have "the stamina to equal his honesty and sense" and George Marshall, "the best public servant of the lot, obviously wants to quit." "And poor HST, a fine man who, in the middle of a stormy lake, knows nothing of swimming," Eisenhower mused, still, "drowning people are forced to look to him as a lifeguard."[33] Truman and the Congress had overreacted, Eisenhower believed. Had the administration taken his advice, the $15 billion Eisenhower originally suggested would have covered the nation's needs, without increasing the deficit, risking inflation, and undermining the American economy. "Such price increases, spiraling indefinitely upward out of anyone's control," Eisenhower wrote, "I am convinced can eventually wreck the nation's security."[34] He worried that a growing national budget, largely the result of increasing expenditures on military hardware, would result in an overall loss of national economic strength. In the end, Truman's failed leadership and poor planning resulted in national budget of $56.9 billion for fiscal year 1952.

Eisenhower's view of the American economy was basic but not simple-minded. From General Fox Conner, Eisenhower learned that democracies such as the United States needed to organize the whole of their industrial and economic base around warfare in order to win any major conflict. By 1935, according to one scholar, Eisenhower had become "one of the country's leading experts on industrial mobilization." As much as anything, this led to his various appointments before and during World War II, including roles in the office of the assistant secretary of war working for industrial mobilization plans. He worked closely with Bernard Baruch, Chairman of the War Industries Board, where he "became a firm convert to Baruch's creed that victory in a future war would depend ultimately upon economic mobilization, a mobilization that would require the government to take control of the nation's economy."[35] In World War II, Eisenhower employed this conception of total war to insure the United States provided proper industrial mobilization to defeat fascism in Europe and the Pacific. All the nation's resources needed proper management and coordination to supply the vast allied armies to defeat ruthless and fanatical enemies. Government had to play a crucial role in this effort.

Once the war ended, however, Eisenhower adopted a view of the American economy which could be characterized as classically liberal. This was not well expressed by Eisenhower as he rarely commented on economic matters not directly related to military procurement or budgets. Labor discord captured Eisenhower's attention in the days after the war, and he did express his economic ideas within that context. In particular, he worried about possible government intervention in a potential strike of 1946. He insisted that strikes would not be a threat if the public understood the nature and danger of the communist threat. "We (our form of government) is [*sic*] under deadly, persistent, and constant attack," he believed, "if this understanding were universal we'd have no strikes; capital and labor would easily solve their difficulties if both knew their very existence depended upon accord." Though "all my sympathies are with the workers," Eisenhower insisted all aspects of management and labor relations required study: "closed-shop, check-off, industry-wide unions, responsible, corporate organization of trade unions (one side). Effective antitrust laws, lockouts, control of raw materials, sound financing – private and government – limiting bureaucratic (other side)." Labor relations laws should be fair and just, Eisenhower believed, but "government should stay out of this field to the utmost extent."[36] A classical liberal on government's role, Eisenhower was also a fiscal conservative. According to William Shannon, "he believed in the absolute primacy of thrift, he wanted to return government functions to the states, he believed deficit financing was a sin, and he believed high taxes and government regulations" smothered free enterprise.[37]

Still, Eisenhower worried about the growing number of government social programs some of which he saw as financially unhealthy and ethically unacceptable. Truman, for example, proposed to the 81st Congress a variety of social measures including federal health insurance, a farm plan, a fair employment practices law, a slum clearance law, and federal aid to education. Congressional Democrats did not possess the majorities to pass any of these pieces of legislation, save the Wagner-Ellender-Taft Housing Act which enjoyed bipartisan support in Congress.[38] Eisenhower was nonetheless appalled. "The trend toward governmental centralization continues – alarmingly," Eisenhower noted. "In the name of 'social security' we are placing more and more responsibility upon the central govt," he lamented, "and this means that an ever growing bureaucracy is taking an ever greater power over our daily lives." "The 'tax and tax – spend and spend – elect and elect' formula is working wonderfully for the shortsighted persons who cannot (or do not desire to) see beyond the next election date," Eisenhower wrote. This same scenario had already created a problem for Columbia. "Taxes leave prospective donors to university income so little in the way of spare income [*sic*] that only the most strenuous efforts keep us going at all," he remarked. When money fell short, the rallying cry was always the same: federal aid to education. "It is a dangerous slogan," he wrote. Even worse, Eisenhower continued, "the proposition is immoral, and its adoption, in this general sense, will lead to statism and, therefore, slavery."[39] Eisenhower reserved this harshest of language for fiscal recklessness.

Things began to change for Eisenhower in October 1950 when Truman again summoned him to public duty and offered Eisenhower the top job at NATO, the Supreme Allied Commander for Europe. If NATO were to succeed, Truman reasoned, the alliance required unassailable leadership from someone committed to a European defensive alliance. Truman expected that Eisenhower would bring immediate credibility and promise to the fledgling organization. Eisenhower accepted and began working to build NATO, all the while staying abreast of American domestic politics. For months, prominent Republicans had urged him to run for president, and in early 1952, after slightly more than a year on the job at NATO, he declared himself a Republican and a presidential candidate.

Eisenhower continued to express frustration with Truman's failure to plan appropriately, to allocate monies judiciously, and to build military strength efficiently. "I know that the men who have made the studies are capable, honest, and patriotic," Eisenhower wrote on 22 January 1952, but "I am well acquainted with some of the countries in which the size of national budgets has stifled initiative and caused great difficulties otherwise." That morning, Eisenhower read in the newspaper of Truman's $85 billion budget request to Congress, including approximately $65 billion for national security and a $14 billion deficit. "There is newspaper speculation to the effect that these budgets will continue to rise," Eisenhower noted. "If this is true (and I cannot believe for a moment that it is), then we are headed for worse than trouble. The effect will be disastrous," he concluded.[40] By 1952, Eisenhower had concluded that Truman, the Congress, the military leadership, and the country had succumbed to growing Cold War hysteria and sought to spend themselves out of danger.

During times of war Eisenhower accepted fiscal policies for the short term which in the long term might do harm to the American economy. "Censorship, price controls, allocation of materials and commodities, and the like are necessary in a great war," Eisenhower confided in his diary. He even accepted that in times of peace "certain of these controls could possibly be applied in unusual and serious circumstances." In both these circumstances, the controls Eisenhower mentioned would be always temporary. Economic controls sustained over the long term to meet a continuing threat to national security, however, could do "serious damage to the system of government set up by our Constitution." To strike a balance between national preparedness on one side and national bankruptcy on the other, the republic needed to anticipate and prepare for national defense priorities rather than to be surprised and reactive, according to Eisenhower. To meet the Cold War threat, Eisenhower believed, "we must devise and follow a system that we can carry on as long as there appears to be a threat in the world capable of endangering our national safety."[41]

Defense preparation constituted one "horn of the dilemma" for Eisenhower. The republic required military power sufficient to meet challenges to its security and to that of the nation's allies. As chief of staff, advisor to James Forrestal, and chairman of the Joint Chiefs of Staff, Eisenhower labored to stabilize the defense budget at $15 billion for several years into the future. According to Eisenhower, "the chiseling and cutting of estimates" by the Congress "was accompanied and made worse by a steadily depreciating value of the dollar." "Thus, in the fiscal years 1947, 1948, 1949, and 1950, the defense fabric continued to shrink at an alarming extent," he continued. The expenditures to allow the nation to wage the Korean War made these budget deficiencies apparent to everyone. Unprepared for the war militarily and fiscally, the nation had overreacted to the outbreak of war and began a military buildup which promised economic troubles down the line.

These economic troubles constituted the other side of the dilemma. "I am afraid that we are risking damage from the other horn of the dilemma," Eisenhower worried, "that is, the danger of internal deterioration through the annual expenditures of unconscionable sums on a program of indefinite duration, extending far into the future." Eisenhower got the impression that the $14 billion deficit for the following year would be the first of many. Expenditures beyond revenue at this level risked significant inflation. "The president told me very solemnly that an aggregate national budget of more than $42 billion would quickly spell unconscionable inflation," Eisenhower remembered of Truman, "today we talk about $85 billion and apparently mean it to be indefinitely prolonged into the future." "National bankruptcy would necessitate a type of control or confiscation of property," he continued, "that would be in utter contradiction to the assurances and safeguards of our Constitution."[42] In short, Eisenhower believed that the result of those deficits might be national bankruptcy and the destruction of the republic.

For the republic to maintain national preparedness for the Cold War indefinitely into the future, the government required military and fiscal discipline to maintain proper economic strength. But, democracies had to undertake military preparation on a defensive basis only, Eisenhower insisted.[43] To insure military strength for defense the republic required careful planning and a conservative, disciplined approach to modernization and growth that provided not only proper force structure and size but also the flexibility to grow, adapt, and advance technologically. The building of economic strength required that the republic not overreact to military threats, maintain planned spending levels even in times of great danger, and build the most strength at the least cost over the long term.

In the midst of the Cold War, greater threats existed to the nation's economy than to her military. "There is no greater probability of war today than there was two years ago; and no one can say for certain that there is any greater probability of deliberately provoked war at the end of this year or of next than there is now," he argued in 1952. Despite the ongoing military effort on the Korean peninsula, Eisenhower was more concerned with Truman's budget follies. Whereas the United States and the free world had met the communist challenge in Korea, the same could not be said of the nation's economic response to the Korean War in particular and the Cold War in general. Eisenhower believed a cumulative loss of economic strength would upset the delicate balance and likely encourage more communist aggression. "We can say only that properly balanced strength will promote the probability of avoiding war," he argued, "in this sense, we need the strength soon – but it must be balanced between moral power, economic power, and purely military power."[44] Any significant reduction of strength in one of these areas risked a loss of cumulative strength that, according to conventional wisdom, encouraged aggression.

Comfortable with America's military position in Korea despite the stalemate, he feared more the rise of the garrison state because of the effect that might have on the nation's strategic position. He believed that lavish defense spending "will actually reduce rather than enhance our chances of preventing a war." This will become reality, Eisenhower argued, "because we will have aroused genuine doubt, both among our own citizens and among our allies, as to the essential stability of the United States economy."[45] For Eisenhower, a shaky economy led either to great skepticism about the United States' ability to defend the free world against communism or to the belief that democracy and capitalism did have fatal flaws and was not capable of providing for the people of the industrial world. The implications of either of those alternatives proved too terrible to contemplate.

At the root of Eisenhower's problem was the fact that defending lives and territory was only one part of his overall defense concept. Without maintaining fiscal discipline during war time, Eisenhower believed that huge expenditures would not serve the purpose of defending freedom, for that would be sacrificed in the land of the controlled economy.[46] Indeed, if defending only property were the central goal, this could be accomplished without much worry or greater risk. Spending could be unleashed, blast and fallout shelters could be built for a great portion of the nation at the government's expense, and both a massive nuclear arsenal and a tremendous conventional force could be built. For Eisenhower, however, America's freedoms and her way of life would be sacrificed in the spending spree. "These methods would almost certainly involve what is euphemistically called a controlled economy," Eisenhower complained, "but which in effect would amount to a garrison state."[47] From controlled economy to garrison state to dictatorial government, the United States would cease to be American and the cost of war would be the reason.

At one point, so disturbed and concerned about the economy of the national security state, Eisenhower wondered if, "in such circumstances, we would be forced to consider whether or not our duty to future generations did not require us to initiate war at the most propitious moment that we could designate."[48] A preemptive nuclear strike would remove the hostile military threat, he reasoned, and eliminate the need for massive military expenditures which might otherwise endanger America's free institutions. Though Eisenhower did not seriously contemplate the possibility of preemptive nuclear war, the economy of the national security state plagued him nonetheless. Following his inauguration as president, he did seek to find a better to way capitalize on what advantages the U.S. already had in an effort to advance all the goals of national security, including fiscal discipline and economic strength. Whereas Truman had not let American security lapse in the military sense, Eisenhower believed Truman's fiscal failings did so in an economic sense.

Eisenhower now needed to decide just how to insure that military strength was not sacrificed for economic strength. Because of his experience with atomic weapons, he concluded that the proper use of atomic weapons might allow the nation to build both equally well. "It would be impossible for the United States to maintain the military commitments which it now sustains around the world (without turning into a garrison state)," Eisenhower wrote later, "did we not possess atomic weapons and the will to use them when necessary."[49] Because Eisenhower saw both the fiscal and military value of the nuclear weapon he formulated the New Look.

c. Security without Bankruptcy

Regardless of Eisenhower's belief in military strength through fiscal discipline, Truman's increased defense budget allowed for the growth of both conventional and atomic armaments and a buildup of military strength. Total expenditures for national defense grew steadily from the post-war low of $16 billion in 1948 to $18 billion in 1950 and $25 billion in 1951. Total military personnel in the United States rose from 1.4 million troops in 1950 to a Korean War high of 3.6 million in 1952.[50] From the paltry beginning in 1945, America's atomic stockpile totaled well over one-thousand weapons and seventy-two megatons of explosive power at the end of Truman's second term.[51] Continuing innovation in military technology, including the thermonuclear bomb and the Redstone missile, supported the growth of American military strength. His objections to the budget notwithstanding, this growth in military strength resulted in part from Eisenhower's work between 1945 and 1953.

In the post-war period, Eisenhower was preoccupied with the political and fiscal aspects of military strategy rather than the technical elements of America's newest and deadliest atomic weapons. Between 1942 and 1953, Eisenhower's appeared to learn very little about atomic weapons beyond the obvious. During World War II, before Operation Overlord, he was briefed by senior War Department officials about the possibility the Germans might use radioactive materials on invading Allied troops. This information did not prompt the general to rethink the landings nor did he alter invasion plans to account for this new information. In fact, his briefing included little information in the way of protection against radiological attacks. For an army the size of the allied invasion force, no suitable protection could be offered, particularly considering that Eisenhower's briefing came less than a month before the 6 June landings. War Department officials waited until the last possible minute to brief Eisenhower, as they likely understood that they could offer no comfort, little reassurance, and above all few specifics about the subject at hand. As chief of staff, as informal chairman of the Joint Chiefs of Staff, and

Atomic Cloud with Soldiers Joking, 1 May 1952 (National Archives)

as supreme allied commander of NATO, Eisenhower required little technical data on the nuclear weapon to do his job.

Up to that point in his military career, Eisenhower had welcomed new technology in his efforts to prepare and wage wars. When the tank emerged as the next revolution in warfare during the Great War, Eisenhower wrote the army's tactical doctrine for that new weapon. He learned the basic workings of the tank, including its armor, its mobility, and its firepower. Atomic weapons were not altogether different for Eisenhower. He did not need to understand the physics of fission, chain reactions, and radioactivity to put these weapons to work. This precise technical information proved largely beyond Eisenhower's intellectual curiosity. He was concerned only about the explosive potential of atomic weaponry and what was required to deliver nuclear bombs quickly, accurately, and decisively.

As chief of staff, Eisenhower's interaction with atomic technology came mostly through his broad role in formulating American atomic policy. Thus, his early understanding of nuclear weapons was not in the realm of technology, but strategy and budgets. He suggested "that there be developed a well considered analysis" and that the military services be allowed to "discuss and justify their plans and programs for the near future and distant future with specific relationship to atomic energy."[52] In the meantime, Eisenhower generally advocated continued modernization of the atomic arsenal if possible and in secret. America needed to continue making progress both on the bomb itself and on delivery methods. From a military point of view, "the maintenance of the highest possible degree of secrecy with respect to the atomic bomb and refusal to give these secrets to any other nation or to the United Nations organization" appeared prudent to Eisenhower.[53]

Lieutenant Colonel Dwight D. Eisenhower, Camp Meade, Maryland, 1919 (Dwight D. Eisenhower Presidential Library)

International control of the atomic bomb was one of the most prominent issues in the discussions between Eisenhower and the Joint Chiefs of Staff. Eisenhower believed that the use of atomic technology by the United States in any future conflict would depend largely upon "action taken by the United Nations to outlaw or control the bomb."[54] In June 1946, Eisenhower's friend Bernard Baruch had delivered America's first proposal for international control of the atomic bomb to the United Nations. Baruch proposed the creation of an International Atomic Development Authority which would be entrusted to control "all phases of the development and use of atomic energy." The United Nations would supervise all peaceful atomic initiatives and once verifiable safeguards were in place, all nations including the United States shall dispose of their bombs and pledge never to build new ones.[55]

The same day Baruch delivered his proposal to the international community, Eisenhower sent his friend a letter. "I completely agree with you that only through effective international control of atomic energy can we hope to prevent atomic war," Eisenhower opened. He then detailed his personal views, not necessarily those of the Joint Chiefs, on Baruch's proposals. He generally concurred with Baruch but he noted the challenge presented by the proposals. Independent and thorough inspections to ensure compliance with atomic disarmament, for example, proved exceptionally difficult, for "no system of inspection can be expected to guarantee completely against the construction of *some* atomic bombs." In addition, Eisenhower noted "the dilemma" of international control of atomic weapons: If nations enter an agreement too quickly and without thorough inspections and guarantees, the international community might find itself "in the position of having no restraining means in the world capable of effective action if a great power violates the agreement." Eisenhower saw something of a paradox. "To my mind, this means, for the present, that to *prevent* the use atomic weapons," he explained, "there must exist the capability of employing atomic weapons against the recalcitrant." In the end, he reasoned, "the problem of controlling, and finally preventing, the use of atomic bombs (and other decisive weapons), thus becomes the problem of preventing war itself."[56]

Still, Eisenhower was not convinced that the atomic bomb brought security. "Bigger and better atomic bombs and their exclusive possession by any one country do not *necessarily* represent the ultimate in present or future possibilities of control by force or threat of force," he wrote. [57] The United States may indeed possess a lead in atomic armaments, but he speculated that other nations would pursue other weapons of mass destruction, namely biological weapons, which might hold even greater potential for destruction. To provide for international control of atomic bombs without similar controls over other destructive devices left open opportunities for catastrophe. His primary concern in this discussion was for the fundamental national interest of the United States. The United States must not enter into any international treaty for the control of atomic energy if the treaty in any way threatened America's national security. This was a "scarcely debatable point." "We can yield much, even certain points of our sovereignty, to reach this solution," Eisenhower noted, but only if the American people can be persuaded that America's ability to defend the republic did not suffer. "To control atomic weapons, in which field we are pre-eminent, without provision for equally adequate control of other weapons of mass destruction," he argued, "can seriously danger our national security."[58]

While serving as president of Columbia University and as NATO commander, Eisenhower had far fewer encounters with nuclear weapons than when he served as chief of staff. Neither from a scientific, technological, nor a strategic standpoint did Eisenhower have much time to think about nuclear weapons. At Columbia, for example, Eisenhower presided over a faculty of distinguished scholars and scientists, including Isidor Rabi, himself a veteran of the Manhattan Project, and yet had virtually nothing to say to them about atomic weapons. However, while at Columbia, Eisenhower also served as an advisor to James Forrestal and as interim Chairman of the Joint Chiefs of Staff. In these various capacities, Eisenhower focused mostly on budget issues, on inter-service rivalries brewing with the Joint Chiefs, and keeping his name out of the political discussions. Otherwise preoccupied, Eisenhower even displayed little concern about Truman's decision to authorize the construction of the hydrogen bomb.

Immediately after work began on the world's first fission bomb in 1942, some physicists including Edward Teller argued that a more powerful bomb, a super bomb, was also possible. This bomb would use a different fuel, hydrogen, and employ the process of fusion, not fission, to create energy. If the scientists who theorized the super bomb were right, the bomb would be thousands of times more powerful than first atomic bomb and indeed all of human civilization, not just cities or nations, could be in mortal danger. Disagreements within the scientific community prompted disagreements within the political community about whether a hydrogen bomb was possible or desirable. Chief among those arguing against the development of a fusion weapon was Robert Oppenheimer. For his part, Oppenheimer doubted the bomb would actually work, but he worried mostly that if the United States constructed a thermonuclear weapon, others would follow and a nuclear arms race with the Soviet Union would follow. Convinced that it could be built and that the communists might already be pursuing it, Teller and others advocated the hydrogen bomb's construction, testing, and deployment. After the Soviet Union tested its first atomic bomb in 1949, Truman decided the United States would build the hydrogen bomb.

Eisenhower's reaction to Truman's decision was skeptical and whimsical. He was not overly impressed nor was he even convinced that the new weapon could be built. "No matter how strong may be that hydrogen bomb," he cautioned, it was "still just an idea."[59] Assuming the bomb could be built, he expressed some concern about the fantastic estimates of the explosive power cited in the popular press and the damage such predictions could do to military planning. All the doomsday talk about the possible destruction caused by this weapon might "be an obstacle to clear thinking and reasonable action." As a practical matter, he inferred, "if we are all to be destroyed in the twinkling of an eye, what is there to do about it?"[60] The important thing to remember, Eisenhower believed, was that the hydrogen bomb "can be produced for good or evil. It is up to us."[61]

Eisenhower soon took a leave of absence from Columbia in January 1951 to become the first NATO commander. In this post, his task in part was to create an integrated fighting force of conventional armies from the nations of Western Europe that would be capable of resisting a possible Soviet military advance across the continent. The North Atlantic Treaty Organization was founded with the premise that the United States alone could not defend Europe against the Soviet Union with a conventional army. On one hand, the American army did not then possess the manpower to repulse a massive Red Army assault. On the other hand, Americans, however internationalist they might be, would never agree to pay the exorbitant cost associated with fielding an American army to defend European interests on another continent. Truman believed that Eisenhower, perhaps more than anyone else, had the authority, the popularity, and the commitment to overcome these problems and make NATO a viable part of the free world's security apparatus in the Cold War. The role of atomic weapons in this effort was initially unclear. American atomic weapons could be used to defend Paris, for example, but Soviet retaliation might strike at Chicago. This was a trade few in the United States would be willing to make. Moreover, the use of tactical nuclear weapons to defend Western Europe proved more complex than originally imagined. The United States could easily decimate advancing Soviet armies with atomic weapons, but the fallout from those weapons might irreparably damage the European continent. Eisenhower's job however was not necessarily to make these types of hard decisions, but to win European approval of NATO first and to build the defensive alliance second. As a result, he did not worry too much about just how atomic weapons would serve NATO. He just knew that they could and must.

In the meantime, Eisenhower became furious about what he saw as the short sightedness of politicians in Washington who had failed to understand the great threat the country faced. "Our country is at stake," he wrote in his diary, "many will give her lip service; few will give her self-sacrifice, sweat and brains!!!" America needed a re-examination of "our whole philosophy of defense in its foreign & domestic aspects." Each defensive asset as well as the whole organization of the military "should be ruthlessly pulled apart & examined in order to get down to the country's requirements." He recommended a dissection of current military spending, including programs such as the B-36 strategic bomber, the heavy carrier, and also the hydrogen bomb. Intelligent men from all sectors of American society should evaluate these programs and others in terms of their "purposes, special & unique capabilities, inescapable need, duplicatory [sic] effort, luxury." Technological advances considered, the U.S. had not built better defenses, Eisenhower argued, but rather only more expensive defenses. "We can have security without paying the price of national bankruptcy," Eisenhower believed, "if we will put brains in the balance." On the other hand, without a "professional examination that will show us where & how to proceed in this armament business, we will go broke and still have inefficient defenses."[62] When North Korea invaded South Korea in the summer of 1950, the reexamination of defense Eisenhower advocated was put on hold as the threat of communism manifested in violence and the United States had to respond.

With the support of the American people to contain communism, Truman and the United Nations sent forces to South Korea to defend freedom against communist aggression in Asia. The North Korean army advanced south in rapid fashion, until General Douglas MacArthur staged a bold landing at Inchon and the allied forces drove the North Koreans back across the thirty-eighth parallel. MacArthur then marched his army nearly to the border with China when Truman ordered a halt. The perceived American threat to China prompted Mao Zedong to send approximately one million Chinese troops over the border into North Korea to drive back U.S. and United Nations forces. The allies fell back into South Korea, and, beginning in 1951, the war stalemated along a front which spanned the width of the Korean peninsula. Despite the financial and human cost of conventional war in Asia and the very real prospect of losing in a stalemate, Truman did not use the atomic bomb against either the North

Korean People's Army or the Chinese People's Liberation Army pushing south. General MacArthur publically argued for the authority to use atomic weapons to relieve his army, take the offensive, and defeat the superior enemy force. His heated rhetoric and the risk of Chinese intervention prompted Truman to caution MacArthur about the growing risk involved in escalating the war.

In consultation but not necessarily cooperation with British Prime Minister Clement Atlee and apparently swayed by MacArthur, Truman began making plans for the use of atomic weapons in the Korean War. Under pressure from members of Congress including Senator Joseph McCarthy of Wisconsin and from the commander of the Strategic Air Command General Curtis LeMay, Truman edged toward decisive atomic force to end the war in 1951. MacArthur submitted plans for the use of twenty-six nuclear weapons against multiple targets in North Korea and China, a blockade of the Chinese coast, and the use of Nationalist troops from Taiwan for an invasion of the Chinese mainland. Although Truman soon fired MacArthur for insubordination, the president ordered atomic weapons to Okinawa for possible use against the Chinese. With the war stalemated, MacArthur fired, and the Soviets watching closely, Truman elected not to order the use of atomic bombings for the third time in his presidency. "I don't think we ought to use this thing unless we absolutely have to," Truman said, "It is used to wipe out women and children and unarmed people, and not for military uses."[63] Eisenhower felt ill at ease with a perceived lack of consistency in Truman's actions.

Eisenhower possessed a broad view of the Cold War which involved not just winning important battles along the way but preparing for the long pull against a relentless enemy. Rather than set some point of maximum danger, he believed in a sustained effort on all fronts to organize for war and for after the war.[64] With a budget now 400 percent above 1946 levels, Truman built more weapons of war to preserve democracy against communism, but proved unwilling to order the use of those weapons. Truman's reluctance to go all out against North Korea meant that the president's increased military spending neither guaranteed victory in Korea nor strength in the long term.[65] For Eisenhower, this simply made no sense. Truman's strategy of limited war would not stop North Korean or Chinese aggression and with every foot of ground gained the communists further doubted the resolve of the United States. For Eisenhower, Truman's ad hoc military increases and a patchwork strategy of limited war and atomic diplomacy had so far failed. The United States required a broader effort on both the economic and military front to deter Soviet aggression. If that should fail, the United States could meet communist advances with a variety of tools, including strong alliances, a counterinsurgency campaign, a powerful military, a strong, vibrant economy, and perhaps nuclear weapons.

This opinion prompted Eisenhower's run for the presidency in 1952 and his reexamination of national security policy in the earliest days of his administration. In the campaign of 1952, Eisenhower muted his criticism of Truman's national security policy. Indeed, the general had been instrumental in the formation of many of those policies and could not enthusiastically challenge Truman without indicting himself to some degree. While Eisenhower campaigned on his personal popularity and command presence, Richard Nixon kept the ticket focused on the winning issues of K1C2: Korea, communism, and corruption. On national security and the Cold War, Eisenhower's most popular campaign pledge was to go to Korea if elected.[66]

Following his election, Eisenhower began the reexamination of policy which ultimately produced a new national security strategy aimed at financial strength. This was possible only through fiscal discipline which in turn was achievable only through the effective management and proper use of nuclear weapons for national security. Eisenhower believed that the mismanagement of the Truman administration regarding the role of nuclear weapons and the fiscal benefits they offered but remained unused contributed significantly to the "mess in Washington" to which he often referred in his campaign. Accordingly, his first steps as president sought not a total revision of American nuclear weapons production, deployment, or even strategy. Rather, Eisenhower intended first to restore fiscal discipline by restraining spending and balancing the budget and doing both without a significant dip in military strength. In July 1953, he asked Defense Secretary Charles Wilson, himself a fiscal conservative like Eisenhower, to help the president find "the most effective employment of available national resources to insure the defense of our country for the long pull which may lie ahead."[67] In that effort, Eisenhower considered current military technology and strategy, including Truman's use or nonuse of the atomic bomb.

One month into his presidency, Eisenhower articulated this emphasis on economic strength explicitly to his administration. "The hope of freedom itself," Eisenhower proclaimed to his national security team, "depends, in real measure, upon our strength, our heart, and our wisdom." That strength was built on free trade and American enterprise, but also on the fiscal responsibility of the government including measured and considered spending, particularly on national security. Eisenhower "was convinced that a freer and a more normal economy would in the long run provide the nation with greater economic strength."[68] He explained that America's problem was "to achieve adequate military strength within the limits of endurable strain upon our economy." "To amass military power without regard to our economic capacity would be to defend ourselves against one kind of disaster by inviting another," he argued.[69] As he later explained in his first State of the Union address in 1953, Eisenhower believed the government's first priority should be "to chart a fiscal and economic policy" which recognized "the inescapable need for economic health and strength if we are to maintain adequate military power." Through spending on New Deal and Fair Deal social programs as well as increased military spending, Truman had created significant budget deficits, the last of which would push America above the $275 million debt ceiling established by Congress. Excessive national debt, Eisenhower believed, risked "the menace of inflation."[70] Moving beyond his words, Eisenhower took steps early on toward economic strength. In February 1953, not even one month into his term, he removed the government controls on wages and salaries in an attempt to stimulate an American economy strained by the cost of war. Two months later, he cut about $5 billion from Truman's 1954 budget which nearly halved the deficit.[71]

In March 1953, he announced that the Secretary of the Treasury George Humphrey would attend all the meetings of the National Security Council. The president wanted to ensure that all examinations of national policy would include a deep consideration of the economics of the matter.[72] Eisenhower expected Humphrey to keep the group grounded on just how national security decisions would affect the nation's economy. At the same time, Humphrey needed to be prepared with economic details so the National Security Council could make better, more efficient, and perhaps more economical decisions when discussing national security. Eisenhower had no illusions of basing national security policy exclusively on the financial cost, but rather he wanted to emphasize that military strength and economic strength could not be divorced and that both must be accounted for when deciding basic national security policy.

For some time, Eisenhower had been concerned about the real costs of national security. "Every gun that is made, every warship launched, every rocket fired," Eisenhower argued in a speech in April 1953, "signifies in the final sense, a theft from those who hunger and are not fed, those who are cold and are not clothed." He also noted that at present, without a change in posture among the Cold War superpowers, the best the world could hope for would be "a life of perpetual fear and tension" including "a burden of arms draining the wealth and labor of all peoples." The result was "a wasting of strength" and a reduced capacity for nations "to achieve true abundance and happiness for the peoples of this earth."[73] He held out some hope that Soviet leadership might change its tune after the death of Stalin, and he intended to jumpstart dialogue between the superpowers. At the same time, Eisenhower could not risk American national security while he pursued openings for peace. He still believed that the United States must plan for a long term conflict with the Soviets. Under the first national security policy for the Cold War, NSC-68, the United States needed to prepare for war continuously and indefinitely out of the fear that the Soviet Union would soon be in a position to launch a decisive first strike against the United States. By 1953, Eisenhower had concluded that the Soviet Union was not yet close to achieving a position of strategic superiority nor would the Soviet leadership risk a general war with the United States. As a result, he believed that the nation's success in the Cold War would depend as much on her ability to sustain her way of life over the long term as on the building of weapons. Economic prosperity was as important as military strength, and national security policy needed to reflect that balance.

Accordingly, Eisenhower created Project Solarium which amounted to a formal reevaluation of the nation's strategic goals in light of the new priorities. The administration set up three separate task forces which would make recommendations for a new national security policy, each of which might better incorporate atomic weapons into U.S. military strategy. Eisenhower understood that in the absence of atomic weapons national security would depend upon building a massive conventional army capable of countering the Soviet Union. This would be tremendously costly not only in terms of the economy but in terms of the ideals of the American republic, which traditionally rejected large standing armies as a threat to democracy and individual liberties. Eisenhower believed the atomic weapon provided an appropriate, perhaps even convenient, answer to this central question of national security in the Cold War. The Solarium team made their recommendation in the fall of 1953 and the members of the National Security Council including the secretary of the treasury, the budget director, the chairman of the Atomic Energy Commission agreed upon NSC 162/2, a paper on basic national security policy which established the New Look.

The New Look had two key elements. The first was military power. NSC 162/2 described the Soviet threat as the primary danger in the larger struggle with international communism. The Soviet Union possessed an inherent hostility to the non-communist world, a sizable military force including atomic weapons, and a desire and means to export communist revolution to the free world. This threat did not diminish as a result of Joseph Stalin's death and there did not appear in the future any foreseeable relaxation of Soviet hostility, militarism, or aggression. The United States then had to be prepared for a long term struggle, one in which the ability to match Soviet military strength would be paramount. The goal was to convince Soviet leadership that they could not be victorious through any amount of aggressive military action. As stated in NSC 162/2, military strength meant "a strong military posture, with emphasis on the capability of inflicting massive retaliatory damage by offensive striking power."[74] This strength would be complemented by strong and committed allies and a sound mobilization base capable of withstanding a Soviet first strike in the event of general nuclear war. To build military strength, the United States needed proper planning, solid intelligence about the enemy, satisfactory manpower, productive scientific research, and reliable internal security. Most importantly, the military strength of the United States needed to be credible, modern, and decisive. Anything short of those goals meant that the Soviets might doubt America's willingness to challenge Soviet forces in Cold War battlegrounds.

Second, Eisenhower planned that the New Look would meet the Soviet threat without "seriously weakening the U.S. economy or undermining our fundamental values and institutions." He insisted that the new policy recognize that any defense against the Soviet threat must include the maintenance of "a sound, strong and growing U.S. economy." Achieved "through the operation of free institutions," this economy would be capable of providing the necessary strength "over the long pull and of rapidly and effectively changing to full mobilization." NSC 162/2 specifically mentioned how "excessive government spending," "persistent inflation" and "repressive taxation" threatened the "strong and growing economy." According to Eisenhower, these ills unnecessarily disrupted the system of free enterprise and risked recession, and the avoidance of these pitfalls meant an increased chance for steady economic growth. "Over the years an expanding national income can provide the basis for higher standards of living and for a substantial military program," the new policy continued.[75]

In the face of the Soviet threat, "the United States must develop and maintain, at the lowest feasible cost, requisite military and non-military strength to deter and, if necessary to counter Soviet military aggression against the United States or other areas vital to its security."[76] If the economy of the United States remained prosperous, satisfactory fiscal policies could be devised to provide sufficient military strength. Indeed, having both meant that each served the other. Neither could be sacrificed under any circumstance or both would fail. For Eisenhower, sustained military strength and promising economic strength were not mutually exclusive. With proper planning and intelligent management, the United States could build both. Eisenhower concluded that conventional military forces – whether those of the United States or her allies or a combination of both – failed in both regards. First, those forces would be exorbitantly expensive, as demonstrated by the quadrupling of defense spending and the doubling of the federal budget in Truman's last three years in office as he tried to force a communist surrender in Korea.[77] Second, this force would not likely be credible enough to deter Soviet aggression in Western Europe in particular. The Red Army was simply too large and too well positioned to be rooted out by any conventional force the U.S. or NATO could field.

Because Eisenhower saw a solution in the atomic weapon, NSC 162/2 reflected the president's faith in the ability of the atomic bomb to provide fiscal discipline and military strength. "Within the free world, only the United States can provide and maintain, for a period of years to come, the atomic capability to counter balance Soviet atomic power," the NSC concluded. Assuming the nation's atomic arsenal included satisfactory delivery systems, atomic weapons were "indispensable for U.S. security." "Such atomic capability is also a major contribution to the security of our allies," the policy added.[78] Eisenhower understood that once both sides have reached "a stage of atomic plenty" each will possess the ability to "inflict critical damage on the other." In fact, the only thing preventing an attack and indeed general warfare was the certain knowledge that major retaliation would befall the aggressor nation. NSC 162/2 referred to the resulting impasse as a stalemate, during which neither side could win and neither side could lose. In accordance with New Look strategy as outlined NSC 162/2, Eisenhower would threaten massive retaliation and accept an atomic stalemate in the short term if he could produce economic prosperity in the long term.

To make the nation's atomic deterrent credible, NSC 162/2 reflected Eisenhower's willingness to use atomic weapons. "In the event of hostilities, the United States will consider nuclear weapons to be as available for use as other munitions," the administration declared.[79] This policy had only one qualifier: the consent of America's allies would be sought in advance when the use would occur within or above allied territory. Beyond that, no restrictions inhibited the employment of the atomic bomb. In accordance with the New Look strategic policy, Eisenhower planned to decrease the funds spent on conventional forces, to increase the production of nuclear weapons, and to invest heavily in research and development in new nuclear weapon delivery systems.

Critics of the New Look abounded. One, Henry Kissinger, believed that Eisenhower had misinterpreted the strategic lessons of World War II. According to Kissinger, history taught the United States government that the maximum development of technology equates to a successful strategy and victory. In the case of World War II, greater industrial production allowed the Allies to win. That lesson did not hold in the Cold War, according to Kissinger. The United States had spent too much time building more and better weapons and left little time to determining a suitable strategy in the new atomic age. This was largely because of the division of armed services and the budgetary restraints forced upon them by the New Look. The result was that each of the service branches clamored for more money and more weapons, convincing Congress that they must have the ability to destroy the enemy completely in order to fulfill their current mission. The strategy then was designed to fit the budget, rather than the opposite, which should be the case.[80] General Maxwell Taylor believed that the New Look grew out of "a desire for budgetary economy" and "the American penchant for simple solutions." Taylor believed that the reduction of armed personnel and the increase in more modern instruments of war, such as atomic bombs and air power, made the U.S. less safe.[81] He later argued that the emphasis on massive retaliation left America with only two options in the event of communist military aggression: to retaliate instantly and massively or to do nothing.

Eisenhower rejected this criticism. He complained that what Kissinger advocated was "both the old and the new" which "would undoubtedly be a more expensive operation than we are carrying on at this time."[82] And cost was as important as any other factor because economic security had a great deal to do with overall strength and deterrence. "I say that in the long run if we spend much more than [35 billion a year for defense] we will actually reduce rather than enhance of chances of preventing a war," Eisenhower argued.[83]

Critics including Kissinger and Taylor characterized Eisenhower's thinking as far too risky. They believed that the president put financial priorities above those of national security. They charged that in his slavish commitment to fiscal discipline, balanced budgets, and reduced government spending, he unnecessarily risked national security. His policies put in jeopardy, they believed, the nation's ability to meet and contain communist advances in the third world. Because Eisenhower had chained the United States to a policy of atomic deterrence via the New Look, they argued, Eisenhower had sacrificed national strategic interests abroad as well as the lives and livelihood of freedom-loving people under siege from communist subversion in distant lands. Atomic weapons could not protect those people and the U.S. would not risk a larger war in their defense. Therefore, the communists could infiltrate and overthrow democratic institutions and the United States would stand idly by as Eisenhower praised his own fiscal restraint.

These criticisms recognized the fiscal aspect of the New Look but concentrated only on the military aspect when judging its worthiness. In this sense, these critics missed the point. They failed to recognize that Eisenhower believed financial strength to occupy equal footing with military strength. "Eisenhower was firmly convinced that the country's economic prosperity was as important to its security as planes and weapons," Sherman Adams later recalled.[84] To build up overwhelming strength in one area without congruent action in the other weakened the republic overall. "To strengthen the military base, while ruining the economic base," Eisenhower told Dean Rusk in 1962, "would be catastrophic."[85] In that weakened state, the U.S. would not be able to meet the Soviet threat. Because Eisenhower believed that America's democratic institutions were rooted in the economic freedom provided by the free market and capitalism, to undermine these sources of strength was comparable to laying down one's arms and surrendering to the enemy.

Eisenhower devised the New Look to lessen the financial burden of the Cold War and allow for fiscal discipline while providing military strength. Atomic weapons greatly served these ends because atomic weaponry could both keep the budget at low levels and deter a major Cold War confrontation. Atomic weapons removed the economy from the war-time footing of the early Cold War and allowed the United States to benefit from a free-flowing market while not sacrificing military strength. In this way, atomic weapons became quite practical and even desirable to Eisenhower. The great danger would be if the United States failed to muster enough strength and became a tempting target for the Soviet Union. "My feeling was then, and still remains," Eisenhower wrote later, "that it would be impossible for the United States to maintain the military commitments which it now sustains around the world (without turning into a garrison state) did we not possess atomic weapons and the will to use them when necessary."[86] Eisenhower's understanding of atomic weaponry in this regard was practical and reasonable. He was not burdened with ethical doubt or by the concerns of his allies, but instead was focused solely on augmenting American strength in the quickest and most pragmatic way. Eisenhower next needed to make sure that any potential communist aggressor understood that atomic weapons would be available for use by the United States under circumstances to be determined by the United States. This required a buildup of military strength through nuclear weapons and a display of America's willingness to use them.

3

Projecting Military Strength

Following the same intellectual path by which he sought to restore America's economic strength, Eisenhower committed early and consistently to the buildup of national military strength through the construction and deployment of atomic and thermonuclear weapons. He believed the United States was fortunate to be able to build a vast nuclear arsenal and he aimed to employ those weapons in every possible manner as a force for good against a ruthless enemy. The president recognized the danger of a massive nuclear buildup and was troubled by the idea of general thermonuclear war. His sincere concern about the fate of the republic and its people in the event of nuclear exchange ultimately did not dissuade him from committing to the nuclear weapon as the primary pillar of national military strength or from brandishing those weapons in crises. Indeed, through the proper management of the nuclear arsenal, nuclear weapons provided tremendous military benefit to the republic, Eisenhower concluded.

Eisenhower believed that the struggle with the Soviet Union mandated that the United States display enough military strength so as not to tempt the communists with weakness. Soviet imperialism in Eastern Europe at the end of World War II and continued communist subversion throughout the world represented a serious threat to U.S. national security. Because Eisenhower believed that waging the Cold War required a responsible buildup of national strength, his faith in the nuclear weapon to serve that purpose was both realistic and practical. He wanted peace in the long term, but he believed the Soviet Union would never negotiate in good faith unless the United States possessed sufficient national strength and demonstrated the willingness to employ that strength as needed. Sufficient military strength would enable the nation to deter enemy aggression if possible and to win a war if necessary. To project this military strength, Eisenhower emphasized the strategic benefits of nuclear weapons. To him, they were available, reliable, and effective and he understood and cared only that nuclear weapons worked well for this purpose. Moreover, Eisenhower committed to build military strength through nuclear weapons and he cared little about which weapons provided the nation that strength. Though he understood the distinction between fission and fusion, between atomic bombs such as those used on Japan in 1945 and thermonuclear weapons, the president's decision to utilize them both for military strength meant that, at least from Eisenhower's perspective, all nuclear weapons were the same. Despite that Eisenhower often indicated trepidation about nuclear war, he refused to describe nuclear weapons as unusable and instead sought every military advantage the nuclear weapon provided. For this reason, he chose first tactical atomic war and later thermonuclear deterrence as the centerpieces of American grand strategy.

a. Simply Another Weapon

In the first military crisis of his administration Eisenhower resolved to end the stalemated Korean War on terms agreeable to the war-weary citizens of the United States. He pursued diplomacy and negotiations, but those had stalled and he had few military alternatives beyond what Truman had already tried. Eisenhower's trump card was the atomic weapon which both the U.S. and the Soviets possessed, but which the Chinese and the North Koreans did not. Truman had ultimately chosen not to use the atomic bomb in Korea, and Eisenhower believed the president had missed an opportunity.

As early as 30 June 1950, while still at Columbia, Eisenhower thought the United States should respond more decisively to acts of communist aggression. "In a fight," Eisenhower believed, "we (our side) can never be *too strong*. We must study every angle to be prepared for *whatever* may happen – even if it finally comes to use of A-bomb (which God forbid.)"[1] After becoming president, Eisenhower, as promised, travelled to South Korea where he saw a stalemated war. Although United States and United Nations forces had recaptured Seoul in May 1951 they had been unable to push North Korean and Chinese forces much further north. "There were no major military movements," Eisenhower later remembered, "but for many months more the war was to grind out painful lists of casualties without significant changes in situation or disposition."[2]

Eisenhower refused to accept the stalemate, but saw only a few options. To stay the course was unacceptable and to seek "an all-out military victory by conventional means" was "the least attractive of all plans." He considered various alternatives to get the communists "to accede to an armistice in a reasonable time" and concluded that his best strategy was a show of strength and possibly a major offensive to achieve the desired ends. This offensive involved an expansion of the war beyond Korea into China, including air strikes against Chinese airfields and a blockade of the Chinese coast, a significant buildup of American and South Korean forces, and "finally, to keep the attack from becoming overly costly, it was clear that we would have to use atomic weapons."[3] Eisenhower did not take lightly the use of atomic weapons, nor did he strike a "cavalier pose toward nuclear weapons," as one historian has suggested.[4]

Rather, Eisenhower first pursued a subtle and gradual escalation of the atomic dialogue. He understood that when talking about the deployment and use of atomic weapons, one must be quite careful.[5] "He was very restrained, especially publicly, in any talk about weapons or military action," Andrew Goodpaster remembered.[6] Sherman Adams also considered Eisenhower a man of deliberation, one who would occasionally hesitate if the situation allowed and if this approach served his interests. Eisenhower believed that the Soviet Union and China properly understood American national strength, but he also thought that a diplomatic and military strategy of projecting that strength was needed to convince those enemies to resolve the stalemated war on the Korean peninsula. Eisenhower decided to use some form of diplomacy which included atomic deterrence if possible and military action through tactical atomic war if needed to bring the war to an end.

Eisenhower's understanding of tactical atomic war was framed by his study of Carl von Clausewitz, the famed Prussian military theorist whose seminal work, *On War*, was standard reading for West Point cadets, Command and General Staff College students, and aides of General Fox Conner. As executive officer to General Fox Conner at Camp Gaillard in Panama, Eisenhower had waded through what one observer called "an intellectual proving ground" during which he read *On War* at least three times.[7] He later recalled his time in Panama as "a sort of graduate school in military affairs."[8] After the Bible, he claimed *On War* had the greatest effect on his life.[9] As president,

Marines Participate in A-Bomb Tests, 22 March 1955 (National Archives)

however, Eisenhower could not always apply the lessons from his training in military history because much of them dealt too specifically with tactical battlefield decisions under specific circumstances in past conflicts. Eisenhower relied on his understanding of Clausewitz to clarify the main issues of the Korean War. On Korea, Eisenhower told a reporter in March 1953, "I would refer you to Clausewitz. He knew even 150 years ago that there were various kinds of wars, and some partake of little more than police action, others get to be great conflagrations. So far as I am concerned, it is a war."[10]

Clausewitz's themes on the nature and purpose of war shaped Eisenhower's understanding of tactical atomic war in the days before deliverable thermonuclear bombs. Key among Clausewitz's ideas was the way in which he connected war and politics. He argued that war was an extension of politics and that a nation-state waged war out of desire to achieve a specific political objective relative to the enemy. That political objective could vary widely within any particular scenario, but the root of the war remained the same: a political goal attainable only through the exercise of decisive force against a hostile or uncooperative power. No doubt Eisenhower understood this most basic principle and his belief in the need for decisive force to achieve the desired objective shaped his view of tactical nuclear war. Eisenhower did not fret too much over the specific type of military force required in the pursuit of the objective, but rather he insisted only that the force be decisive. All other factors aside, when the state decided to enter a military conflict no effort must be spared. If the cause was worth violence, then it was worth any amount of necessary violence to achieve the political goal. To Eisenhower this seemed an average solution.

Eisenhower often sought a middle of the road or average solution which to him meant to avoid the extremes, to reject a best-and-worst-case-scenario analysis, and to use common sense in war and peace. "The nature of the war itself had to be clearly understood," Eisenhower believed, "if we were to attack intelligently the problem of bringing it to an honorable end."[11] "The struggle is to apply common sense," Eisenhower wrote to a friend in July 1953, "to reach an average solution."[12] In seeking average answers to problems, political or otherwise, Eisenhower often fell back on historical or philosophical maxims. In the case of Korea, for example, Eisenhower applied Napoleon Bonaparte's interpretation of individual genius. Napoleon believed that in times of war, when everyone around was panicking, to find the average solution, calmly and resolutely, made a man a genius. He believed that the average approach to the Korean problem was to consider all options in search of an armistice and peace.

Eisenhower also believed that atomic weapons should "be treated like other weapons and that the taboo on the use of atomic weapons be abolished."[13] He planned to make few if any distinctions between atomic and conventional armaments; to do otherwise splintered unnecessarily U.S. military strength into usable and unusable weapons, effectively weakening the country overall. Eisenhower's first advisor for atomic policy, Lewis Strauss, wrote that the president expressed exactly that sentiment to British Prime Minister Winston Churchill in Bermuda. "The President touched upon his belief that

Atomic Cannon Test, Frenchman's Flat, Nevada, 23 May 1953 (National Archives)

atomic weapons were now coming to be regarded as a proper part of conventional armament," Strauss wrote.[14] "Tactical atomic weapons," Eisenhower later confirmed to his national security team, "have come to be practically accepted as integral parts of modern armed forces."[15] By May 1953, Eisenhower considered the fission bomb "as simply another weapon in our arsenal."[16]

Eisenhower believed that the average solution to the Korean conflict meant taking all necessary steps to force enemy capitulation to U.S. demands. Through his Secretary of State John Foster Dulles, Eisenhower hinted that the United States might expand the war with atomic weapons but stopped short of threatening or guaranteeing military action. In late spring 1953, while on a diplomatic mission in South Asia, Dulles conveyed to Indian Prime Minister Nehru that should the stalemate continue with no new negotiations or should the enemy launch an offensive, the United States would employ its full arsenal of weapons in order to bring the war to a conclusion. Of course, Dulles' message was not so clear. "In India and in the Formosa Straits area, and at the truce negotiations at Panmunjom, we dropped the word, discreetly, of our intention," Eisenhower later explained. "We felt quite sure it would reach Soviet and Chinese Communist ears," he continued.[17] The U.S. ambassador to India, Chester Bowles, remembered a vague, but clear threat of atomic war. Unless an agreement was soon reached, "the grim logic of the situation would finally compel the United States to seek to win by new offensives." "In other words, if the Communists continued to defeat all efforts to secure an armistice," Bowles wrote, "we would not deliberately launch World War III, but we would continue to expand the Korean War until we had won it."[18] This was classic Eisenhower.

Though Eisenhower decided perhaps early on that he would use atomic weapons in Korea, he saw no benefit at the start of his administration in clearly displaying his true intentions to the enemy. Indeed, General Andrew Goodpaster, Eisenhower's friend and aide, remembered that "he ultimately never told anybody whether he would or not, not even within the administration." Goodpaster was not sure himself whether Eisenhower had even made a decision on the matter, but he was certain that Eisenhower intended to keep his options open. As Goodpaster noted, Eisenhower wore a poker face within his own administration as well as for his friends and enemies abroad. Indeed, Eisenhower was a formidable bridge and poker player and he often used poker analogies to describe the world of international conflict. Goodpaster believed without equivocation that Eisenhower applied basic lessons learned from games to his decision making process. "He was a great poker player," Goodpaster remembered, "and he did think of things in poker terms." "He put on a mask of ambiguity," he continued, "in the sense that you did not show your hand to the other fellow." "One of the things he always talked about was getting inside the other man's head," Eisenhower's friend remembered.[19]

To continue the analogy, Eisenhower held many more chips than his enemy, in the form of military assets, and intended to force the enemy into a decision either to bet everything he had on a single hand or to fold his hand and stay to play again. Eisenhower projected his readiness and willingness to push all his chips into the pot, and he intended to see what the enemy was willing to risk to win the prize of Korea. This strategy was only available to Eisenhower if the United States operated from a superior military position. He had a significant stockpile of atomic weapons and the means to deliver them. At this opportune moment, when the enemy could not be completely sure just how aggressively Eisenhower intended to play the game, Eisenhower chose to project confidence in the

President-Elect Eisenhower in South Korea, 4 December 1952
(Dwight D. Eisenhower Presidential Library)

strength of his hand to see if the enemy felt as confident in their own. He predicted that the enemy would not call his bluff, but if they did, he was prepared to employ his atomic arsenal as the most obvious, practical, and decisive step toward achieving the overall goal of the ending the conflict. "If you're ever found making a bluff that you're not prepared to follow up," Eisenhower continued, "then your word will be worthless in the future."[20] If the enemy called his bluff and the president wavered or faltered, the enemy would win the hand over the president's bluff and would never again respect Eisenhower's words or his show of strength. Accordingly, Eisenhower needed to display enough military strength to convince the enemy to reexamine his strategic goals. He also needed to be prepared to back it up.

Eisenhower believed that this projection of strength could bring a successful conclusion to the war. In technical terms, convincing the enemy that atomic bombs might soon be employed did not create deterrence, for the hostilities had already begun. Instead, Eisenhower tried to make known America's willingness to use all measures to end the war. "We could not go on the way we were indefinitely," Eisenhower routinely reminded his advisors, and he hoped to make that point equally clear to the Soviet Union, China, and North Korea.[21] To this end, he underscored the importance of "deliberately impressing our enemies that these weapons were now conventional usage in our armed services."[22] He hoped "to handle the matter in such a way as, on the one hand, to impress the enemy with our determination, without, on the other hand, unduly alarming our allies or our own people."[23]

Through the spring of 1953, Eisenhower increased the pressure on America's enemies on the Korean peninsula to bring the war to an end. He ordered a strategic redeployment of the naval forces which, since 1950, had been stationed in the Straits of Formosa to guard against attack by the People's Republic of China or Taiwan against the other. That is, he ordered the navy out of the straits where they had patrolled for three years. "This has meant, in effect," Eisenhower remarked, "that the United States Navy was required to serve as a defensive arm of Communist China." The Chinese had attacked South Korean forces in Korea, engaged in a war with the United Nations, and refused to negotiate in good faith for peace on the Korean peninsula. Eisenhower withdrew the fleet accordingly and suggested at minimum that the U.S. would no longer shield the People's Republic of China from the Chinese nationalists on Taiwan. "This order implies no aggressive intent on our part," Eisenhower told those listening, "but we certainly have no obligation to protect a nation fighting us in Korea."[24] Eisenhower later said that this "put the Chinese Communists on notice that the days of stalemate were numbered; that the Korean War would either end or extend beyond Korea."[25] If "military advantage dictated such use," he concluded, the United States planned to employ American firepower to her best advantage in current and future Cold War contests.[26] His warning was neither unnecessarily inflammatory nor confrontational, but muted and matter of fact. At that point in 1953, Eisenhower did not fear that the limited use of tactical weapons would necessarily lead to a general war, or a large-scale exchange of conventional, atomic, and thermonuclear weapons between the United States and the Soviet Union. The American thermonuclear weapon was still primitive; the first deliverable thermonuclear bomb would not be tested by the United States until more than a year later, on 1 March 1954 in the Castle test series in the Pacific Ocean. With only fission devices available, Eisenhower believed that a tactical atomic war could be fought and won. His allies were not so sure.

British Prime Minister Winston Churchill had his doubts about the desirability of tactical atomic war. In late winter of 1953, Churchill sought a guarantee from Eisenhower that the British would be consulted in advance of the United States' decision to employ atomic weapons. Churchill feared mostly for his own civilian population, not for those of South Korea or North Korea. He later argued that "one good nuclear bombing" could destroy his "small crowded island" and this catastrophe might very well be provoked by the introduction of atomic bombs on the battlefield in Korea.[27] He even went so far as to argue that an atomic bombing of North Korea and China by the U.S. would be the beginning of the end. "There will be nothing left but to take a pill and end it all," Churchill remarked.[28]

Eisenhower sympathized with the British position because of "the exposed position of Britain in the event of general war" but interpreted Churchill's request for consultation as a request to allow the British to prohibit the use of atomic weapons in Korea by the United States. Eisenhower "declined to give such a commitment" on the use of tactical atomic weapons. He promised to "take every possible step to consult with Britain," but he stopped short of the making the commitment Churchill desired.[29] At an earlier National Security Council meeting in 1953, Eisenhower had already "ruled against any discussion without allies of military plans or weapons of attack."[30] Eisenhower would not ignore his friends but neither would he compromise the integrity of his atomic striking force by providing others with a veto on his authority to employ all force necessary to protect U.S. national security. He would not sacrifice the atomic pillar of U.S. military strength for the sake of allies who had not committed any significant conventional forces to the battlefield. "I earnestly assured Winston that I had no intention of acting rashly," Eisenhower wrote, "saying that I merely wanted our friends to know that past limitations on our actions, in the event of a heavy attack on us, would not necessarily be observed."[31]

At the same time, Eisenhower doubted that Churchill's suicide scenario would come to pass because the North Koreans and the Chinese would not be willing to accept an escalation of violence. He thought that the communists in Asia believed their invasion of South Korea would be swift and successful. "It is quite probable that the Communists expected, when they made their attack, a cheap and easy victory," Eisenhower later wrote, "believing that neither the United States nor any other Western power would assume the risk of general war in order to defend that newly independent country." The communists had miscalculated, Eisenhower believed. So far under Truman, the United States had not committed to use the force necessary to win in part because the use of atomic force risked the outbreak of a wider atomic war between the superpowers.[32] Eisenhower did not share this view or this specific fear. "The tactical use of atomic weapons against military targets," Eisenhower told his Joint Chiefs of Staff later, "would be no more likely to trigger off a big war than the use of twenty-ton 'block-busters.'"[33] Violence was violence, Eisenhower reasoned, and atomic bombs held only as much chance of igniting

John Foster Dulles, Winston Churchill, Dwight Eisenhower, and Anthony Eden, 25 June 1954 (Dwight D. Eisenhower Presidential Library)

a larger war as did the large conventional bombs the United States currently employed in combat.

Furthermore, Eisenhower explained to Churchill that the timing and nature of the American tactical atomic response to renewed war in Korea likely precluded a Soviet nuclear response. What Eisenhower initially planned was "not the bombing of Chungking or Peking but the pursuit of attacking aircraft to their bases and the destruction of enemy supplies and troop concentrations."[34] Because Eisenhower would limit his response to tactical and not strategic targets, the Soviets would have little cause for a major retaliation against the United States and her allies. He anticipated instead that the Soviets might respond to attacks with tactical strikes of their own against "the almost defenseless population centers of Japan" from which U.S. attacks would likely originate. This scenario, rather than the Churchill's doomsday version, seemed more likely, but not quite as terrifying to Eisenhower. Though it weighed on his mind, the Soviet retaliatory threat did not impact his conclusion that the United States would expand the war if necessary.[35] He was not immune to Churchill's concerns, but he had other priorities beyond the view of his allies.

Eisenhower anticipated that some in the world would object to the use of tactical atomic weapons. "The use of even small atomic bombs," he later wrote, "could scarcely fail to result, for a while, in a worldwide feeling of revulsion against the United States." But the sentiment "might be lessened if these relatively small weapons were used solely against military installations, minimizing fallout and civilian casualties."[36] Still, he seemed frustrated with those who questioned the idea of tactical atomic war in Korea. "If they objected to the use of atomic weapons," Eisenhower told his National Security Council, "we might well ask them to supply three or more divisions needed to drive the Communists back, in lieu of use of atomic weapons."[37] Tactical atomic weapons could end the war, and, "if people raised hell when they contemplated these results the thing to do would be to ask them to volunteer for front-line action in a continued Korean war."[38]

Even so, Eisenhower was not completely convinced of the tactical value of the atomic bomb in a ground campaign. "My own idea is that if this hellish contrivance is really effective against ships," Eisenhower had quipped in 1946, "it will be from some type of under water use rather than from air bursts."[39] Later in his deliberations over Korea, he even doubted whether atomic weapons would destroy concrete pillboxes or crater runways sufficiently. Unsure, Eisenhower nonetheless had specific suggestions about the uses of tactical atomic weapons in the Korean conflict. Less than a month after his inauguration, he suggested the Kae-song area as "a good target for this type of weapon" though he did not specify precisely why.[40] He asked his military advisers "as to whether or not a test had been made at Bikini as to the effectiveness of a penetration type of atomic weapons." Though his advisors disagreed, Eisenhower held fast to the idea that atomic weapons would be effective "against the dugouts which honeycombed the hills along which the enemy forces were presently deployed."[41] General Lawton Collins, Chief of Staff of the Army, suggested that atomic weapons could be used in a more direct manner. Mustard gas could drive "the enemy out of his caves and tunnels" and then "these troops would be effective targets for our tactical atomic weapons."[42] Eisenhower accepted that "to drive the Communists back" without the atomic weapon might require "three or more divisions."[43] This was an undesirable alternative because of the inevitable cost in lives and treasure. Atomic weapons could do the job better, cheaper, and without spawning a larger war, he ultimately concluded.[44]

Eisenhower began making clear publicly the United States' willingness to use whatever military strength available to end the Korean War. Eisenhower's veiled threat reached the enemy, and the combatants signed an armistice in the summer of 1953. Though historians do not always agree, Eisenhower himself appeared never to doubt that the likelihood of facing an atomic attack by air helped to convince the enemy to sign and honor an armistice.[45] Eisenhower expressed gratefulness that the United States possessed an atomic arsenal which he believed to be capable of deterring the enemy from aggressive action and suitable for use in a limited war. The use of atomic weapons was nothing unusual or overly dramatic to Eisenhower, but rather a singular act of warfare necessary in the Cold War. Eisenhower made the end of the Korean War a priority but refused to exaggerate the use of atomic weapons. For a man fond of the sayings of Shakespeare, Eisenhower must have believed that using atomic weapons against enemy troops in Korea was much ado about nothing.

Robert Divine has argued that no one knew for certain, then or now, whether Eisenhower planned to use atomic weapons in Korea. This, he argued, was the genius of the man.[46] There was nothing mysterious about him, however. The president's public hints about the use of atomic weapons in the Korean War were sincere, and, though he hoped to avoid it, he was poised to use atomic weapons in that conflict. All the evidence suggests that Eisenhower planned to use atomic weapons. On 20 June 1953, he approved the transfer of complete atomic weapons to the military for distribution to military bases on land and at sea.[47] He consulted his advisors and his allies about the possible consequences of an atomic strike, and through John Foster Dulles he issued a warning to the enemy. The only evidence to support the idea that Eisenhower would not use atomic weapons was that in fact he did not.

Eisenhower stressed the utility of the atomic weapon as a pillar of American military strength. He emphasized the value of atomic weapons as both a satisfactory counterbalance to the communist conventional forces and as a viable option for tactical warfare. For Eisenhower, America's atomic arsenal had become a central element of U.S. military strength and in projecting that strength he needed to demonstrate a willingness to use atomic weapons to achieve U.S. goals. Not to use all those tools at his disposal to bring the Korean War to an end, Eisenhower believed, was nonsensical, irresponsible, and dangerous. Accordingly, he sought to project military strength to force an armistice, and, if that failed, to employ American military strength in defeating the enemy in Korea. The increasing progress on thermonuclear weapons both in the United States and behind the Iron Curtain, however, threatened to alter fundamentally the way wars would be fought. Eisenhower understood fission weapons as simply a new version of the old, and it only made sense to use them when necessary. But as Eisenhower came to understand the new thermonuclear weapons, he saw that the wars of which Clausewitz wrote and in which Eisenhower was steeped might soon be a thing of the past.

b. On Thermonuclear War

Eisenhower's understanding of the origins of World War II convinced him that military strength discouraged enemy aggression.[48] The early days of the Cold War confirmed that belief. Still, Truman refused to order the most formidable piece of American military strength, the atomic weapon, into action to defend the free world.[49] As president, Eisenhower undertook a buildup of American military strength through atomic weapons which took final form in the New Look. As previously argued, the New Look was intended first to allow for fiscal discipline and economic strength through an increased reliance on atomic weapons as cheaper, better alternatives to a vast conventional force. The successful test of a deliverable thermonuclear weapon in March 1954 required a strategy for incorporating megatons of explosive power, not merely kilotons, into the American national security plan.

Eisenhower ultimately opted for a policy that was often called massive retaliation. This doctrine stipulated that the United States would retaliate instantly and decisively against communist aggression anywhere in the world at any time. Implementing the massive retaliation doctrine suggested an end to long-term and expensive commitments of conventional armies in faraway lands such as Korea. In addition, the plan for massive retaliation offered to the Soviet Union a warning that the Cold War would not be fought under conditions set by the Soviet Union. Eisenhower intended to retake the initiative from the enemy and to determine the circumstances under which the United States would wage the Cold War in the future. In this way, Eisenhower emphasized massive retaliation as a means to project U.S. military strength and thereby either deter or win the next war.

Operation Ivy Mike was the world's first test of hydrogen bomb by the United States on 1 November 1952, just three days before the election of Dwight Eisenhower as President of the United States. (National Archives)

The formal announcement of the transition to massive retaliation as a strategy came from John Foster Dulles in a speech to the Council on Foreign Relations on 12 January 1954. In his speech, Dulles explained that the Soviet Union had built a Cold War strategy premised on America's inability to meet Soviet moves in many areas of the world at once. According to communist theory, the United States lacked the strength to meet Soviet threats without succumbing to national bankruptcy. Soviet strategy, according to Dulles, aimed at subversion in multiple vulnerable areas at once, overextending the capitalists, and then striking the decisive blow. As Dulles observed and the National Security Council later articulated, "the way to deter aggression is for the free community to be willing and able to respond vigorously at places and with means of its own choosing." To those allies who might fall victim to "the mighty land power of the Communist world" the United States promised the support of her "massive retaliatory power."

This strategy provided several benefits for American national security. First, the enemy would no longer be able to determine the timing and location of potential conflicts because the United States intended to deter Soviet advances with the threat of massive retaliation.[50] Second, the policy allowed the United States to meet any aggression effectively at a sustainable cost. With a $50 billion national security budget and a total deficit of $20 billion for fiscal years 1953 and 1954, Eisenhower had landed on a policy which afforded the United States the ability first to deter and then to counter communist aggression in many places over the long term. For Eisenhower, a buildup of nuclear

President Eisenhower and Secretary of State Dulles, 14 August 1956 (Dwight D. Eisenhower Presidential Library)

weapons coupled with effective management of those weapons properly prepared the American economy and the military for the long-term struggle with the Soviets.[51]

While formulating this policy, Eisenhower came to two separate but equally important conclusions. First, Eisenhower did not believe that peace was possible with the Soviet Union. He believed that Soviet leaders were inherently deceitful and, at least in 1954, he doubted that the Soviets would uphold their end of any diplomatic bargain struck between the superpowers. Second, Eisenhower concluded that general war between the United States and the Soviet Union with thermonuclear weapons was unlikely. He accepted as policy that the United States would never strike first with nuclear weapons, and he concluded then that the only danger of general thermonuclear war with the Soviet Union was through communist aggression. Regardless of the circumstances, Soviet leadership acted only out of consideration for their selfish and imperialistic concerns, Eisenhower believed. NSC 162/2 reflected his belief: "Present estimates are . . . that the USSR will not deliberately initiate general war during the next several years, although general war might result from miscalculation."[52] Through Eisenhower's first term, neither atomic war nor thermonuclear war would have benefited the Soviet Union, so they refrained from risking or conducting either.

If the Soviet leaders would not negotiate in good faith to solve Cold War problems and if they did not plan to strike first, the United States would be in for a long struggle. In that long struggle, the United States needed strength to defend the nation's interests and those of her allies. Accordingly, in the months after the end of the Korean War, Eisenhower adopted a policy of massive retaliation and intended his thermonuclear arsenal to serve one grand strategic goal: deterrence. Eisenhower believed a policy of massive retaliation would take away any remaining Soviet inclination to launch a surprise nuclear attack. He believed that the more destructive a weapon becomes, "the more value you place on the element of surprise in war." At Pearl Harbor, the United States was surprised by an enemy attack. Now, the president reasoned, the next Pearl Harbor-style attack might be carried out with atomic and thermonuclear weapons: "then you will see something of what the element of surprise has come to be." The only defense against the surprise nuclear attack was "a strong retaliatory power" designed to prevent that attack from ever happening, the president concluded.[53] Whereas limited war with tactical atomic weapons might be possible and desirable in the future, the goal of deterring major Soviet aggression through a rigid strategic policy seemed the only responsible choice for the republic. This was especially true because the nation's ability to wage war was inherently compromised by the very principles of the republic, including separation of powers, civilian control over the military, and checks and balances upon the three branches of government.

The Korean conflict confirmed for Eisenhower that the Soviet Union and China intended to use force to achieve their imperialistic goals in Asia and elsewhere. But the Korean conflict also demonstrated to Eisenhower that, in the atomic age, any conflict always possessed the potential to change quickly from a conventional war to a nuclear one. This had certainly been the case on the Korean peninsula where the stalemate had convinced Eisenhower that decisive force was needed to end the war and the nation's atomic arsenal could provide that force. He understood that the use of American atomic weapons would have likely resulted in retaliatory use of similar weapons by the Soviet

Union. But that was before a deliverable thermonuclear bomb with a yield more than a thousand times those of the original atomic bomb.

Eisenhower and Secretary of State Dulles routinely disagreed over whether massive retaliation was a suitable long-term strategic posture. The pair diverged mostly over the dramatic and catastrophic consequences of a policy of massive retaliation and the nature of modern war.[54] In particular, Eisenhower doubted whether war with thermonuclear weapons was even war at all. The president relied on his understanding of Clausewitz to grasp the essentials of modern warfare, noting its tendency to become absolute. As James King noted in 1957, no combatant would settle for defeat in any conflict if they still had weapons available to use. Eisenhower similarly concluded that any limited war would quickly escalate as one side inevitably faced defeat. Limited war would quickly become general war and general war with thermonuclear weapons effectively nullified the Clausewitzian notion of war to serve political ends. No political objective could be served by thermonuclear war as neither combatant nation would survive the conflict in any form that would resemble its prewar state; no political objective could thus be won. In the hopes of deterring war altogether, Eisenhower accepted this risk in adopting massive retaliation.[55] By contrast, Dulles believed limited war remained possible and indeed desirable to avoid the gradual chipping away of democracy and freedom by communists who would exploit every weak point to their own advantage. For Dulles, massive retaliation offered too little flexibility to meet these types of small, limited threats. But Eisenhower was convinced that the threat of atomic war and then thermonuclear war provided the greatest deterrent to Soviet aggression.

For his part, Eisenhower thought much about thermonuclear war, and he concluded that any nuclear conflict would be a long and costly affair. He disagreed sharply with many of his military planners who believed that a thermonuclear war would involve only an initial destructive exchange of weapons lasting from three days to a few weeks. After that, the war would end and reconstruction would begin, they argued. Eisenhower believed that nuclear war would likely last up to four years. "Those who argued that a future thermonuclear war would be won or lost in a period of thirty days were crazy," Eisenhower quipped.[56] "The notion that such a war would last for only thirty to sixty days was just about as specious as the idea of a race between himself and Secretary Humphrey to the moon," Eisenhower joked.[57] "The war wasn't going to be over in a couple of days," Eisenhower cautioned his staff in January 1954, "the continuous war effort that followed the initial strike was of great importance also."[58]

After the initial exchange of thermonuclear weapons, Eisenhower anticipated that the conflict would evolve into a conventional war similar to World War II. In fact, he cited the first two world wars as evidence of a prolonged conflict. In those conflicts, combatants believed that the enemy could not afford, economically or physically, to fight a sustained conflict. That presumption proved false in those cases as it would in any future thermonuclear war.[59] Eisenhower believed that the initial nuclear exchange perhaps lasting as long as week would be followed months and years of sustained conventional military conflict between what remained of the combatant nations. In the first strike and subsequent retaliatory strikes, enemy missiles and bombs would focus redundantly on the most valuable targets assuming that at least some of those bombs would miss the mark. The thinking was that it was better to guarantee complete destruction of those targets than to waste weapons on smaller, relatively unimportant targets. As a result, communities of all sizes without significant industrial, military, or political centers would be left in relatively good condition and in position to wage the second part of the general war.

Those less valuable targets would escape direct nuclear annihilation because of the nature of thermonuclear war, Eisenhower concluded. He knew that the enemy's first strike would be his only sizable strike. The surety of the enemy's counterattack meant that if any weapons were not initially used by the aggressor then those bombs or missiles would be left vulnerable to the immediate and inevitable enemy response. Not to use those weapons at the outset meant the nation might not be able to use them at all. Therefore, the logic of thermonuclear war held that the first strike would be massive, complete, and aimed at total victory. At the same time, Eisenhower knew that at the first sign of an enemy bomber or missile attack the United States would instantly launch its own massive retaliatory strike. "If we really get into a war we should get off our striking power as quickly as possible," he said in 1959.[60] In the unlikely event the United States ever struck first, he extrapolated, the enemy would also respond with a massive counterattack. The nature of this early conflict meant that the outbreak of nuclear war would witness a rapid and complete spasm of attacks. The enemy's initial strike would target the most strategic sites available including the United States' own nuclear stockpile because the enemy would understand that the inevitable American response meant that he would have very little or no capacity for a second strike. The nuclear spasm at the onset of war would be as quick as it would be exhaustive. But, according to Eisenhower, neither attack would be decisive because many non-strategic areas would be left intact.

How to plan for this next stage was a question that troubled Eisenhower. To conclude that all human civilization would suffer total destruction after the initial series of thermonuclear strikes meant there was little need for further discussion or planning. In a July 1957 meeting of the National Security Council, for example, Robert Cutler, Assistant to the President for National Security Affair, briefed Eisenhower on "Situation Assumption No. 9," a surprise nuclear attack on the United States which resulted in 50 million casualties. Just after Cutler began, Eisenhower interrupted, asking "why he felt it was necessary to go any further, since by this time we would all be dead." The room broke out in laughter. In his serious moments, Eisenhower struggled with the difficulty of how his administration could plan for a thermonuclear war.[61] As a military man whose instincts were to plan for war-time eventualities, Eisenhower regretted that "for the period which followed the first exchange, there was virtually nothing that could be realistically planned in advance."[62]

Eisenhower insightfully recognized that all recent planning for general war often ignored a glaring contradiction. All planning, including those estimates which supposed an attack resulting in tens of millions of casualties, accepted that the United States would emerge in a poor position from which to rebuild. In a number of NSC meetings, he "asserted many times that if we assumed too much damage there would be little point in planning, since everything would be ashes."[63] How could the United States possibly survive this catastrophe, and, if no possibility existed, why initiate a whole line of questions and answers for this eventuality? Planning for a worst-case attack scenario held no practical value for Eisenhower. A massive and catastrophic attack complete with "ultimate damage" promised to leave so much destruction that the nation might not be able to recover. "We ought, rather, to plan on the basis of a situation from which we could emerge in time," Eisenhower insisted.[64]

Eisenhower's long military career had taught him the value not of plans themselves but of the planning process. To his advisors and others he would often repeat an old saying which held that "plans are worthless but planning is absolutely invaluable."[65] Eisenhower believed that military engagements rarely develop as anticipated and so the best laid plans often became obsolete after the first unanticipated development. The act of planning, however, produced expert knowledge of the enemy's force, the terrain, and other logistical factors, which allowed for fluid and successful battlefield adaptation. In this way, planning proved far more useful than plans. For a general thermonuclear war, however, neither plans nor planning had great value. No amount of contingency planning could improve a combatant's situation once the war had begun and no nation could win a general war given the numbers of casualties estimated by many within the administration. If a nuclear war began, no change in tactics, operations, or strategy would negate the simple reality that the nation faced certain, massive destruction from the enemy's nuclear strike. In the slim hope of surviving this damage and living to fight another day, national leaders needed to launch as many of their own weapons against the enemy before those same weapons were all destroyed by the incoming attack. To do otherwise guaranteed both terrible destruction and utter defeat. This paradox bothered Eisenhower. All of his military training and experience in a sense had been voided because the thermonuclear weapon invalidated the basic nature of Clausewitz's type of war. General thermonuclear war exposed the uselessness of plans and planning, removed the political goal of a military conflict, and negated the concept of military victory with which Eisenhower was so familiar.

Accordingly, Eisenhower advocated as much thoughtful and realistic planning for a nuclear exchange as possible. He commissioned studies to ascertain how much destruction the nation might suffer from a thermonuclear strike. From those studies, he came to learn that in the event of general war the physical destruction would be enormous. But he was not prepared to accept even the most erudite estimates of casualties and destruction. Not until the end of his presidency after the U-2 spy flights provided a more accurate glimpse of Soviet capability could the United States better estimate the destruction to be expected from a Soviet first strike. Meanwhile, through most of Eisenhower's two terms, estimates came in from a variety of sources on the damage to be expected from nuclear war. In most cases, official government studies of nuclear war which Eisenhower saw in one form or another predicted casualties between 25 and 50 million Americans. Out of population of around 160 million, between fifteen and thirty percent of Americans would be killed or injured in a nuclear exchange, studies suggested.

For example, in March 1956, the National Security Council requested a formal study of the social and psychological effects of nuclear war upon human beings. The study was completed in November and titled "The Human Effects of Nuclear Weapons Development." Dr. Frank Fremont-Smith chaired the panel which wrote study. The result was a grim summary of the effects of a nuclear attack on the United States that anticipated casualties of around fifty million. These heavy casualties, the panel explained, would undermine public support for the government and might result in the disintegration of the national government. This scenario might be avoided, the committee advised, if the public was prepared emotionally and psychologically for the tremendous destruction and death that would assuredly result from nuclear war. A program of "involvement" might very well increase national unity in the event of war, but only if the proper steps were taken in advance. The panel recommended solutions aimed at producing a better informed public which would be less likely to suffer paralyzing grief during and after an attack. A magnificent effort of public information and preparedness had to be made by the government to avoid an apocalypse.[66]

Eisenhower's reaction to this report was measured. With no degree of overstatement, he remarked that the report correctly concentrated on "the most serious problem which had ever faced the world." He told the National Security Council that he "was searching desperately to find the best thing for us to do at the present time in order to minimize the terrible results of a nuclear attack on the United States." He was "certain that this could not be achieved by simply ignoring the danger." At the same time he concluded that "this was a terrible kind of problem" which could not be solved "by talking of maintaining six divisions abroad." "It would seem that the only sensible thing for us to do was to put all our resources into our SAC capability and into hydrogen bombs," the president noted. Eisenhower also remarked during the same meeting that the report "emphasizes again the vital need for an effective disarmament program."[67]

Another government-initiated report which likely crossed Eisenhower's desk was titled "Survival of Population Following a Massive Nuclear Exchange" and was surprisingly positive about the ability of the United States to survive and recover from a nuclear attack. A group of scholars assembled through Stanford University produced the report in July 1958 and generally maintained an upbeat tone. This was largely because the study assumed a Soviet nuclear attack which did not target American oil refinery equipment or petroleum storage. Therefore, the committee concluded that the United States would be able to begin the recovery process quickly and successfully because of the availability of petroleum which was necessary for just about everything, including food production and transportation, communication, and industrial and agriculture services.[68] The group noted however that the anticipated Soviet attack would require only minor changes to destroy these petroleum capabilities. The statistics, charts, and general conclusions were far more depressing. They described a nation completely destroyed and in total disarray. Without petroleum, the nation had virtually no chance for beginning the process of successful recovery. Beyond the physical destruction in lives and property, the American way of life would be destroyed as well. "It would literally be a business of digging ourselves out of ashes, starting again," Eisenhower noted.[69]

That same year, the Department of Defense conducted a top secret study which was later published under the title *The Emergency Plans Book*. The study presumed a Soviet nuclear attack primarily from submarine-launched ballistic missiles and intercontinental bombers. Seven days after the initial attack, blast and radiation would have killed or fatally injured 25 million Americans. Another 25 million casualties had the hope of recovery. One in five of all Americans would die, the report concluded. The first priority of the government would be to protect the remaining population from residual radiation. Given the depleted state of health care, the destruction of food sources, and the severe disruptions to monetary, communication, transportation, and power systems, this would be difficult. The economy would suffer from complete paralysis, and government control, especially at the federal level, would be severely compromised. A return to normal seemed unlikely in the near future, if at all.[70]

After reading these kinds of studies, Eisenhower came to believe that "our great fundamental problem will be how to mobilize what is left of 165 million people and win a war."[71] "All of our initial effort would have to be devoted to keeping a government running," he reminded his staff. Where only local governments remained, Eisenhower debated the imposition of martial law, as Abraham Lincoln had done in a time of another great national crisis. After all, the retired general understood, "you could not put Federal troops under the command of a Mayor."[72] Also like Lincoln, Eisenhower agreed with Attorney General Brownell that the government would need to suspend the right of habeas corpus.[73] From government studies such as those of 1958, Eisenhower understood that the federal power would be displaced and ineffective at best or fatally crippled at worst. In any case, the ability of the federal government to continue the war or to begin reconstruction soon after the first thermonuclear exchange would be greatly compromised. Local authorities would have to do the job as the federal government recovered.

Eisenhower also understood that this new governmental reality would not allow for free, representative government, particularly in the days and months immediately following the beginning of nuclear hostilities.[74] Though some of the people might likely survive, the constitutional republic would be compromised by the demands of recovery in a postwar environment. According to Eisenhower, "even assuming that we would emerge from a global war today as the acknowledged victor, there would be a [*sic*] destruction in this country that there could be no possibility of our exercising a representative free government for, I would say, two decades at the minimum."[75] Eisenhower accepted that this kind of national emergency meant temporarily sacrificing the ideals of the American republic in an attempt to preserve and protect the remaining Americans. National chaos would require a dictatorship and government by decree. "We would have to run this country as one big camp," Eisenhower noted, "severely regimented."[76] The government would do its best to preserve free institutions of government, Eisenhower reasoned, but the nation would be "in no position to count on it or plan on it, in view of the catastrophic nature of the third world war if it should come."[77] Americans would be lucky if they survived, Eisenhower remarked, and they would likely have to accept also the loss of personal property rights and significant restrictions on individual freedoms as necessary evils.[78]

Eisenhower further believed that the rehabilitation of the country as described in government plans would be gradual and deliberate, but also that those plans needed to be aimed at winning the war. Severely devastated areas of the nation would be beyond help in the early days. Those areas would have to be neglected temporarily while the most attention would be paid to those areas which were "relatively undamaged." In the heavily damaged areas so few would survive that no amount of immediate action taken towards recovery offered even moderate prospects for success. "We would not be able for a long time," Eisenhower reasoned, "to move into the devastated areas in order to get people into hospitals."[79] At the same time, the destruction of industrial, military, and political centers meant a certain crippling of the nation's hospitals. Only the most remote and isolated hospitals would remain, and those hospitals would be the least prepared to handle the large numbers of seriously wounded people.[80] Neither would stockpiling of national resources such as medical supplies serve the republic after the war. Eisenhower doubted that the United States could stockpile enough materials to satisfy the demands of the postwar environment. Besides, any stockpile of provisions large enough to serve a significant percentage of the population would likely be destroyed in the initial nuclear attack anyway.[81] Eisenhower was convinced that national triage was needed to preserve what was left of the population so as to win what remained of the war.

Still, Eisenhower struggled to plan for the post-war period because he believed that the human mind could not contemplate the devastation of that war. This failure of imagination deeply bothered Eisenhower. All his previous military experience allowed him to consider and to anticipate the worst-case scenario; therefore, he could guard against it. Never before in human history were the stakes so high as in the thermonuclear era, and Eisenhower could not imagine the consequences of a thermonuclear war between the United States and the Soviet Union. No study could accurately anticipate the destruction because there was simply no basis for comparison or analysis. "Our imagination could not encompass the situation which would result from an attack on this country involving the explosion of 2000 megatons," Eisenhower believed.[82] For a man of great optimism, stubborn moderation, and discipline such as Eisenhower, this future was unfathomable. "We are in fact talking about something the results of which are almost impossible to conceive of," he told his staff.[83] Nuclear war would be "so terrible that the human mind cannot comprehend it."[84] Nuclear war would be an "unmitigated disaster" and a "catastrophe."[85] It was "unthinkable."[86] "Casualties of the magnitude being talked about would mean that civilization could not be rebuilt in a century – or even two centuries," Eisenhower predicted.[87] He mused that nuclear war might even bring the end of human civilization.[88]

This failure of imagination paradoxically contributed to Eisenhower's decidedly moderate view of nuclear war. Eisenhower was neither a doomsday prophet nor a simple optimist. His view of a possible nuclear war was above all pragmatic and realistic. He could not afford to assume the worst because any apocalyptic scenario would make his job and that of the American government moot on this important issue. If there was no possibility of recovery from the war, there would be nothing left for Eisenhower to do except, of course, to avoid that final war. This he tried to do but he could not guarantee that the enemy would do the same. Eisenhower anticipated that the targets of a Soviet attack would be industrial, political, and military centers. When he also factored in the short duration of the nuclear exchange, he concluded that about half of the American population would survive the war. This view represented the high end of projected casualties for thermonuclear war, but it was not entirely a pessimistic one. Rather, Eisenhower's view was a middle-of-the-road perspective which allowed both for the worst horrors imaginable and the opportunity to recover and rebuild. One out of two killed or severely injured was not exactly hopeful, but neither did it necessarily mean the end.

Eisenhower held the belief that a future general nuclear war would produce no winners and only losers. According to Andrew Goodpaster, Eisenhower maintained that "nuclear wars are still loseable" or rather that "one side may lose a little more than the other." But the president rarely entertained this "esoteric discussion of winability" and instead argued that everybody involved in the conflict would suffer so much destruction as to be incapable of declaring victory.[89] "We are in the era of the thermonuclear bomb that can obliterate cities and can be delivered across continents," Eisenhower told the Republican National Convention in 1956. "With such weapons, war has become, not just tragic, but preposterous," he continued, "With such weapons, there can be no victory for anyone."[90] With a wealth of military experience, he "now realized that in this atomic age a war could no longer be won because it would bring destruction to both sides."[91] He repeatedly argued that nuclear war would not last thirty to sixty days, but instead would continue until the war had reached some indescribable state of destruction. The only thing likely to spare the United States, the Northern hemisphere, and human civilization from nuclear Armageddon would be the limits of human endurance. "There was obviously a limit – a human limit – to the devastation which human beings could endure," Eisenhower believed.[92] He often asked others informally to study the precise limits of American endurance in the event of nuclear devastation, but the president never received a satisfactory answer.[93]

Eisenhower's understanding of the nature and consequences of nuclear war shaped his thinking on the desirability of blast and fallout shelters for the American public. He was most familiar with blast shelters or bomb shelters such as those used by citizens of allied cities during attacks by German bombers and rockets during World War II. These shelters were no deeper than ordinary basements and were not equipped to sustain human life for more than a few hours or a day at most. American families could dig their own blast shelters at little cost or could convert underground basements into blast shelters without much effort. Blast shelters only needed to provide immediate, short-term protection from nearby explosions and flying shrapnel. Fallout shelters which would be required by potential survivors in a thermonuclear war were more elaborate and more expensive. Fallout shelters required greater physical protection from blast, from radiation, and from fallout. They needed to be built deeper into the earth and required heavy locking outer doors. Most important, they needed to be large enough and comfortable enough to seal multiple people and sufficient provisions inside for a week or longer without resupplying or even opening the door. Eisenhower himself appeared to make no distinction between blast and fallout shelters and seemed to believe the two were the same. Regardless, shelters became the key component of any civil defense measures discussed in Eisenhower's administration

In the spring of 1953 after the Upshot-Knothole nuclear test series, Eisenhower endorsed basic and local civil defense measures to protect American citizens from nuclear blasts and fallout.[94] "The bulk of the responsibility [for civil defense] rests upon the locality and the private citizen," Eisenhower later told Henry Luce, and "unless the private citizen does become interested and has a definite sense of responsibility for himself and family, there is little that government, by itself, can do."[95] "For certain obvious strategic targets – such as New York City, Chicago, or Gary, Indiana," the federal government would augment civil defense measures such as shelters, but local governments bore the primary burden of civil defense.[96] Eisenhower encouraged the federal government to educate the citizenry on the best use of locales already available to them which might provide some protection against blast and fallout. Citizens on the fringe of a potential blast area should take advantage of underground structures, such as basements and cellars, which provided more protection than remaining above ground. These structures served best as blast shelters and offered little protection against fallout. Nevertheless, this was the best and most practical step for citizens lacking a private shelter. It was cheap, easy, convenient, and somewhat effective. Eisenhower also encouraged individual citizens with some disposable income to construct their own shelters.

Fallout Shelter, 1957 (National Archives)

The federal government could offer support for state and individual civil defense efforts, but Eisenhower never wavered from his conclusion that the federal government could not embark upon a massive civil defense program which would have involved primarily the construction of fallout shelters. Specifically, he had three concerns. First, a shelter program sufficient to protect a majority of Americans reached far beyond the responsibility of the federal government. The United States government must not implement a program to protect Americans and their property from the consequences of nuclear war, Eisenhower reasoned, simply because the government did not do so in conventional conflicts. In fact, just the opposite was true: the government did not provide protection for the citizenry in previous wars, but instead the government asked Americans to provide protection for the whole community by putting their sons in the armed forces. The construction of federal shelters strayed in the opposite direction. A federal shelter program took responsibility for defense of the citizens of the republic away from those citizens and placed it solely in the hands of the vast federal bureaucracy.[97]

Second, Eisenhower also feared the larger psychological consequences of building large numbers of shelters and of actually using them. He even worried about the preparations already in progress to provide for all three branches of government, including himself as head of the executive branch, to descend into shelters at the necessary moment. "One trouble with the idea of key officials going into underground structures was the morale problem of the public," Eisenhower remarked.[98] The building of a shelter to provide protection from a possible nuclear war threatened to create "a defensive or pessimistic attitude" which might make it more difficult to convince Americans of the need to maintain proper military posture. Morale must be kept high, despite the likely horrors of war, Eisenhower insisted. He cited the example of an officer whom he had fired when he found the gentleman hiding in a wine cellar in Normandy after the Overlord invasion.[99] Defeatism and pessimism had no place in a nation at war, and shelters might very well contribute to that sentiment. Indeed, the very notion of encouraging individuals to build shelters worried Eisenhower. "If we provide incentives to individual shelter construction, it must be done without hysteria, must be accepted as routine," he noted.[100] The nation balanced on a knife's edge, Eisenhower waxed pragmatic, between "providing some degree of confidence through the medium of a shelter program while at the same time not scaring our citizens to death by too elaborate a program."[101]

The president worried also about the consequences of building his own personal shelter. Eisenhower "had long been undecided as to whether or not it would be a good thing for the president to build such a shelter and thus set an example to other people." He worried that "if he went ahead and built such a shelter, the effect would be to scare other people to death." In an NSC meeting of December 1958, Eisenhower queried Federal Civil Defense Administrator Leo Hoegh about an American citizen who had reportedly built himself "an extremely comfortable, commodious, and safe blast shelter at a cost of only $15,000."[102] Eisenhower wondered how deep the shelter was and how it was so cheap to construct. Eisenhower was intrigued and joked that he could afford a decent shelter only "if he got a good job after he ceased to be President." Of course, he understood that many others could not afford to build this level of protection and inevitably would turn to the federal government for help.[103] He favored all efforts to encourage private construction, but what then for those who can not afford it? Are they to be left on their own in the event of a nuclear war? Underground structures remained an option for those Americans, but Eisenhower seemed to regard that option as insufficient. Eisenhower decided against building his own private shelter during his presidency "for fear of the public hysteria that such might cause."[104]

Nonetheless, he did approve the top-secret construction of massive fallout shelter under the Greenbrier Resort in White Sulphur Springs, West Virginia in 1958. The shelter was located about two-hundred fifty miles from Washington and was accessible by car, train, or plane. The site was situated far enough from Washington to escape a nuclear strike on the capital but close enough to get key government officials inside before the bombs fell. Unknown to the general public until 1992 the bunker could protect all three branches of government from nuclear war and fallout for an extended period of time. Eisenhower understood that some effort had to be made to protect the federal government from the war for purposes of post-war recovery, but that effort also had to be kept secret from the public.

After he left office, Eisenhower revisited the idea of building a fallout shelter. He thought building a fallout shelter as a private citizen might not receive as much as attention from the public as it would have while he was in office.[105] In retirement, Eisenhower seemed to find some humor in either the uselessness of shelters or the impossibility of providing them for all Americans. "But even if I were persuaded that the building of a shelter would be good," Eisenhower told his golfing buddy Freeman Gosden from Augusta, "I would most certainly insist that it would have to be ample to take care of all

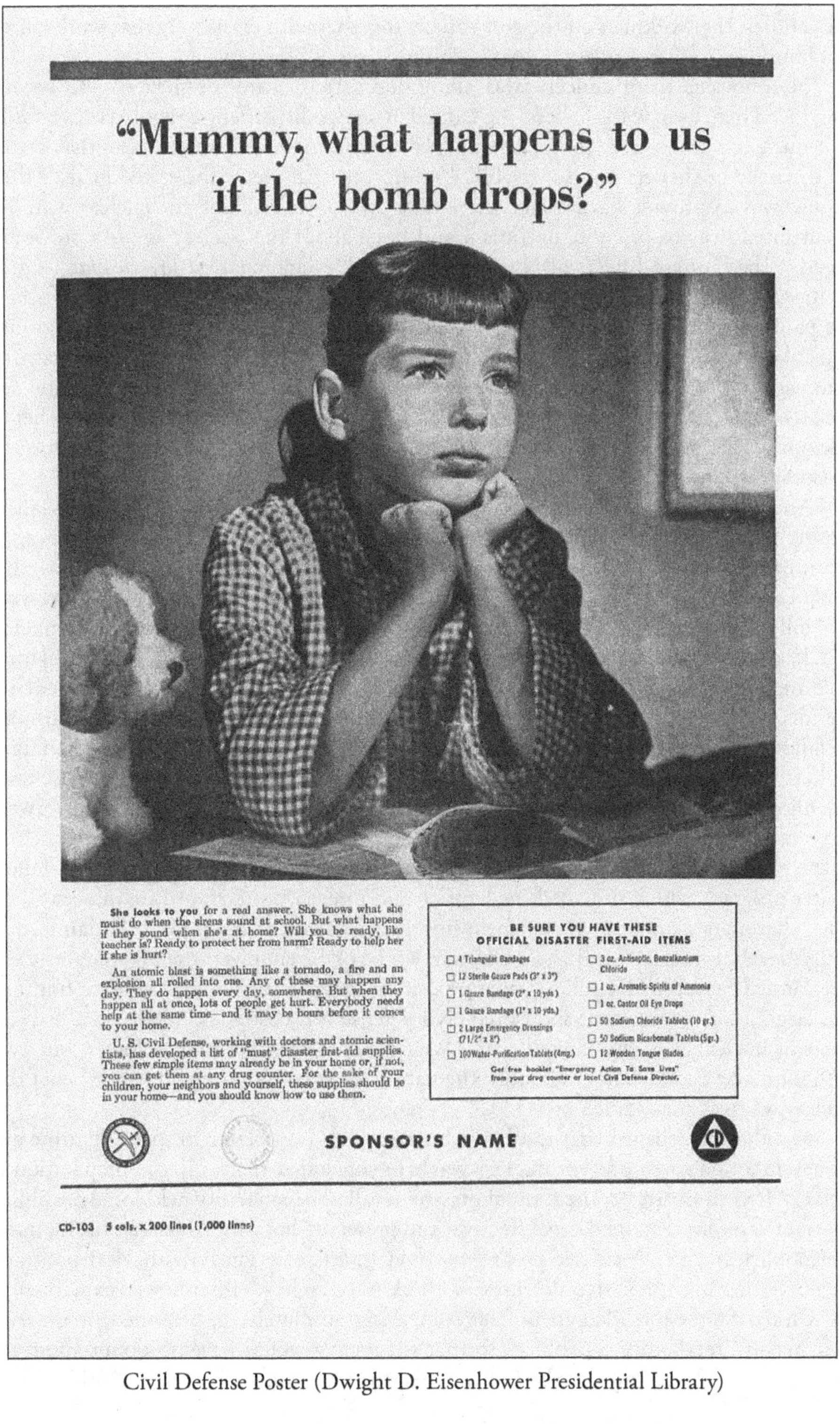

Civil Defense Poster (Dwight D. Eisenhower Presidential Library)

the caddies, the workmen on the golf course, together with everybody that works in the clubhouse, including waitresses, maids, janitors, and all the rest."[106]

Eisenhower's third concern was about the actual utility of shelters. He became convinced that, even with shelters, the United States would suffer tremendous devastation in a nuclear war. A variety of scientific studies commissioned by the executive branch on the issue of shelters and survivability reinforced that view. The stated goal of these studies was to provide hard quantitative data on the survivability of nuclear war. The latent intent was to promote optimism and hope about the nuclear age. As previously noted, "The Human Effects of Nuclear Weapons Development" study, despite its grim theme, proved surprisingly optimistic on the issue of recovery. "We share a firm belief," the panel argued, "that the prospect is not a hopeless one." "Our pioneer background and inheritance predispose us to count hardships as a challenge and fortify us against complacency. We are resourceful people," the panel proclaimed, "inventive no less socially and politically than technologically." American inventiveness and belief in freedom were the "genius of American life," and through this genius, the committee insisted, the United States could survive even the worst nuclear disaster.[107]

Another more influential finding which addressed the issue of shelters was the Gaither report. Titled officially "Deterrence and Survival in the Nuclear Age," the Gaither report recommended that the Eisenhower administration make preparations to strengthen America's continental and civil defenses. Among these improvements was a five-year, $25 billion program for fallout shelters. Eisenhower took issue. In the event of nuclear attack, the president learned, fallout shelters might save 35 percent of the population. "We are talking about the complete destruction of the United States," he concluded. The president thus opposed the Gaither committee's recommendation to build vast numbers of fallout shelters because in any nuclear exchange millions would die and fallout shelters would provide minimal protection for a limited number of people.[108] Echoing Eisenhower's own conclusion, Vice President Nixon argued that the difference between forty million dead Americans and sixty million dead Americans was inconsequential in the grand scheme of the United States.[109] Why divert billions of dollars to a fallout shelter program which provided inadequate and uneven protection, Eisenhower asked, when that money might be better spent improving America's economy and maintaining a high level of nuclear readiness to deter a war? For Eisenhower, the answer was clear. The United States held a solid strategic position, despite the Gaither report's findings, and large-scale, government-sponsored civil defense was costly and ineffective.[110] In the event of nuclear war, the United States would suffer horrific physical losses, but even without major civil defense measures, the nation must remain hopeful in the belief that nuclear war was survivable.

Eisenhower believed that the United States would do better to spend its time and money in an effort to prevent nuclear war. He concluded that only the preparation of active defense measures in the form of massive retaliatory capability held some possibility for deterring war, remained cost-effective, and preserved hope for America's future in the thermonuclear age. "A shelter program would interfere seriously with vital programs for strengthening the active defenses of the United States," Eisenhower explained. If the United States intended to protect something absolutely, he reasoned, it must be "our massive retaliatory capability" so that the enemy would have no doubt about the consequences of war and thus be less inclined to risk a confrontation.[111] Working from this rationale, the president implemented the policy of massive retaliation which built upon the great power of the newest nuclear weapons and allowed him to project military strength to America's enemies. He chose a logical and pragmatic policy of nuclear deterrence. He had confidence the Soviet Union did not seek a general war with the United States, and he pledged that the United States would never launch a first strike. Instead, with some understanding of nuclear war, he placed his faith in the strength of nuclear weapons with the belief that only strength could bring peace.

c. Taking Appropriate Military Action

Following the end of the Korean War and the implementation of the New Look, Eisenhower faced a crisis in Asia in September 1954 when the People's Republic of China (PRC) began shelling two small islands, Quemoy and Matsu. Located in the Taiwan Strait close to the mainland of China, Quemoy and Matsu, like other islands in the vicinity, remained disputed by both parties. Chiang Kai-shek's Nationalist government on Taiwan, then known as Formosa, claimed the two islands as its own and even garrisoned a small number of troops on each island. Mao Zedong and the People's Republic of China continued to insist that Quemoy and Matsu belonged to the PRC and Chiang's occupation of those islands and Taiwan as well was both illegal and temporary. To protect Formosa, the U.S. Navy had occupied for some time the straits to repel a Chinese attack against Taiwan but also to deter a Nationalist attack against the People's Republic. In February 1953, Eisenhower removed the naval blockade which the United States had held in the Taiwan Straits in the days since the beginning of the Korean War. Beijing perceived the removal of the blockade as a signal of America's intent to unleash Chiang and to begin the rollback of communism in Asia. Soon after the blockade's removal, Chiang began moving the first of 75,000 troops to Quemoy and Matsu in preparation for battle. Believing that Chiang Kai-shek was developing closer relations with Washington, Mao ordered the People's Liberation Army to begin began shelling the two islands on 3 September 1954. PLA airplanes also attacked the Tachen islands, another set of disputed territories near the Chinese mainland.

The evidence seemed to support Mao's view that Washington and Taipei were growing closer. Shortly after the shelling began in September 1954, but nine months after John Foster Dulles announced the policy of massive retaliation, the United States helped form the Southeast Asia Treaty Organization (SEATO). Similar to NATO, SEATO intended to resist the spread of communism in Southeast Asia. Mao was convinced that Chiang intended to use those islands as launching points for an invasion of mainland China. Mao believed, moreover, that Chiang would not take this risky action without the permission and backing of the United States. In an effort to deter U.S. interference in what he considered in an internal affair, Mao ordered the shelling. He anticipated that this action would put pressure on both Taipei and Washington and also expose to the world the American plot to interfere directly in the affairs of a sovereign nation, namely the People's Republic of China.[112] In January 1955, Chinese forces seized Yijianshan Island approximately 200 miles north of Taiwan and the Nationalist garrison there was destroyed. Military clashes between China and Taiwan increased in the early part of 1955 including fighting on Quemoy, Matsu, and along the coast of mainland China. To Eisenhower, Chinese communists were becoming increasingly hostile and aggressive.

The Taiwan Straits crisis of 1954-55 was the kind of crisis with which Eisenhower was familiar. The danger of wider war always existed in areas where national interests were at stake and where potential combatants failed to recognize the great risks involved. To Eisenhower, World War II was clearly the product of one man's drive for power, but both World War I and the Korean War came about as a result of miscalculation. In the case of the Great War, Eisenhower understood that "a prince was murdered; there began to be an exchange of notes back and forth; and I believe that there was a miscalculation of what Russia, France, and Britain would do, and that created that war." In Korea the situation was not altogether different but certainly simpler: "I feel that the Korean conflict started because of our failing to make clear that we would defend this small nation, which had just started, in a pinch."[113] Miscalculation by the aggressor nation in these two cases resulted in a larger war than originally intended by the aggressor nation.

In Taiwan, Eisenhower feared another "powder keg" war. "To my mind, the danger of Communists beginning a global shooting war is not too imminent," Eisenhower told a friend in 1952, "at least as long as we are not taking into account the danger of a 'powder keg' war."[114] "Wherever there is any kind of fighting and open violence in the world," Eisenhower told journalist Chalmers Roberts at a press conference, "it is always sort of a powder keg."[115] He believed that even the smallest spark, such as the murder of a prince or misunderstood intentions could ignite a powder keg which would then explode into a greater war. The Taiwan Straits crisis held the potential to create that spark. "As long as actual fighting persists anywhere," Eisenhower said of the Taiwan Straits, "there is always the danger that some hot bullet will hit a powder keg."[116] Given this view, he sought to make clear the United States' intentions regarding Taiwan and the surrounding islands.

Eisenhower was not anxious to get into war and he resisted those who seemed eager to do so. The Joint Chiefs of Staff repeatedly argued to Eisenhower the great importance of Quemoy and Matsu to the stability of the military situation in the Straits. They believed that holding the islands was of great military value in the larger Cold War struggle. Eisenhower did not agree, and he cautioned his military advisors on the consequences of placing great value where it did not belong. The president was not willing to risk a larger war over these strategically unimportant islands. If the United States decided to attack the Chinese forces bombarding the islands as well as other Chinese forces in the region to relieve pressure on Chiang, Eisenhower believed that the attack could not be limited. Those strikes would be first steps only, he thought, and the following steps would likely involve atomic weapons.[117] But the president did not intend "to use the A-bomb in any 'border incident,'" rather it "was to be reserved for a major Communist attack."[118] If the United States were to expand the war with atomic weapons over Taiwan, the president reminded his advisors, "we're not talking now about a limited, brush-fire war. We're talking about going to the threshold of World War III. If we attack China, we're not going to impose limits on our military actions." Even more, he continued, general war would likely follow, and the logical enemy for such a war was Russia, not China. The United States would attack there as well.[119] Eisenhower wanted to avoid that scenario, and through late 1954 he believed avoidance of a larger war in Asia was still possible.

The crisis over Taiwan quickly worsened. The bombardment which began in September in the Straits continued through the fall. On 1 November 1954, Eisenhower learned that the Chinese Communists had expanded the bombing to the Tachen Islands;

an island group north of Taiwan. Meanwhile, the shelling of Quemoy and other small associated islands continued, as did the buildup of Chinese troops opposite Taiwan.[120] Chinese Foreign Minister Zhou Enlai continued to speak of the liberation of Taiwan, and on 23 November 1954, the government of China announced guilty verdicts and long prison sentences for American airmen shot down during the Korean War. At the same time, Eisenhower received little help in avoiding war from Taiwan's President Chiang Kai-shek who predicted a war in the near future and appeared to relish that likelihood. The crisis continued to escalate into the next year. On 10 January 1955, the PRC conducted air raids against the Tachen islands and eight days later they overran the small island of Ichiang, seven miles north of the Tachens.

Though he still saw none of these areas as worth the risk of war, at the urging of John Foster Dulles, Eisenhower shifted his policy. In January 1955, the United States agreed to an evacuation of the Tachen Islands, which the president believed would be difficult to defend, but also pledged to hold those areas then in friendly hands, including Quemoy and Matsu.[121] In a message to Congress on 24 January, Eisenhower explained just how and where the United States intended to meet the communist aggression in the Taiwan Straits. The president cited the continuing availability of the Seventh Fleet and reminded the Congress of the Mutual Defense treaty between the U.S. and Taiwan then under consideration by the Senate. He recited the series of aggressive military actions by China and noted that "the Chinese Communists themselves assert that these attacks are a prelude to the conquest of Formosa." While waiting for the United Nations to act appropriately, Eisenhower requested Congressional authorization for "the use of the armed forces of the United States if necessary to assure the security of Formosa and the Pescadores."[122] In addition to providing support to Taiwanese forces, the United States "must be alert to any concentration or employment of Chinese Communist forces obviously undertaken to facilitate attack upon Formosa, and be prepared to take appropriate military action."[123] Congress agreed, and Eisenhower signed the Formosa resolution on 29 January 1955 which afforded him authority to take the military action he deemed appropriate within the confines of the resolution.

Eisenhower hoped that a strong Congressional resolution would help to reduce the likelihood of a powder keg war. He asked for and received from the Congress a resolution which "would make clear the unified and serious intentions" of the United States. The president believed that a clear statement of American intentions and goals would "reduce the possibility that the Chinese Communists, misjudging our firm purpose and national unity, might be disposed to challenge the position of the United States, and precipitate a major crisis which even they would neither anticipate nor desire." He further wanted to "remove any doubt regarding our willingness . . . to engage in whatever operations may be required" to preserve the freedom of Taiwan and the world.[124] The president wanted to guarantee that war did not occur "through mistaken calculations on the other side." "The purpose is honestly and hopefully to prevent war," Eisenhower explained.[125] Specifically, the resolution allowed the president to "to employ the Armed Forces of the United States as he deems necessary for the specific purpose of securing and protecting Formosa and the Pescadores against armed attack." With the resolution, Congress approved in advance those measures the president judged "to be required or appropriate in assuring the defense of Formosa and the Pescadores."[126] Meanwhile, Eisenhower continued to explore the possibility that the United Nations might help mediate the conflict but China and the Soviet Union had so far refused to cooperate.

The evacuations of the Tachens began on 4 February 1955 and the reinforcement of the Matsus followed. "What we have done has apparently been interpreted by the Chinese Communists merely as a sign of weakness," Eisenhower wrote Winston Churchill two weeks later.[127] John Foster Dulles agreed. After returning from Southeast Asia on 8 March 1955, Dulles told the president that "the Chinese Communists are determined to capture Formosa. Surrendering Quemoy and Matsu won't end that determination." Dulles told Eisenhower that he estimated the United States' chance of going to war was fifty-fifty. "If we defend Quemoy and Matsu, we'll have to use atomic weapons," Dulles continued, "they alone will be effective against the mainland airfields." Eisenhower agreed with Dulles' analysis and considered atomic war with China.[128]

With tensions increasing, the press caught wind of a possible American atomic attack and sought to discover Eisenhower's thinking on how the situation might develop. The United States has been "active in producing various types of weapons that feature nuclear fission ever since World War II," Eisenhower reminded a reporter. Without revealing under what specific circumstances these weapons might be used, the president did explain that tactical fission weapons, not thermonuclear bombs, worked best against military targets. "In any combat where they can be used on strictly military targets and for strictly military purposes," he remarked, "I see no reason why they shouldn't be used just exactly as you would use a bullet or anything else." Eisenhower did add a caveat: "I believe the great question about these things comes when you begin to get into those areas where you cannot make sure that you are operating merely against military targets. But with that one qualification, I would say, yes, of course [fission weapons] would be used." If he decided to use force in a war, Eisenhower continued, "then I know of no reason why a large explosion shouldn't be used as freely as a small explosion." Still, he ridiculed "the indiscriminate use of [thermonuclear] weapons" as illogical. "What would you have left?" the president rhetorically queried. During his press conference the following week, Eisenhower used the term atomic to apply to all fission and fusion weapons. Clearly, "the indiscriminate use atomic weapons" might leave nothing standing. At the same time Eisenhower also noted that "the concept of atomic war is too horrible for man to endure and to practice."[129]

For his part, British Prime Minister Winston Churchill argued against the use of atomic weapons to defend Quemoy and Matsu. The United States need not defend them at all, Churchill told Eisenhower, because the effort would simply not be worth it. Going to the brink over non-essential areas which proved vital only to the ego of Chiang Kai-shek and not the free world made little sense to Churchill. In principle Eisenhower agreed and hoped Chiang Kai-Shek would come to realize how unimportant some of the disputed areas were. For Churchill, waging nuclear war seemed an unacceptable alternative to referring the matter to the United Nations and giving the People's Republic of China the benefit of the doubt over whether Mao intended to invade and reclaim Taiwan.

Eisenhower, however, believed that the risk of a larger war was small. Indeed, he appeared unconcerned about possible Soviet entry even if the war expanded.[130] The U.S.S.R. would likely send supplies into China to assist, but the president concluded that Kremlin leaders would ultimately decide not to risk the PRC falling victim to "the bombing that we *could* conduct against her mainland."[131] Eisenhower had already concluded that large-scale atomic attacks against China would likely be paired with attacks against what he called the logical enemy, the Soviet Union.

Still, Eisenhower routinely refused to commit either to the use or non-use of atomic weapons to resolve the Taiwan Straits Crisis. He well understood that wars often failed to follow a predictable pattern and that he could not and would not predict just how the United States would meet an unknown series of future events. "So I think you just have to wait," he concluded, "and that is the kind of prayerful decision that may some day face a president."[132] Eisenhower wanted to take all the time he was afforded before committing. As he told Speaker of the House Sam Rayburn on 20 March 1955, "we have not made that decision and will not make it until we know the circumstances surrounding any given attack."[133]

Ultimately, the large-scale Chinese attack upon Taiwan which would have likely prompted an American atomic response never came. On 23 April 1955, at an Asian-American conference in Bandung, Chinese Foreign minister Zhou Enlai publicly expressed China's desire not to go to war with the United States over Taiwan and suggested that China would pursue liberation of Taiwan through peaceful means. The PRC stopped the shelling of Quemoy and Matsu on 10 May 1955 and an informal cease fire fell into place on 22 May 1955. A few days later, China announced the release of the American airmen imprisoned for their participation in the Korean War. Although the area would flare up again in 1958, the first Taiwan Straits Crisis had ended and the region calmed.

Eisenhower remembered the Taiwan Straits Crisis of 1954-55 as "one of the most serious problems of the first eighteen months of my administration." He saw the crisis as an opportunity to learn from previous mistakes, to repair lost credibility, and to put to work his vision of Cold War conflict in the nuclear age. "The mistaken communist notion that under no circumstances would the United States" assist South Korea, for example, led in part to that conflict. This time, Eisenhower resolved that "no uncertainty about our commitment to defend Formosa should invite a major Chinese Communist attack."[134]

Eisenhower intended to build the nation's capacity to retaliate instantly and massively and to project that strength in order to eliminate enemy doubt about American resolve. He hoped the projection of strength was all he needed. "It was the threat that he was primarily talking about," Andrew Goodpaster remembered, "Now behind the threat there has to be the reality, but he always put the stress on the threat."[135] When asked if he would use atomic weapons in a general war in Asia, Eisenhower answered that he would. "I hoped this answer would have some effect in persuading the Chinese Communists of the strength of our determination," Eisenhower later wrote.[136] If this show of strength should fail to prevent aggression or to stop a war, "then they would know that if their use of conventional force in fact threatened our vital interest, we would not be limited, that the threat of nuclear attack would exist."[137] He told his advisers that, as in Korea a year before, if the Chinese pressed the attack and threatened Taiwan, the United States would respond with sufficient force to drive the Chinese back. U.S. conventional military power hardly had this capability, and atomic weapons would be used, first at the tactical level and then beyond as needed.

Eisenhower believed that only satisfactory and indeed overwhelming military strength could provide a deterrent to aggressive action, and he further concluded that only nuclear weapons provided that level of force. The U.S. Seventh Fleet offered only the flimsiest of military protection to Taiwan from an invasion of the People's Republic of China and vice versa. With SEATO in existence and with a mutual defense pact in place between the U.S. and Taiwan since March 1955, the United States committed not only its conventional force to the area but the whole of its nuclear options as well. By 1955, Eisenhower sought to make all interested parties aware that the defense of Taiwan was perhaps more vital to the United States than the Soviet Union or China realized. If the enemies of the United States underestimated the lengths to which the United States would go to defend Chiang Kai-shek's nation, they risked a far larger general war. Eisenhower intended to force the communist powers to decide as to what goals they hoped to accomplish and at what cost. He used a strategy of massive retaliation to raise the stakes of the Cold War and simultaneously make sure that a larger war was far less likely. For Eisenhower, the crisis proved to be a successful test of his nuclear policy.

Eisenhower intended for his nuclear strength to be a legitimate, practical, and ultimately decisive strategic weapon. He rejected the advice of the British who, he believed, "had not as yet fully grasped the importance of atomic warfare."[138] He employed the New Look and the doctrine of massive retaliation to deter enemy aggression through the threat of nuclear war and also as an appropriate strategy to achieve military victory should deterrence fail. He did not take the use of nuclear weapons lightly, particularly not after the development of the thermonuclear bomb, but he did not attach much special significance to those weapons either. The historical record showed that Eisenhower did not just avoid nuclear war during his administration, but he avoided large-scale conventional war as well. For Eisenhower, only nuclear weapons, tactical and strategic, atomic and thermonuclear, created the military strength necessary to achieve this goal. He did not have much interest in the science of fission or fusion, nor was he burdened by the weight of moral arguments against the use of nuclear weapons that troubled many scientists in the United States and his British allies. Through military strength, Eisenhower hoped either to preserve the peace or win the war. In either capacity, the nuclear weapon proved both useful and good.

4

Supporting Industrial Strength

On 11 June 1955, two months before the start of the International Conference on the Peaceful Uses of Atomic Energy in Geneva, Switzerland, Eisenhower spoke at the centennial commencement of Pennsylvania State University. The topic of his speech was the promise of nuclear power: "In ten short years the curtain has been pushed aside sufficiently to afford glimpses that have aroused atomic hopes commensurate with the awful dimension of atomic fears." The atomic hopes of which Eisenhower spoke included electrical power through fission as well as the use of radioactivity and radioactive isotopes to explore "new horizons in medicine, agriculture, and industrial processes." Unfortunately for the United States, "those few evil men" in Soviet Union and other communist nations sought to "use command of this energy for their control of human destiny."[1] To combat those men, Eisenhower believed he could increase the industrial strength of the United States through the peaceful application of nuclear energy.

With the vast natural and human resources of both the Soviet Union and the People's Republic of China, the communist world seemed poised to creep into a position of industrial dominance. Large reserves of coal, iron ore, uranium, natural gas, petroleum and other natural resources, and foodstuffs such as wheat and rice seemed to have given the communists the upper hand in promising lasting prosperity for future generations. In addition, communist centralized planning such as Stalin's successive five-year plans aimed at the goal of significant industrial development in a relatively short amount of time. Engaged in a great Cold War, the United States could not allow her enemies the same advantage in industrial output that they possessed in manpower and landmass. To meet that challenge, Eisenhower believed that the United States needed to seize upon her great intellectual and entrepreneurial resources, the newest of which was nuclear technology, to support American industrial strength.

Additionally, Eisenhower lamented the prospect of a future filled with fear as a result of advances in atomic science. He well understood that the nuclear weapon's military value grew from the fear the weapon could instill in the enemy as well as the damage the weapon could cause. But, the acquisition of the nuclear bomb by America's enemy forced upon Eisenhower a reconsideration of the overall value and prospects of the weapon. He regretted that the bomb seemed not to inspire any hope for the future but only fear of the destruction of nations and peoples by atomic attack. As president, Eisenhower sought to reorient nuclear technology toward peaceful and hopeful purposes. A National Security Council analysis reflected the president's view: "Atomic energy is an integral part of the new and tremendously constructive technology of western civilization. Developments in the use of atomic energy for peaceful purposes can in the foreseeable future have immense practical and economic benefits. Our national atomic energy activities are and should be increasingly related to other areas of governmental and industrial activity."[2] Specifically, Eisenhower imagined that the creation of power through controlled fission and fusion could serve to help relieve the great demands for power placed upon American industry. He sought revisions to the Atomic Energy Act of 1946 to provide private companies with the fissionable material and financial assistance in order to make electrical power from atomic technology available to the American public and the world. He also pushed for a variety of other applications such as the nuclear-powered peace ship and Project Plowshare which sought industrial uses for nuclear explosions. With these applications Eisenhower was convinced that he could transmute nuclear technology into hope for the republic.

The president believed that the use of nuclear technology for national industrial strength fit well with his other initiatives to build economic and military strength. For Eisenhower, to put the atom to use in these ways was obvious, practical, and effective. From the beginning of his presidency, he celebrated the civilian industrial applications of nuclear power. He routinely advocated for the use of atoms for peace in several different ways at the same time that he championed the military application of the same technology. Because the industrial application of nuclear power served U.S. national interests as well as those of the developing world, Eisenhower believed that this peaceful application further convinced the world of his desire for peace. Moreover, Eisenhower's discovery of what he believed was a suitable and desirable place for nuclear weapons technology in domestic life further committed the United States to a long-term relationship with nuclear energy and nuclear weapons. Beyond use in military conflicts, the citizens of the republic under Eisenhower saw nuclear technology become part of their everyday lives.

a. A Wasting of Strength

Americans such as Eisenhower struggled to adapt to the new atomic age. Historian Paul Boyer argued that Americans experienced a variety of feelings during the American atomic monopoly, or the period between the end of World War II and the explosion of the first Soviet atomic bomb in 1949. "The initial response of the American people to the atomic bomb, then, was shaped by two intertwined cultural moods," Boyer argued, "intense fear and a somewhat unfocused conviction that an urgent and decisive public response was essential."[3] Boyer focused on the cacophony of voices offering unique visions of the atomic future. The initial fear of atomic destruction felt by some Manhattan Project scientists immediately after Hiroshima juxtaposed with the prospect of a great atomic utopia among others. "Along with the shock waves of fear, one also finds exalted prophecies of the bright promise of atomic energy," Boyer wrote.[4]

Indeed, the practical applications of atomic energy seemed limitless in the late 1940s. Rudolph Langer of the California Institute of Technology described the atomic age as "an era of unparalleled richness and opportunities for all." According to Langer, atomic energy would heat and cool underground houses, provide quick, easy, travel, by ground or by air, upon machines powered by uranium, and create light for underground living and for growing fruits and vegetables to sustain human life. Microwave ovens would cook the food instantly and thoroughly.[5] Physicist John J. O'Neill speculated on the availability of cheap electrical power for all Americans, on atomic vitamins, on beams of radioactivity to mine and smelt metals, and of atomic-powered airplanes, ships, automobiles, and rockets.

Like radical technologies of the past such as gunpowder or steam power, Eisenhower believed atomic power through nuclear fission was inherently harmless. The atom "wears no nationality and recognizes no frontiers," Eisenhower believed, "it is neither moral nor immoral." "Only man's choice can make it good or evil," he argued.[6] "These discoveries in the field of science present in themselves no threat to man," the president told the National Assembly of United Church Women. "Like other scientific developments," he explained, "they are susceptible to good or evil use, depending upon the intent of the individual or group possessing them."[7] In this way, nuclear technology was neither entirely wicked nor entirely benevolent. For this reason, when he came to the presidency in 1953, Eisenhower believed that atomic energy, however dangerous in the form of a bomb, could be trusted to civilian entities which sought to provide power for profit. He believed that private companies and individuals must be given access to atomic fuel and technology with which they could produce energy from fission for the market. In February 1954, he submitted to Congress his recommendations for amending the Atomic Energy Act of 1946, the nation's first atomic energy law which was born in the early days of the Cold War when secrecy was paramount, the United States' relationship with the Soviet Union was rapidly deteriorating, and American policymakers labored to decide just how the atomic weapon would be used in current and future Cold War struggles.

The project to build the atomic bomb was a government operation from the start. Beginning in 1942, the War Department, under Secretary Henry Stimson, built a laboratory in the New Mexico desert as well as a network of production facilities to manufacture all the necessary ingredients for an atomic bomb. In addition to the site at Los Alamos, uranium and plutonium production facilities were built in Tennessee and Washington State. Reactor research took place in Chicago at the Metallurgical Laboratory, later the Argonne National Laboratory, and explosives research and bomb preparation took place in California and New Mexico respectively. From 1942 to 1945, the United States government poured over $2 billion into research and development in the Manhattan Engineer District to build an atomic bomb. The Manhattan Project, as it was called, included also a number of private citizens and companies. J. Robert Oppenheimer took leave from the University of California to assemble a team of respected scientists from university campuses and research laboratories across the nation and the globe. What they shared was a quest for scientific knowledge in service of the allied powers. The same was true for the numerous companies involved in one phase or another of the bomb project, including the Dupont Corporation that built the Hanford site along the Columbia River in Washington State. Other private companies provided necessary supplies and service in a variety of production processes. In sum, the building of the atomic bomb depended upon a combination of individual citizens, universities, private corporations, and government.

But, the United States government was the dominant partner. "Stated in its simplest terms," the author of the U.S. Army history of the Manhattan Project reported, "the achievement of an atomic bomb resulted from the highly successful collaboration of American science and industry carried out under the direction and guidance of the U.S. army." Only the United States government through the Army, Vincent Jones wrote, "could provide the administration, liaison services, security, and military planning essential to the success of a program requiring ready access to scarce materials and manpower, maximum protection against espionage and sabotage, and, ultimately combat utilization of its end product."[8] This combination of partners built and tested the atomic technology later used with such stunning success in the war against Japan in August 1945.

Fresh out of the war and into the atomic age, those who had built the atomic bomb now argued over who would control it. Great momentum developed quickly for the military to manage atomic weapons. President Truman's Secretary of War Robert Patterson believed that control of the bomb must be placed in the hands of military men who "would be representative of all that is best in our national life – men of demonstrated wisdom and judgment who would accept appointment not because of any emoluments that might attend their membership but rather because of a profound recognition of the significance of atomic power to the future of civilization." Congressman Andrew May, Chairman of the House Military Affairs Committee, and Senator Edwin Johnson, ranking member of the corresponding Senate committee, introduced legislation which would fully entrust the military with the responsibility to preserve and protect the nation's atomic secrets and establish American atomic policy. Secretary Patterson, General Leslie Groves, Vannevar Bush, Head of the Office of Scientific Research and Development, and James Conant, President of Harvard University and chair of the National Research Defense Committee, all testified before Congress in favor of the May-Johnson bill.[9] The opposition to the May-Johnson bill featured a coalition of politicians and former Manhattan Project scientists, including the newly created Federation of Atomic Scientists.

Immediately after the war, some scientists who had labored to build the bomb now organized to make the public aware of the power of the new weapon. These scientists felt a moral obligation to ensure proper use of their creation. They argued that atomic energy was far too important and too powerful to be left in the hands of the military exclusively and that the military had in fact hampered the bomb's building because its excessive secrecy restricted the flow of scientific information.[10] These scientists also argued that in keeping with the traditions of the republic civilians, not the military, should control the tools of war including the atomic bomb. The debate continued in Congress through the fall of 1945, with hearings in both chambers. In the end, the scientists won the debate when Senator Arthur Vandenberg of Michigan killed the bill in committee.

Senator Brien McMahon of Connecticut proposed new legislation on 20 December 1945 that addressed the concerns of both the scientists and the military, but which vested the control of atomic power in the United States in civilians. McMahon's bill ultimately became the Atomic Energy Act of 1946 and it established a civilian-controlled Atomic Energy Commission. The five-member commission had sole responsibility for and possession of atomic weapons and before these weapons could be delivered to the military, the Commission needed agreement and explicit presidential approval. The president alone possessed the authority to decide if and when to use the bomb.[11]

The Atomic Energy Act of 1946 laid out six broad goals related to the research, production, control, and application of atomic energy. These goals were: 1) To encourage private research and development in atomic fields so as to achieve maximum progress; 2) To provide for the free exchange of basic scientific information and, whenever possible, related technical information; 3) To study the social, political, and economic effects of atomic energy; 4) To establish solid federal research in atomic energy; 5) To provide for "government control of the production, ownership, and use of fissionable materials to protect national security and to insure the broadest possible exploitation of the field"; and 6) To create an international policy concerning atomic energy. In addition, the authors of the Act allowed sufficient opportunities for Congress to modify the legislation pending future developments in the field of atomic energy.[12] The act made clear distinctions between the prerogatives of the federal government and the role of the private sector in atomic research. While the private sector including the scientific community, universities, and industry would participate, the federal government held a monopoly in the production and control of fissionable materials. Congress and the president granted the federal government primacy in the field of atomic energy and confirmed that national security and secrecy took priority over all other considerations.

For his part, army chief of staff Eisenhower supported the McMahon Bill. "I became very actively involved in the discussions both with the Senate Committee and with several members of the Government," Eisenhower explained to Secretary Patterson, "my position has been that the terms of the McMahon Bill are acceptable to the General Staff."[13] Eisenhower believed "that the security interests of the United States can be protected sufficiently under that bill" and it "gives us plenty of authority all the way through to protect our position until there is something else done."[14] He noted also that President Truman had already expressed his general approval of the Atomic Energy Act and that left the military "no recourse but to continue in our stand that it is acceptable to us."[15] The Act was passed by Congress, signed by the president in 1946, and went into effect on 1 January 1947.

In the eight years between the adoption of the first Atomic Energy Act in 1946 and President Eisenhower's request for revisions in early 1954, the atomic energy industry in the United States grew significantly. The United States plowed forward making both uranium and plutonium bombs, enlarging the atomic arsenal. When the Soviet Union exploded its own atomic bomb in 1949, President Truman authorized the full-scale pursuit of the fusion bomb which commenced in earnest under the direction of Edward Teller and resulted in the first thermonuclear detonation in 1952. The Soviets began their quest for the hydrogen bomb immediately after the Americans. For purposes of the Cold War and the new nuclear arms race, the United States now required more-than-adequate numbers of both types of weapons, fission and fusion; in pursuit of nuclear superiority, the amount of money, facilities, tests, and secrecy all grew. The production of atomic materials accelerated and the number of available atomic weapons grew as well. Despite the concerns over national security and the growing atomic infrastructure, the idea persisted that atomic energy must benefit mankind and not simply forecast its destruction. From 1947 until the time of Eisenhower's inauguration, the quest for atomic power for industrial and public purposes made slow but steady progress.

When Eisenhower assumed the presidency in January 1953, he expressed deep concern that so much initiative, effort, money, and resources had been poured into a technology intended only for destructive use. Speaking before the American Society of Newspaper Editors in April 1953, Eisenhower highlighted his worry. In the eight years since the end of World War II, he told his audience, fear and force had dominated the global community. The Soviet Union had turned the world down the path of dread with only a few options open to the United States and the free world. "The worst to be feared and the best to be expected can be simply stated," he asserted, "The *worst* is atomic war."[16] The best seemed only slightly better: "a life of perpetual fear and tension; a burden of arms draining the wealth and the labor of all peoples; a wasting of strength that defied the American system or the Soviet system or any system to achieve true abundance and happiness for the peoples of this earth." He cited the price in detail. "The cost of one modern heavy bomber is this: a modern brick school in more than 30 cities. It is two electric power plants, each serving a town of 60,000 in population. It is two fine, fully equipped hospitals. It is some 50 miles of concrete highway." One fighter plane cost 500,000 bushels of wheat; one destroyer cost homes for 8,000 people. "The sweat of [the world's] laborers, the genius of its scientists, the hopes of its children" were sacrificed on "a cross of iron" leaving behind the hungry and cold people of the earth with no hope for salvation. Living "under the cloud of threatening war," Eisenhower complained, was "not a way of life at all."[17]

Eisenhower then proposed initial steps toward reducing "the burden of armaments now weighing upon the world." He hoped to agree with Soviet leaders to limit the numbers of weapons and he advocated "international control of atomic energy to promote its use for peaceful purposes only and to insure the prohibition of atomic weapons."[18] This would allow America "to dedicate our strength to serving the *needs,* rather than the *fears,* of the world."[19] While he expressed a desire to reduce both expenditures on and numbers of atomic weapons among the world's nations, he argued that atomic technology should serve peaceful and hopeful purposes as well. Just as atomic fission brought the risk for great death and destruction so too did it bring the opportunity for peaceful rewards. So far, the world had seen only the dark side of atomic technology, and the growing Cold War between the United States and the Soviet Union made the threat of atomic destruction more likely. The president saw a cruel irony: "In the minds of most people this new energy was equated with the atomic bomb, and the bomb spelled the erasure of cities and the mass death of men, women, and children." He despaired that the bomb's "awesome destructiveness overshadowed its potential for good."[20]

The death of Soviet leader Joseph Stalin, the advent of the thermonuclear weapon, and the growing likelihood that the next war might be the last war prompted Eisenhower to search for an alternative atomic future which involved the exploitation of atomic technology for the greater good. "The free world is still overwhelmingly strong as compared to the Iron Curtain countries," he told an Iowa crowd, "in the people we have, in their levels of intelligence and understanding, in their skills, in agriculture, and in industry; in their free adherence to a cause, rather than in regimented adherence to a government."[21] Despite the ominous applications of atomic technology, Eisenhower believed that by employing fission and fusion properly, in civilian power plants as well as for other peaceful purposes, the nation could augment her strength, serve the cause of peace, and do so without wasting American intellectual and scientific resources.

b. To the Constructive Purposes of Man

Throughout his presidency, Eisenhower placed a high priority on the development of atomic energy for electrical power and sought to create a balance between atomic weapons for national security and atomic energy for economic and industrial development. In that effort, he believed that private industry should be given every opportunity to succeed in the realm of atomic power because private industry could do so more effectively, more quickly, and at less cost to the American taxpayer. Accordingly, Eisenhower instructed Lewis Strauss, the Special Assistant to the President for Atomic Energy Affairs from 1953 to 1959, to work with the Atomic Energy Commission to prepare amendments to the Atomic Energy Act of 1946 in order to allow for the private development of atomic power. According to Richard Hewlett and Jack Holl, Eisenhower sought "to break the government monopoly" on atomic energy and "to find some redeeming value in nuclear technology."[22]

For Eisenhower, the Atomic Energy Act of 1946 hampered progress in the development of private atomic power. Tight restrictions on the flow of scientific and technical knowledge greatly limited any entity other than the U.S. government from making any headway in developing atomic power. As army chief of staff Eisenhower had supported the Atomic Energy Act because he believed it provided the military with the means to promote American national security. But as a civilian executive he concluded that "in order to strengthen national security through a sound industry, it is essential that Government ownership of production facilities" be terminated.[23] Eisenhower wanted the Commission to provide advice, assistance, and incentives to private companies pursuing atomic energy.[24] To accomplish this, he knew that the law needed to be changed.

As Strauss prepared those revisions, Eisenhower took his argument about the need for peaceful atomic energy and the growth of industrial strength to the United Nations in December 1953. "The United States knows that peaceful power from atomic energy is no dream of the future," he noted. "Who can doubt, if the entire body of the world's scientists and engineers had adequate amounts of fissionable material with which to test and develop their ideas," he queried, "that this capability would rapidly be transformed into universal, efficient, and economic usage." To this end, he hoped "to hasten the day when the fear of the atom will begin to disappear from the minds of people." He offered proposals aimed at creating an international bank of fissionable material and suggested the application of atomic energy "to the needs of agriculture, medicine, and other peaceful activities." "A special purpose would be to provide abundant electrical energy in the power starved areas of the world," he directed. Eisenhower concluded that the "contributing powers would be dedicating some of the strength to serve the needs rather than the fears of mankind."[25]

Two months later, Eisenhower again spoke to his nation about the promise of atomic power and the heretofore unrealized dream of cheap energy for America and the world. "The destiny of all nations during the twentieth century will turn in large measure upon the nature and pace of atomic energy development here and abroad," Eisenhower told the Congress. Yet so far, the "rich possibilities" for atomic energy remained unfulfilled. Though "economic industrial power from atomic energy" was clearly within reach, restrictions placed on the community of atomic scientists had impeded the proper development of atomic power. The United States had so far seen little return in the quest for the peaceful atom because only the government was allowed to pursue scientific and technological discovery. Eisenhower wanted to make good use of "the enterprise, initiative and competitive spirit of individuals and groups within our free economy" to make the dream of atomic energy a reality. He believed that peaceful applications of atomic energy "can be developed more rapidly and their benefits more widely realized through broadened cooperation with friendly nations and through greater participation by American industry."[26] He sought to create a favorable climate in which American private industry could capitalize on atomic energy to give strength to the United States and the free world. Private initiative would expand opportunities for exploration and innovation in atomic energy, and private corporations would find financial interest in the pursuit of the best way to provide atomic energy to consumers. According to the administration, medical, agricultural, and industrial applications of atomic energy would soon follow.[27] After private industry found atomic energy to be a profitable and responsible business model, the federal government could slowly cut back its own atomic energy efforts, saving taxpayer dollars, and reducing the size of the federal bureaucracy.[28]

To give the new initiative a jumpstart, Eisenhower recommended that the Atomic Energy Commission supply the necessary materials and services at cost to private manufacturers.[29] "I asked the Congress for legislation to permit the private manufacture, ownership, and operation of atomic reactors," Eisenhower remembered, "under licensing systems administered by the Atomic Energy Commission."[30] Under Eisenhower's direction, Strauss worked with the Atomic Energy Commission and the Joint Congressional Committee on Atomic Energy, and particularly with Congressman W. Sterling Cole and Senator Bourke B. Hickenlooper, to agree on the proper language to achieve the desired result. In the end, the proposed revisions reflected a consensus between the Eisenhower administration, the Atomic Energy Commission, and the Joint Congressional Committee.[31] The Congress approved the changes, and the president signed the new atomic energy law on 30 August 1954.

The revised legislation established that "the development, use, and control of atomic energy shall be directed so as to promote world peace, improve the general welfare, increase the standard of living, and strengthen free competition in private enterprise." To achieve these goals, Eisenhower aimed to create "a program of conducting, assisting, and fostering research and development in order to encourage maximum scientific and industrial progress"[32] In the distribution of fissionable material, "preference shall be given to those activities which are most likely, in the opinion of the Commission, to contribute to basic research, to the development of peacetime uses of atomic energy, or to the economic and military strength of the Nation."[33] Under the new law, the Atomic Energy Commission could grant licenses to private companies to construct and run electrical power plants fueled by nuclear materials. The Commission would not be allowed to build nuclear reactors with the purpose of selling the resulting power to the public. Instead, the Commission would supply the license and the fissile material, and private companies would invest in construction and maintenance of the plant itself and in distribution of the electrical power produced. These companies could then earn profits and pay dividends to stockholders. The time had come, Eisenhower argued in his statement at the signing of the new law, for the "initiative and resources of private industry" to be put to work in the national atomic energy program.[34]

Eisenhower also pursued amendments to the Atomic Energy Act because he wanted greater authority to share nuclear information with the British.[35] The new legislation removed the restrictions on sharing information with America's allies, specifically Great Britain. According to historian John Baylis, Eisenhower believed the United States owed Great Britain something for holding off the Nazis for so long during World War II as well as for British help in developing the bomb. More importantly, a strong, stable, nuclear-equipped Britain would go a long way toward making the rest of Western Europe better prepared to defend against a Soviet invasion. The United States could not alone afford to defend Western Europe indefinitely, Eisenhower believed, and the quicker Europe turned into a "third power block," the sooner the United States could improve its domestic economic situation.[36]

But, the primary goal of the amended law was private nuclear power. Eisenhower understood that the peaceful applications of atomic power could also provide strength in the form of inexpensive, private nuclear power for both America and the developing world. "As I sign this bill," he told the nation, "I am confident that it will advance both public and private development of atomic energy – that it will thus lead to greater national strength – and that programs undertaken as a result of this new law will help us progress more rapidly to the time when this new source of energy will be wholly devoted to the constructive purposes of man."[37] Greater national strength was Eisenhower's priority, a goal more quickly achieved by allowing the entrepreneurial spirit of American industry to work freely. The new act created a more liberal atomic marketplace where individuals and industry could compete to produce electrical power through splitting or fusing atoms. The country suffered from a lack of atomic opportunities, and "by enlarging opportunities for peacetime development," Eisenhower proclaimed, "we accelerate our own progress and strengthen the free world."[38] He hoped that appropriate legislation would release the stored energy of American innovation and propel the United States into that era of progress and peace. By amending the original Atomic Energy Act only a year into his first term, Eisenhower sought to achieve the connected goals of achieving civilian nuclear power and supporting America's national strength. One week after the signing of the new Atomic Energy Act, Eisenhower presided over the groundbreaking ceremony for the construction of the Shippingport Atomic Power Plant in Pennsylvania. Shippingport would not be the best example of private atomic power as Eisenhower envisioned it, but it would be a start.

In the late summer of 1953, the Atomic Energy Commission adopted a five-year program that was intended to get the ball rolling on nuclear power plant production in the United States. This program included five separate plant projects, three of which were under direct government control, two at the Argonne National Laboratory and one at Oak Ridge. As the only example of private development, North American Aviation, with financing from the Commission, pursued a fourth project, a sodium-graphite reactor. The fifth reactor project was a pressurized-water reactor.[39] For this project the Atomic Energy Commission solicited bids from private industry to work with the Commission on what later became Shippingport. The Commissioners accepted the bid of the Duquesne Light Company of Pittsburgh in part because the company offered to absorb about $30 million worth of associated costs. According to Hewlett and Holl, "Duquesne offered to provide the site, build the turbogenerator plant, and operate and maintain the entire facility. The company also agreed to assume $5 million of the cost of developing and building the reactor, which Westinghouse would design and the Commission would own."[40] In addition to building the reactor, the government would provide the fissile material. In the end, Shippingport was a "government project with only a limited role for private industry."[41]

In his remarks at the groundbreaking on 6 September 1954, Eisenhower described the goal of the Shippingport Plant. Although the plant was not a purely private venture, the United States had moved closer to the goal of private electrical power by an atomic reactor. The initiative opened "new avenues to constructive employment, to prosperity, to respite from burdensome toil," he explained. The atom had become man's "mighty servant and tireless benefactor" and brought mankind one step closer to "the ancient dream of a new and better earth."[42] Eisenhower made the dream even more palatable as he dedicated the Shippingport Plant in Pittsburgh from his summer home in Denver through the wave of an "atomic wand" which set a bulldozer in motion from thousands of miles away.[43] A little over three years later on 2 December 1957, the Shippingport reactor reached near-critical mass. Two weeks later, Shippingport reached full power and began producing 60 megawatts of electricity. It was the first full-scale atomic power plant to operate in the United States.[44]

Overall, Eisenhower's efforts to achieve civilian atomic power produced substantial results. Various experimental reactors began operating during Eisenhower's second term, including the experimental boiling water reactor, BORAX III, in Arco, Idaho in July 1955 and the Sodium Reactor Experiment in Santa Ana, California in July 1957. Construction had begun on pressurized-water reactors by Yankee Atomic Electric in Massachusetts, by Consolidated Edison of New York, and by Pennsylvania Light and Power in Liberty, Pennsylvania. In addition, Rural Co-Op Power Association of Minnesota began construction of a boiling-water reactor. Nuclear superheat reactors, organic-cooled reactors, sodium-cooled fast reactors, gas-cooled reactors, and heavy water reactors were soon in design, under construction, or operating from California to Illinois. Pathfinder Northern States Power Company of Sioux Falls, South Dakota, Pacific Gas and Electric of Humboldt, California and a host of others sought to create atomic power for the American people.[45] At the close of Eisenhower's second term, ten atomic power plants operated in the United States. Between the U.S. government and private industry, twenty-two more plants were in the early stages production, and universities across the nation operated thirty teaching reactors.[46]

Eisenhower sincerely believed in the benefits of atomic power for the nation. His efforts to spur the development of inexpensive electrical power from atomic reactors was not a gimmick, nor was it meant as a distraction from the potential horrors of atomic war.[47] The president believed that atomic science and technology provided the U.S. a marvelous opportunity to increase the efficiency of electric power and at the same time to reduce the cost. He also believed that inexpensive electric power might remake the landscape of the United States. According to Eisenhower, both businesses and citizens in rural areas across the nation could now benefit from affordable power. American industry required reliable electrical power. Without a steady supply, machines go idle, production ceases, and business collapses. Even worse, any interruption in industrial production meant similar consequences for the American economy as a whole. Slows in production could translate into unemployment, inflation, and depression. Eisenhower did not foresee an immediate crisis, but thought the prudent approach was to diversify America's electrical infrastructure with atomic power. Facing a determined and rising enemy in the Cold War, the industrial strength provided by atomic power would serve to augment America's cumulative national strength.

c. An Era of Progress and Peace

In addition to civilian atomic power, Eisenhower believed that atomic technology could provide industrial strength in a variety of other ways. Though none of these other nuclear initiatives bore fruit during or after his term in the way civilian atomic power did, Eisenhower envisioned something akin to the atomic utopia first imagined in the days after Hiroshima and before the Soviet atomic bomb. As Paul Boyer noted, scientists, politicians, philosophers and others believed in those early days that atomic technology could be put to great use in everyday life and the result would be a more comfortable and more convenient world. "We live in one of the great ages in the story of mankind," Eisenhower told the nation in November 1957. "For millions of people science has removed the burden of backbreaking toil. For other millions the hope of a good life is being translated into a definite promise," he continued.[48]

On 7 November 1957, only a few hysterical weeks after the launching of the earth's first artificial satellite, *Sputnik I* by the Soviet Union, Eisenhower spoke to the American people on the subject of science and national security. He boasted of America's military strength and cited several examples of scientific developments that served the nation. Ballistic missiles, nuclear-powered submarines, atomic depth bombs, aircraft, and artillery pieces were all either powered by or dependent upon an atomic weapon for their deterrent effect. Soviet aggression forced America to build this magnificent arsenal, Eisenhower lamented. Though *Sputnik* suggested that the Soviets possessed superior satellite technology and "are quite likely ahead in some missile and special areas," the overall military strength of the free world proved far superior. But freedom required that the United States continue to match and indeed beat the communists "in military power, general technological advance, and specialized education and research." Scientific research and development made this military strength possible, and Eisenhower promised the nation "to put current scientific discovery at the service of your defense."[49] He also forecasted the long range investments required to insure the nation did not fall behind in "over-all strength." According to Eisenhower, his "scientific friends" argued that a failure to place high priority on scientific education risked the future of America's freedom. He announced changes and new initiatives. Most of these involved America's ballistic missile program, but they also included the creation of the Special Assistant for Science and Technology and ultimately the President's Science Advisory Committee. "I am not forgetting that there is much more to science than its function in strengthening our defense," he remarked.[50]

A critical need, Eisenhower explained, was to give "higher priority, both public and private, to basic research."[51] He believed this investment in time, resources, and effort would foster a healthy and robust scientific community. American citizens who specialized in scientific disciplines held long-term promise for the nation's intellectual future. "Talent and quality are vital to our national strength," he explained, "they are the ingredients needed to carry us onward and upward to higher peaks of achievement in science as well as in the non-material world of the mind and the spirit."[52] Certainly American scientists would be able to make contributions to military strength as they had in the past, but Eisenhower also imagined a strong scientific community contributing to general prosperity and peace. In this effort, he planned to strengthen America's commitment to basic scientific research.

Though he did not often articulate precisely what he thought the United States would gain from this research, he did suggest that basic science and the resulting intellectual and scientific growth contributed much to America's overall strength. Eisenhower told the nation that the first task confronting America in 1958 was "to ensure our safety through strength." He noted the "potential resources on other non-military fronts to help in countering the Soviet threat: education, science, research, and, not least, the ideas and principles by which we live."[53] "And in all these cases," he continued, "the task ahead is to bring these resources more sharply to bear upon the new tasks of security and peace in a swiftly changing world."[54] He sought a doubling of National Science Foundation money to support basic science and to improve science education.[55] More specifically, he planned for nation-wide testing to insure success among high school students, incentives for students to pursue scientific studies, more money for laboratories, a rejuvenated teaching program for math and science, and fellowships for promising young teachers in science fields.[56] "With this kind of all-inclusive campaign, I have no doubt that we create the intellectual capital we need for the years ahead," Eisenhower concluded.[57] With some modifications, additions, and subtractions, the Congress endorsed Eisenhower's vision, and, on 2 September 1958, less than one year after *Sputnik*, the president signed the National Defense Education Act.

Eisenhower's concern about the state of basic science in the United States also led him to elevate science into a position of power within his own administration. In late 1957, Eisenhower appointed James Killian, President of the Massachusetts Institute of Technology, to the newly created position of Special Assistant for Science and Technology. Killian became also the first head of the President's Science Advisory Committee (PSAC). Eisenhower expected Killian, supported by the Committee, to advise him and the National Security Council directly on those scientific matters that had an impact on national security issues. The president wanted independent and unfiltered technical advice to allow him to manage better the scope of America's resources for the Cold War. He wanted to understand the differences in competing missile systems, for example, to determine which programs could be cut to save the already growing security budget without a loss of national strength. He also needed advice on research and development in the Department of Defense and for negotiating a ban on nuclear testing.[58]

Both the National Defense Education Act and the President's Science Advisory Committee brought basic science to the highest levels of government and solidified Eisenhower's commitment to fulfill the great promise of the atomic age. To Eisenhower, a new atomic lifestyle seemed both desirable and within reach, and a future atomic utopia might finally realize the most abstract and greatest dreams of many Americans. These dreams included cars, planes, trains, and ships running on small amounts of uranium or plutonium and requiring no refueling. Many believed that atomic technology also would bring heretofore-unthought-of products and services to serve mankind. Others imagined a wealth of everyday industrial applications for atomic energy which would benefit from limitless, cheap, and safe power. Eisenhower saw multiple applications for atomic energy and believed that each could contribute to the industrial strength of the United States.

One project which served both industrial and psychological goals was the atomic-powered peace ship, which Eisenhower proposed to his staff in May 1955. The president imagined an atomic-powered merchant vessel which would serve both as a tramp steamer and a harbinger of the peaceful atom throughout the world. The steamer could carry cargo from port to port across the globe and offer "exhibits of peaceful uses of atomic energy to be viewed by the people of each country in the ports visited by the ship."[59] An atomic reactor would provide power for the vessel which could crisscross the world's oceans without stopping to refuel for a period of up to two years. In addition to its payload of industrial and commercial goods, the atomic peace ship might also be constructed to carry passengers. Eisenhower dreamed of luxurious quarters for VIPs who could see firsthand the peaceful uses of atomic power.[60]

In a press conference of 31 May 1955, Eisenhower explained the value of the peace ship. "It is true, as I visualize it, it will be a peaceful ship with many an exhibition really of American culture, of the arts and industry," the president explained. "On top of that, I would hope that it would actually carry cargo as it went around the world on unscheduled runs, be ready to pick up such cargoes it could, so that everybody could see it performing a useful service in the world," he continued. The peace ship would also serve as an exhibition of American industrial know-how.[61]

Eisenhower lobbied Congress to approve funding for the atomic peace ship because he considered it a valuable venture both for its psychological value and for its industrial applications for the future.[62] He believed that "apart from the psychological and political advantages of such a ship, we would almost certainly learn a lot of practical value from the construction and operation of such a nuclear-propelled ship."[63] This might translate into the building of many nuclear-powered vessels. If, in the future, atomic reactors powered all steam ships, international trade and commerce would be greatly served by the reduced costs and increased pace of global shipping. Eisenhower had so much faith in the overall value of the atom peace ship that the project made it onto the Republican Party Platform for the 1956 election. "We should proceed with the prompt construction of the Atomic Powered Peace Ship in order that we may demonstrate to the world, in this as in other fields, the peaceful uses of the atom," the Party agreed.[64] The atom peace ship was ultimately funded and built under the Eisenhower administration. Christened the N.S. *Savannah* by Mamie Eisenhower in 1959, the ship steamed under atomic power for ten years between 1962 and 1972 almost exactly as Eisenhower had envisioned: a cargo and passenger ship complete with exhibits showcasing the promise of nuclear power.

Beyond the peace ship, Eisenhower envisioned other industrial tasks for atomic weapons, many of which stemmed directly from Project Plowshare. As early as 1955, Manhattan Project veteran and unofficial "father of the hydrogen bomb" Edward Teller excited Eisenhower with the possibility that clean atomic bombs might be used for a variety of peaceful purposes.[65] Along with other scientists, including Herbert York and Harold Brown, Teller convened a classified conference of top national scientists at the Lawrence Livermore National Laboratory in California in February 1957. At the conference, scientists explored other possibilities for nuclear explosives including the creation of diamonds, the search for oil, and landscaping on a massive scale. Eisenhower and Atomic Energy Commission Chairman Lewis Strauss accepted the arguments of Teller and allowed the unnamed initiative to grow in the months after that February conference. Isidor Rabi had skeptically commented to Harold Brown that nuclear scientists like Brown and Teller now wanted to beat their bombs into plowshares, alluding to a passage in the biblical book of Micah.[66] Not until after July 1957 was the project with these lofty goals named Plowshare.

Plowshare advocates believed that the project's success depended primarily upon the availability of clean nuclear weapons. In theory, clean bombs would produce little or no radioactive fallout because they would produce no residual radiation. Fission reactions produce energy in several forms. Blast comprises approximately 50 percent of that energy while thermal radiation or heat comprises another 35 percent. Fast neutrons or prompt radiation makes up 5 percent with the remaining 10 percent coming from residual radiation. This residual radiation is responsible for fallout. Thermonuclear reactions do not produce residual radiation inherently, but because fission reactions are needed to prime the thermonuclear bomb, both fission and fusion weapons produced radioactive fallout. Clean bomb advocates held that clean versions of both fission and fusion weapons would produce energy in only two forms: 20 percent blast and 80 percent prompt radiation.[67] No residual radiation meant no radioactive fallout. If a fallout-free atomic explosion were possible, it would open up a range of potential industrial uses as the proximity of the explosion to civilian populations would not matter nearly as much.

The idea of a clean nuclear bomb intrigued Eisenhower. On 24 June 1957, Teller, Ernest O. Lawrence, and Mark Mills visited the president in the White House on the invitation of Strauss.[68] Only ten days earlier, the Soviet Union had publicly proposed a moratorium on nuclear testing, and Eisenhower was considering accepting the Soviet offer. For the scientists, the principal goal of the meeting was to persuade Eisenhower to continue nuclear testing in the United States. They argued that recent progress indicated how close scientists had come to developing a clean nuclear weapon. They told the president they had already succeeded in producing an "over 90 percent clean" weapon and needed only "six or seven years" to reach 100 percent clean.[69] To stop now, according to Lawrence, would be a "crime against humanity."[70]

The scientists apparently convinced Eisenhower at least for the time. "No one could oppose the development program [the scientists] had described," the president remarked.

Launched in 1962, the N. S. *Savannah* was the world's first nuclear-powered passenger ship. (National Archives)

He recognized that the delicate international situation he might create if the United States hesitated to stop nuclear testing when the Soviets had already done so. The prospect of clean nuclear weapons and peaceful applications of atomic technology warranted a reorientation of public opinion regarding nuclear testing. Eisenhower became convinced that in order to continue development of peaceful nuclear technology nuclear testing needed to continue despite the risk to American disarmament and test ban efforts. He proclaimed that he would not allow America to be "crucified on a cross of atoms" for failing to stop nuclear testing.[71]

To continue the required testing, Eisenhower needed to convince the world that no new harm to humanity would come from the clean tests.[72] Eisenhower wanted to make the three scientists available to the press, and he instructed Press Secretary Hagerty to make it happen.[73] For his part, if asked at his next press conference why the U.S. had so far refused to stop testing, Eisenhower would "simply say that our tests are projected to clean up weapons and thus protect civilians in the event of war."[74] In a press conference two days later on 26 June, *The New York Times* wanted to know Eisenhower's thinking on the suspension of nuclear testing.[75] He recounted his meeting with Teller and Lawrence and repeated the assertion about the successful tests of 90 percent clean bombs and the likelihood of 100 percent clean bombs in "four or five years." He recited the arguments of his scientists and connected nuclear testing directly with the progress on the peaceful development of atomic science. "So you realize that when you are making these agreements to stop [nuclear tests]," Eisenhower explained, "you are not doing something that may not have an adverse effect, finally, on what we hope to get out of this." Eisenhower wanted to get "the best out of this new science for the peaceful uses of mankind" and accordingly, he argued, "we should go right ahead with the plan" to continue testing until an acceptable agreement with enforceable safeguards was successfully negotiated.[76]

Despite his enthusiasm for clean bombs and the possibility that they might limit civilian casualties in a thermonuclear war, he doubted publicly that clean bombs should even be used as weapons. "If you had this clean, completely clean, product," the president told John Scali of the Associated Press, "I should think that in building of tunnels or, you might say, moving mountains, and that sort of thing, you could have many economical, useful, peaceful purposes for the thing." "Of course," he continued, "you wouldn't want to deny civilization the opportunity of using it" by incorrectly classifying it as a weapon.[77] Eisenhower's hope in the clean nuclear bomb grew from his meeting with Teller, Lawrence, and Mills into seventy-seven nuclear tests in the first ten months of 1958.[78] Eisenhower endorsed Plowshare wholeheartedly and according to his scientific advisor, George Kistiakowsky, he thought Plowshare was "terribly important."[79]

Eisenhower was further convinced by the success of a particular nuclear test in the late summer of 1957.[80] Rainier, one of the last shots of the Plumbob test series, detonated at 1900 feet underground and yielded only 1.7 kilotons. Willard Libby, Nobel prize-winning chemist and Atomic Energy commissioner, testified before a Senate Subcommittee that the blast bumped the mountain up about six inches and no radioactivity escaped.[81] "There was no mushroom cloud, no fall-out radioactive or otherwise," Strauss gleefully remembered.[82] Not only did Rainier seem clean, but the technical evaluation of the Rainier shot confirmed for Strauss that underground nuclear tests would be difficult to detect. In short, the success of Rainier suggested that it might possible to conceal atomic explosions underground.[83] Like Teller, Strauss believed that if a country insisted on testing despite agreeing to a moratorium, the Rainier shot proved they could do so without detection. Rainier seemed to support the belief that a nuclear test moratorium could benefit the Soviet Union and that the United States should avoid an agreement and continue testing out of a desire to improve America's defense capability.[84]

Beyond this, Strauss found in Rainier another reason to continue nuclear testing. The test demonstrated that clean underground nuclear explosions could advance the goals of Plowshare.[85] Without the contaminating effects of radioactive fallout, nuclear explosions held great potential for moving earth and clearing land for a variety of industrial applications. Plowshare excavation projects involved the blasting away of earth to construct harbors, build highways, open pit mines, and allow for the construction of dams. Nuclear explosions might also create massive holes for natural gas and oil storage.[86] In addition, to liberate petroleum reserves from the earth, nuclear blasts might fracture stubborn oil shales in places such as Colorado, Utah, and Wyoming.[87] These projects greatly intrigued Eisenhower, particularly the possibility that nuclear explosions might provide an inexpensive means of recovering oil. At a PSAC meeting in July 1958, Eisenhower questioned Dr. Wolfgang Panofsky whether the Committee had considered atomic weapons for the recovery of oil from tar sands.[88] The following October, Eisenhower pressed the issue of using atomic explosions to recover oil in a National Security Council Meeting.[89]

One Plowshare project involved the use of atomic explosions to dig a new Central American canal to connect the Atlantic to the Pacific Ocean. This second canal would be under American control like the one in Panama but, unlike the Panama Canal, it would be dug and built at sea level. This would eliminate the need for la complicated system of locks. The Panama Canal was built above sea level because of the presence of a huge amount of tough rock immediately below the canal's location. To build the new canal, Plowshare advocates estimated that twenty-six nuclear bombs totaling 16.7 megatons of explosive power would be able to blast away the rock and debris and eliminate the need for locks.[90] "From a remark of the president, I gather that he intends to address the UN General Assembly," Kistiakowsky remembered, "and at that time (September) announce that we are going ahead with the Plowshare program for digging a second Atlantic-Pacific canal through Mexico, which has agreed to the project."[91] Eisenhower authorized a detailed study of the project that was completed and presented to him in 1960. Proposals for the Isthmian Canal suggested several possible locations, all of which promised a financial benefit for the nation. In 1947, the cheapest estimates for digging this canal ranged up to $2.3 billion. With Plowshare, a sea-level canal through Panama would cost $770 million and another through Colombia about $1.2 billion. Plowshare might save the United States between $1.5 billion beyond the economic advantages of multiple, American-controlled routes from one ocean to another.[92]

For Eisenhower, Plowshare held the potential for even more industrial uses. At the Second International Conference on the Peaceful Uses of Atomic Energy in Geneva in September 1958, American scientists, including Teller, brought with them a short film titled "Industrial Applications of Nuclear Explosives." One potential industrial use, the film suggested, was the construction of an "instant harbor" in an unidentified coastal area using 1.4 megatons worth of nuclear explosives.[93] "The world needs more harbors and canals," Teller wrote in 1962, "There is much too little protection for big ocean-going vessels along the western shores of South America and Africa." "More water transportation, because it is the cheapest form of transportation, would speed the development of backward countries, would increase trade, and would strengthen ties between people," Teller concluded.[94] Not only did America require the industrial strength for the Cold War augmented by Plowshare, but "Plowshare was *needed* as a tool of Third World development in order to prevent the spread of Soviet communism."[95]

Between the Soviet proposal to stop testing in June 1957 and the American moratorium in October 1958, Plowshare planning continued. With Eisenhower's blessing, Strauss pursued and won larger budgets for Plowshare through the end of June 1958, including $6 million for Fiscal Year 1960.[96] Scientists at the Lawrence Livermore National Laboratory sought early on to take the experiments out of the lab and into the field for full-scale demonstration. In late 1957, scientists chose a remote coastal location in northwest Alaska to excavate an instant harbor with nuclear explosives. The project was named Chariot. The particular location at the mouth of Ogotoruk Creek on Cape Thompson was chosen because a deep water port was possible in that location. Additionally, the area around Cape Thompson was composed of solid bedrock, not permafrost, allowing for the immediate and relatively simple construction of railroads, roads, pipelines, and large-scale industrial sites.[97] According to the Atomic Energy Commission, "the absence of harbors on the northwest coast of Alaska close to important large-scale mineral deposits has in the past hampered development of such deposits."[98] Nuclear excavation provided both the opportunity to extricate these mineral resources and to ship them out to markets quickly and cheaply via a new harbor. Teller explained to skeptical crowds that Livermore Scientists and the Atomic Energy Commission wanted "not just a hole in the ground, but something that will be used."[99] Eisenhower delighted in "the wonderful prospects of this project" and despite the testing moratorium still desired "to proceed with this type of experimental development work."[100] Unfortunately for Eisenhower, the scientific community did not develop soon enough the clean bomb technology that Teller had promised, and Project Plowshare never developed as advertised, particularly after funding cuts through the 1960s and 1970s. Nonetheless, Plowshare represented precisely what Eisenhower envisioned of atomic energy for industrial strength. To Eisenhower, clean nuclear technology could provide greater opportunity for industrial development, from the recovery of oil stores and mineral resources to the construction of instant harbors and underground natural gas storage. These and a host of other potential excavation-related uses buoyed Eisenhower's faith in the industrial promise of nuclear science.

In the end, Eisenhower's attempt to use atomic energy to support industrial strength produced mixed results. On one hand, he created the National Science Foundation to encourage and fund basic science in the nation. He and the Congress sought to improve dramatically math and science education in the United States through the National Defense Education Act. Eisenhower intended this investment to produce the high quality of teachers and students needed to challenge Soviet scientific power in the Cold War. The proliferation of units in the national laboratory system and the increased prominence of science in public life bolstered basic and applied scientific research in the United States. Rapid advances in technology and a thriving scientific community resulted. Eisenhower intended all of these efforts to serve the public good and more specifically to serve the cause of strength in the Cold War. In addition, Eisenhower oversaw the construction and maiden voyage of the N.S. *Savannah*, an atomic-powered cargo and passenger ship. Per Eisenhower, the ship served the cause of peace through a demonstration of the peaceful applications of atomic energy as well as through global trade and commerce. On the other hand, Eisenhower's efforts also met failure. Scientists and engineers were unable to develop a clean nuclear weapon, and as a result, the various applications envisioned in the Plowshare project proved unfeasible. Plowshare survived the Eisenhower presidency but never achieved the full results he desired.

Eisenhower believed that the scientific advances of the atomic era promised great opportunities to support American industrial strength. He imagined a world not unlike the most utopian atomic fantasies described in the days immediately following the end of World War II in which atomic energy was to provide limitless energy for industry. He understood that this industrial energy served to increase America's overall strength, and, in the midst of a Cold War with an immoral and expansionist enemy, strength was one trait of which the nation could not have too much. For Eisenhower, the atom supported the nation's industrial strength through the successful creation of civilian atomic power. In addition, American industry benefited from the major investment made by Eisenhower in atomic research. The president believed his scientific investment would return a variety of industrial applications, all of which would buttress American industrial power. In general, he believed that atomic energy must serve humanity in ways unrelated to weapon production. He accepted that atomic weapons served a great purpose as guarantors of national security and peace in an age of great fear and uncertainty. This primary function however must not deter the United States from pursuing peaceful and positive applications of atomic energy. To balance the negative function of atomic weapons for deterrence, Eisenhower pursued positive value in atomic energy. "The beneficent use of atomic energy is human service," Eisenhower believed, and he expected "atomic energy development, public and private, to play a full and effective part in leading mankind into a new era of progress and peace."[101]

5

Bolstering Moral Strength

Eisenhower sought also to use nuclear technology in keeping with his own and the nation's religious foundation. He believed that nuclear weapons retained a certain righteousness that befitted and benefitted the American republic, was sustained by a religious faith, and characterized by moral behavior. According to Eisenhower, the nation needed this moral strength to wage and to win the war with atheistic communism. "If we are to be strong," Eisenhower told the Freedoms Foundation in December 1952, "we must be strong first in our spiritual convictions."[1] He had few doubts about America's military strength against the Soviets, but, according to historian Richard Immerman, other "problematic variables in the national security equation" existed. Those variables included economic production, trade with the third world, allied relations, domestic morale, and "even less tangible, more spiritual considerations."[2] "The United States does not rely on military strength alone to win the peace," Eisenhower told the Canadian Parliament in 1953. "Our primary reliance is a unity among us forged of common adherence to moral principles," he continued, "this reliance binds together in fellowship all those who believe in the spiritual nature of man, as the Child of God."[3]

The United States needed strength for the long pull against communism, Eisenhower believed, and proper moral conviction provided the kind of sustainable strength required. "The spiritual powers of a nation – its underlying religious faith, its self-reliance, its capacity for intelligent sacrifice – these are the most important stones in any defense structure," he told the nation in 1957.[4] National strength, he continued, grew from "the ability of free men to rule themselves when they are informed" and free men and free forms of government depend "on some deeply felt religious faith."[5] Accordingly, he sought to increase American national strength for the Cold War by improving America's moral standing in the eyes of the world with the positive and peaceful use of atomic technology. These uses included the pursuit of disarmament, an effort to end to nuclear testing, and the promotion of Atoms for Peace.

Eisenhower's commitment to nuclear weapons as a means to peace was as sincere as was his commitment to wage war with thermonuclear weapons if necessary. To Eisenhower, the two initiatives were neither unrelated nor contradictory. Rather the quest for peace through threat of war has existed from time immemorial and is symbolized by the annual awarding of a peace prize named after the man who invented dynamite, Alfred Nobel. Nobel's belief that dynamite might bring an end to war was not too dissimilar for Eisenhower's hope that nuclear weapons might also make war unwinnable and thus undesirable. Until others saw the nuclear war the same way, Eisenhower emphasized the moral correctness of the use of nuclear weapons for American national strength and security. He believed that to advocate peace while building for war was not paradoxical but responsible. It was not radical thinking, but common sense, not shameful but pious. "I believe there is no mutual antagonism between a nation's faith in God and her determination to defend herself against attack," Eisenhower wrote. He

Dwight and Mamie Eisenhower leave church services at the National Presbyterian Church on 20 January 1953. (Harry S Truman Presidential Library)

quoted the Gospel of St. Luke: "When a strong man, armed, keepeth his palace, his goods are in peace."[6]

a. A Crusading Religion

As president-elect in December 1952, Eisenhower advocated faith as a means to wage the Cold War. "Now, it seems to me that if we are going to win this fight we have got to go back to the very fundamentals of all things," Eisenhower explained, "and one of them is that we are a religious people." Even those "silly" people who denied the existence of an Almighty nonetheless lived in a "religious civilization," he continued, simply because "the Founding Fathers said it was a religious concept that they were trying to translate into the political world." In the middle of the Cold War, the republic needed strength to defend the nation against the scourge of communism in this great "ideological war." Strength would demonstrate to other nations that "our leadership is not one of imperialism, but is one of purity. It is one of integrity, with a belief in the dignity of man."[7] The calls for moral strength reverberated throughout Eisenhower's two terms. "I patiently explain over and over again," Eisenhower wrote to a friend in 1956, "that American strength is a combination of its economic, moral, and military force."[8]

Eisenhower's emphasis upon moral strength stemmed in part from his own religious faith. Robert Linder and Richard Pierard have argued that Eisenhower's childhood religious experiences included Bible readings, moral piety, and steady church attendance.

According to Pierard and Linder, Eisenhower was not baptized as a child because his parents belonged to a Christian sect called the River Brethren which believed in baptism only of believers. His parents later joined the Jehovah's Witnesses, but young Dwight apparently did not follow. After that, Linder and Pierard concluded that "the evidence is far too sketchy to render a firm judgment" about his faith. During his time at West Point and through World War II, Eisenhower held a "transdenominational faith" not unlike that "propagated through the military chaplaincy."[9] His religious faith was later reinforced by his belief in the goodness of the Allied cause during World War II and he understood the war against Nazi tyranny to be a moral fight, a sentiment so strong he titled his memoir of the war years, *Crusade in Europe.*[10] He believed that the freedom of individuals "was a value derived from their status as children of God" and that the Nazis sought to destroy that freedom and replace it with quasi-religious adherence to the nation.[11] Later, Eisenhower would attribute a similar creed to the communists who abolished religion.

Before 1952, Eisenhower did not subscribe to a specific religious denomination. He attended chapel occasionally while in the army but never joined a church or established ties with a religious community. He considered himself "very earnestly and seriously religious" but never described himself as anything more precise than a Christian. "I have always sort of treasured my independence," Eisenhower told a friend, "because I like to note the differences in several Protestant denominations." After the election of 1952, Eisenhower was baptized a Presbyterian and joined the Presbyterian Church. "It is much easier to say 'I am a Presbyterian' than to say 'I am Christian but I do not belong to any denomination,'" Eisenhower explained.[12] Indeed, when Eisenhower spoke of religion before and after his baptism, he made few distinctions among persons of differing faiths. "Our form of government has no sense unless it is founded in a deeply felt religious faith," Eisenhower argued just after his first presidential election, "and I don't care what it is."[13]

Eisenhower's professions of faith during his presidency typify what scholars such as Pierard and Linder have called American civil religion.[14] According to Robert Bellah, the American sociologist who coined the term, American civil religion referred to a specific kind of religious faith, unique to the United States, in which the secular values embodied in the Declaration of Independence and the Constitution are recognized, respected, and celebrated as if they were divine and where secular American experiences are equated with Judeo-Christian ones.[15] Pierard and Linder took the concept further and have considered the role of presidents within the context of American civil religion. They have described President Eisenhower's civil religion as pastoral in nature. They argued that Eisenhower believed his political and indeed religious role was to lead the American republic and its citizens to national greatness. He yearned to steer the nation through the difficult early years of the Cold War and growing American global responsibility. The Republican National Committee went so far as to call Eisenhower "the spiritual leader of our times."[16] Immediately before delivering his first inaugural address, Eisenhower read a prayer for those in attendance: "Almighty God, as we stand here at this moment my future associates in the executive branch of government join me in beseeching that Thou will make full and complete our dedication to the service of the people in this throng, and their fellow citizens everywhere."[17] After the inauguration, Eisenhower the pastor convened his new administration with a prayer and a speech in which he asked for God's help in guiding the people of the United States.

The Cold War brought a new dimension to Eisenhower's civil religion, specifically an anti-communist element. The battle against communism, Eisenhower argued, did not result from a difference of political ideology alone but also religion. Whereas the United States was founded upon Christian values of peace, love, and forgiveness, atheism spread by Soviet communism rejected such values and led to moral depravity, violence, pestilence, and dictatorship. Pierard and Linder asserted that Eisenhower's personal faith "emphasized God as the wellspring of individual and national strength, government as resting on a spiritual foundation, faith as a public virtue, and the utilitarian nature of religion in the apocalyptic struggle against communism."[18] Eisenhower's moral campaign against communism was rooted in his belief that humans were born free, and any individual or institution seeking to destroy that freedom did so in defiance of God's will.[19]

During the Cold War, Eisenhower's faith helped him understand what he saw as the central moral difference between a society such as the United States in which the value of individual life was rooted in a belief in the Almighty and one such as the Soviet Union where life was rooted in atheistic materialism. "Basic to our democratic civilization are the principles and convictions that have bound us together as a nation," he told graduates of the Naval Academy in June 1958. "Among these are personal liberty, human rights, and the dignity of man," the president continued, "all these have their roots in a deeply held religious faith–in a belief in God." More importantly, he argued that "These are the truths with which we must combat the falsity of Communist materialistic doctrine . . . Free world respect for them and Communist disdain for them are the very core of the struggle between Communist imperialism and Western freedom."[20]

Eisenhower believed that the greatest threat to those divine rights was the spread of international communism from its source in the Soviet Union. "Atheism substitutes men for the supreme creator," he told a television audience in 1954, "and this leads inevitably to domination and dictatorship." "It is because we believe that God intends all men to be free and equal that we demand free government," the president continued.[21] Because the communists were atheists, he believed that they operated without a moral compass, without proper respect for the lives of others, and without concern for the future of their own world. "All our laws are rooted in values very different from the Soviets'," he concluded, for example, "we speak of 'good faith'; they believe, as part of their creed, in any form of deceit and treachery which advances the cause of Communist domination."[22] He concluded in 1954 that "the future is shadowed by mushroom clouds and menaced by godless men addicted to force and violence and the continuance of anarchy among nations."[23]

Though he often chided the Soviets for their unthinking atheism, he maintained his conviction about the basic nature of humanity. As Joseph Stalin lay dying in March 1953, Eisenhower helped craft a letter to the Soviet people. "The thoughts of America go out to all the peoples of the U.S.S.R.," the president wrote. "They are children of the same God who is the Father of all peoples everywhere," he continued. "Regardless of the identity of government personalities," Eisenhower concluded, "the prayer of us Americans continues to be that the Almighty will watch over the people of that vast country and bring them, in His wisdom, opportunity to live their lives in a world where all men and women and children dwell in peace and comradeship."[24] Still, the absence of religion among communists in general and Soviet leaders in particular made them an unstable adversary. The president did not believe that he could anticipate Soviet actions or account for Soviet thinking on matters of life and death because the Soviet atheistic world view contrasted so greatly with his own. "We have no basis for thinking that they abhor destruction as we do," Eisenhower told the Joint Chiefs of Staff in 1956.[25] As president, he could do very little to change this situation, but he could take the moral high ground in the struggle with the communists.

Eisenhower believed that the nation needed to muster enough moral strength to challenge the communist threat. "And because of the threat imposed by a militant and aggressive atheism," he explained, "I believe that the strengthening of all phases of our moral and spiritual foundations has a profound significance for the actual security of our nation."[26] The building of moral strength did not involve an iteration of Christian doctrine as part of a missionary impulse to convert the non-Christian world. Rather, Eisenhower believed that national moral strength developed from a combination of secular American political rights such as speech, suffrage, and property and basic Christian values such as peace, love, and forgiveness. This blend manifested in a desire to preserve the natural right of men to be free and in the pursuit of peace for all of God's creatures. It was confirmed by a universal hope for a bright and better future. Throughout his presidency, when Eisenhower spoke of spirituality, religion, or faith in the context of national strength, he referred to this general mix of secular and religious values and described nothing more specific than basic human morality and social responsibility inspired and sustained by a lasting faith in an Almighty god. Within this context, Eisenhower believed that the United States could use nuclear weapons and nuclear energy to make peace among men and to foster hope for the future of the atomic world.

b. An Indispensable Platform

The increasing tension of the Cold War, the subsequent arms race between the Soviet Union and the United States, and the pursuit of nuclear weapons by Great Britain, France, and China created a stable if uncertain system of nuclear deterrence among the superpowers. Nuclear weapons and their delivery systems improved during the 1950s and by the end of the decade, the United States and the Soviet Union possessed enough firepower to destroy one another completely. As the Cold War intensified, both sides understood that neither side could attack the other and expect to achieve victory without suffering catastrophic damage themselves. The fear that any nuclear attack would prompt a devastating counterattack and certain destruction on both sides discouraged either superpower from initiating the next great war. This system was known as deterrence.

For Eisenhower, deterrence was the byproduct of the great scientific and technological achievements of the period. "We continued to build an overpowering military establishment," Eisenhower remembered, "as the only feasible defense against the menace and probings of international Communism."[27] Despite the need, Eisenhower still thought that "the building up of large arsenals was just absurd on both sides."[28] The arms race and deterrence which resulted seemed likely to continue on "into the indefinite future" with little prospect for anything other than a paralyzing fear among the peoples of the world.[29] "Because each side possesses weapons of incalculable destructive power and with extraordinary efficiency in means of delivery," Eisenhower understood, "world fears and tensions are intensified."[30]

He recognized that the United States suffered from a "hysterical fear" of nuclear war, but he worried that the enemy might not share that sentiment indefinitely.[31] If the fear dissipated, deterrence would falter, which would lead to a catastrophic nuclear war. It was also possible that the fear itself might encourage the enemy to launch a first strike under the presumption that an effective surprise attack might eliminate or seriously weaken any response. Deterrence depended upon each side responding rationally to danger, and the system allowed no room for error. This balance of fear always seemed precarious, and, as a result, Americans lived in fear of nuclear annihilation.

Deterrence over the long term seemed both necessary and unacceptable to Eisenhower. He hated that deterrence bred fear and uncertainty. At any one point, nuclear deterrence preserved the peace, but over the long term deterrence offered no prospects for lasting peace. As Eisenhower prepared his nation for the long pull economically, militarily, and industrially, he concluded that deterrence was not compatible with his vision for the Cold War. Deterrence then became equally as immoral as fiscal irresponsibility. Still, he accepted deterrence in the short term. He found it difficult to resist this convenient if hazardous answer to the Cold War's nuclear dilemma, and he saw no immediate desirable alternative. While the problems inherent in deterrence, the increasing tension of the Cold War, and the global consequences of general war weighed heavily on Eisenhower's mind, he reluctantly concluded that only from the "indispensable platform" provided by deterrence could he pursue disarmament and peace.[32]

For Eisenhower, general disarmament, or reduction of nuclear and conventional weapons to a certain low level, was attractive for several reasons. First, a reduction of armaments would spare the superpowers the unbearable cost of building and maintaining massive nuclear stockpiles. The saved resources might then be directed inward on the domestic economy or outward on developing nations where imperialism and its legacy had retarded economic and political development. Second, Eisenhower believed that disarmament would reduce the great fear which dominated international relations. "If nations, large and small, feel compelled to produce costly weapons of war because of alleged or genuine fear of attack," he reasoned, "these fears would be lessened and cost markedly reduced if trustworthy agreements on levels of military power could be achieved."[33] He believed arms reduction or general disarmament might achieve the genuine international stability which offered a far better chance at preventing the catastrophic war which the world needed so desperately to avoid. Eisenhower "felt that if arrangements of this kind could be made they would bring stability and lessen the chance of nuclear war occurring," Andrew Goodpaster remembered.[34] The president insisted that the United States "find a way to arrest the development of weapons of massive destruction and to ultimately do away with them." "This objective seemed paramount in his mind," John McCone remembered "and he related it to a real fear of an ultimate catastrophe to civilization."[35]

As a step in this direction, Eisenhower appointed Minnesota Governor Harold Stassen as his first Special Assistant on Disarmament on 19 March 1955. When asked by the press about his thinking behind the creation of Stassen's new job, the president replied that "the concept is very simple." The United States has spent "billions and billions" of dollars to build and maintain "these sterile, unproductive agencies we call defense units and organizations" which served only the negative purpose of security through fear.[36] "Fear begets fear," Eisenhower lectured, and the arms race gathered momentum. The president sought to break the deadlock. So far the varying disarmament proposals from the State Department, the Defense Department, and others in his administration had failed because they were uncoordinated.[37] "To the members of the Cabinet, accustomed to long and futile discussions on the subject, disarmament was something as theoretical and abstract as calculus," Sherman Adams remembered. "But to Eisenhower and Stassen," Adams continued, "disarmament was a real and urgent necessity of today, the only means of gaining peace and security."[38] The president expected Stassen to work with the State Department, the National Security Council and other involved executive branch institutions to develop a unified policy for disarmament.[39]

To hold the moral high ground in the disarmament initiative and to make progress toward an agreement, Eisenhower believed that honesty and openness were the keys. This seemed to be the only way to convince the Soviet Union of American good will and to pursue serious disarmament discussions. This was far easier said than done, and his failure to penetrate the depth of Soviet secrecy crippled his disarmament talks from the beginning. By the time of Stassen's appointment, Eisenhower had already tried several times to reduce the fear of war by opening the dialogue on disarmament. In addition to the "Chance for Peace" speech, Eisenhower had also labored on a speech a month before designed to explain the realities of the nuclear weapon to the public. Under the direction of C. D. Jackson, the drafting process for a candid speech on nuclear weapons began in March 1953.[40]

Special Assistant to the President Bryce Harlow outlined and drafted a speech originally titled "Age of Peril" but which was renamed "The Safety of the Republic." Harlow wrote of the billions of dollars spent on weapons research, of American nuclear weapons equivalent to 500,000 tons of TNT, and of one American weapon which exceeded the total amount of explosive power unleashed on Germany during World War II. Subsequent drafts circulated through the White House, the Atomic Energy Commission, the Pentagon, and the State Department through the spring of 1953. Those drafts "have since been characterized by a single word 'BANG!'" reporter John Lear wrote, "because they pictured the frightful wounds a H-bomb could inflict upon the United States."

Jackson presented early drafts to Eisenhower, who rejected all of them as too frightful.[41] A State Department version dated 16 June 1953 contained the following cryptic passage: "The most important problem for our national defense today is the fact that even now the Soviet Union could drop atomic bombs on this country and that within the next two years, under certain conditions, may be able to deliver a crippling atomic surprise attack against us."[42] A draft dated 22 June 1953 replaced the section quoted above ("the most important problem") with the following: "The fact of transcendent importance for our national security today is that the Soviet atomic stockpile has now reached to point where if delivered on target in the United States – I repeat, if delivered on target – could injure this country gravely, both in material damage and in loss of life." If they were given the time to resupply and rearm, the Soviets would be capable of delivering another attack which would "hurt us so critically so that our ability to carry on the war thus forced upon us would be substantially impaired."[43] Eisenhower remembered that, upon seeing the final drafts of the Candor speech, "Jackson and I agreed that the exposition left the listener with only a new terror, not a new hope."[44] The president wanted a speech which "provided the opportunity to tell America and the world about the size and strength of our atomic capabilities – and yet to do it in such a way as to make the presentation of an argument for peaceful negotiation rather than a story told in an atmosphere of truculence, defiance, and threat."[45] He ultimately settled upon the idea of encouraging nuclear nations to contribute fissionable material to the United Nations which would use the material for nuclear power. This later became the Atoms for Peace program.

A related attempt at disarmament was the president's Open Skies proposal of July 1955. Open Skies was intended to involve a frank and full exchange of military capabilities which would hopefully eliminate the secrecy on both sides which had contributed so greatly "to the fears and dangers of surprise attack." From there a system of inspections and monitoring could be implemented to guarantee compliance with any future agreements on disarmament. To Eisenhower it was a necessary first step. "The successful working out of such a system," Eisenhower believed, "would do much to develop the mutual confidence which will open wide the avenues of progress for all our peoples."[46] He hoped an agreement might instill "a spirit of non-aggressiveness on both sides and so to create a fresh atmosphere which would dispel much of the present fear and suspicion."[47] When Eisenhower spoke about Open Skies in his remarks at the Geneva Conference of 1955, he spoke broadly of faith.

The heads of the United States, the Soviet Union, Great Britain, and France convened in Geneva, Switzerland in July 1955 to discuss lingering Cold War problems. Eisenhower joined with British Prime Minister Anthony Eden, Premier Edgar Faure of France, and Soviet Premier Nikolai Bulganin to consider issues such as East-West trade, international security, and the arms race. Eisenhower delivered remarks to the delegates about his new vision for international security through disarmament on 21 July. To safeguard the republic after World War II America needed great strength, he explained. The nation rearmed and built alliances "in a partnership for peace and for mutual security." Since then, the Cold War had begun and the danger of nuclear war had grown. He believed that the preservation of peace through the building of nuclear arms had devolved from merely ironic to paradoxical, from bizarre to catastrophic. Working toward peace, Eisenhower then concluded, no longer meant only building for war. He announced his pursuit of disarmament to "lighten the burdens upon the backs" and to "ease the fears of war in the anxious hearts of people everywhere."[48]

The complicating matter in any disarmament negotiation was verification. On one hand, the Soviet leader Bulganin and his successor Nikita Khrushchev insisted on preserving as much as possible the closed nature of Soviet society. They feared any disarmament verification apparatus that included on-site inspections or listening posts. Any agreement, the Soviets argued, needed reliable verification but must not reveal Soviet state secrets or provide a window into the regime for western spies. On the other hand, both Eisenhower and the Congress worried that without proper verification the Soviets would cheat on any deal and augment their own military strength as America foolishly abided by the terms of a treaty. For Eisenhower, the United States bargained in good faith, but the Soviets did not. The president saw the dilemma clearly: "all disarmament proposals stumble over the seemingly insuperable obstacle of Soviet opposition to any kind of inspection. Since they have so often proved faithless to their word, we cannot consider any move that does not provide for adequate inspection and safeguards."[49] Accordingly, Eisenhower insisted on rigid monitoring and inspections. He told the National Security Council "that any agreement would have no effect and would not be signed unless an inspection system had been agreed upon, set up, and tested."[50] By early 1957, the United Nations General Assembly had referred the matter of disarmament to the U.N. Disarmament Commission where Open Skies and the Soviet counterproposal languished for the rest of Eisenhower's second term. As the President's Special Assistant for Disarmament, Stassen continued to work directly with the Disarmament Commission, the Soviets, and the British to take a sound first step toward an agreement.[51] The president understood the difficulty in reaching an agreement with members of his own administration, Congress, and other nations. "There is, however, no alternative to continuation of the effort," Eisenhower reminded Stassen, "with all the intelligence and patience that we can bring to bear on the matter."[52]

Beginning on 18 March 1957, the major powers began a series of meetings in London under the banner of the United Nations Disarmament Commission. Eisenhower earlier succeeded in opening a dialogue with the Soviet Union about a reduction in nuclear armaments, and the Soviet leadership expressed a willingness to discuss the matter further. Within this promising climate, the London talks began. Soviet and American delegates labored over the issue of verification as the central issue of any disarmament deal. The president needed a guarantee of Soviet compliance with any agreement to placate all doubters. The American delegation, which included Eisenhower and Stassen, "worked very hard to find a position in the disarmament area that is as liberal and broad-gauged as elementary considerations of security would permit."[53] In June, the Eisenhower administration settled on a State Department paper that outlined the United States' position on the first phase of disarmament. Nations willing to agree to that paper would pledge "to cooperate in designing, installing, and maintaining effective inspection systems to verify compliance." They would further agree that each nation's compliance with the agreement would be conditioned upon effective operation of those inspection systems. Under this proposal, agreeable parties pledged not to use nuclear weapons unless vitally necessary and "to devote all future production of fissionable materials exclusively to non-weapons purposes." The deal included trust-building measures such as the creation of initial inspection zones and a temporary nuclear test ban. On disarmament, the United States suggested that three months after the conclusion of an agreement the parties disclose "inventories of fixed military installations and numbers and locations of military forces and major designated armaments (including nuclear weapons delivery capabilities but excluding nuclear weapons)" within the inspection zones. One year after the agreement, the United States and the Soviet Union would transfer "specific quantities of designated types of armaments, substantial in amount, significant in kind" to internationally managed storage sites.[54] Discussions and negotiations dragged on throughout the London talks.

The president exchanged letters first with the Soviet leader Bulganin and then with his successor Khrushchev pleading with them to change their intransigent attitude toward disarmament negotiations. He reiterated past overtures, including Open Skies, and became increasingly frustrated at Soviet unwillingness to conclude even the most basic agreement to reduce the danger of nuclear war. U.S. disarmament proposals made since 1953 had either been ignored or rejected outright by the Soviet Union, and

Eisenhower labored to maintain his optimism. "For several years we have been seeking a dependable ending to the accumulation of nuclear weapons stockpiles and a dependable beginning of the steady reduction of existing weapons stockpiles," Eisenhower wrote to Khrushchev in April 1958. "However," Eisenhower continued, "the Soviet Union continues to reject the concept of an internationally supervised program to end weapons production and to reduce weapons stocks."[55]

Despite his efforts, the president knew his disarmament accomplishments were "meager, almost negligible." "No matter how deeply preoccupied my associates and I became with other urgent situations," Eisenhower later wrote, "never for a day was there absent from our minds and organized work the search for some kind of agreement that would mark a first, even if only a small, step toward a satisfactory disarmament plan." Disarmament had been a moral imperative for the nation, he believed. "To lighten the burdens of armaments" meant "to lessen the likelihood of war," and "any progress would be an important step toward the ultimate goal of establishing a universal peace with justice and freedom."[56] Fear compelled governments to amass tremendous military power, Eisenhower believed, but that fear had not entirely destroyed the hope for peace. The building of armaments by both the United States and the Soviet Union created a system of deterrence which for the time at least was preventing war. But Eisenhower refused to accept the moral bankruptcy of succumbing to fear and relying on deterrence forever.[57] "Hope is more difficult to kill than men," Eisenhower wrote, "and humanity is not ready spinelessly to accept the cynical conclusion that war is certain to recur, that the law of the jungle must forever be the rule of life."[58] Only though the economic, military, and industrial strength provided for the United States by the nuclear weapon could Eisenhower negotiate a reduction or elimination of armaments and bolster America's moral standing. "In the meantime, and pending some advance in this direction [of disarmament], we must stay strong," Eisenhower wrote in his diary, "particularly in that type of power that the Russians are compelled to respect – namely, destructive power that can be carried suddenly and en masse directly against the Russian economic structure."[59] His quest for peace through deterrence supplied the United States with moral strength as America demonstrated her desire to remove the paralyzing fear which had long defined the Cold War.

c. Some Basis of Hope

Eisenhower pursued a cessation to nuclear testing as a step toward disarmament and peace. While he valued nuclear testing because of its contribution to the buildup of U.S. military strength through improved nuclear weapons and to industrial strength through the development of clean nuclear weapons to be used in Project Plowshare, Eisenhower also emphasized the building of moral strength and America's continued testing of nuclear weapons soon began to strain the world' faith in the United States. How could the United States continually prepare and test new nuclear weapons while at the same time claiming to be working towards peace, some wondered? Eisenhower recognized and attempted to address the testing dilemma. On one hand, Eisenhower hoped to stop nuclear testing to demonstrate to the world the United States' steadfast commitment to peace and her hopeful vision for the future. On the other hand, he sought to ease the growing controversy both inside and outside the United States over nuclear fallout from testing. Eisenhower lamented the harmful human effects of fallout in the

Operation Cue tested the effects of an atomic blast on typical suburban houses and household items, 5 May 1955. (National Archives)

United States and the South Pacific, but was never fully convinced that nuclear fallout was as dangerous as critics suggested. The real danger of nuclear testing, he believed, was increased international tension, a continuing arms race, and a greater likelihood of nuclear war between the superpowers. To Eisenhower, fallout was an unfortunate political issue which unnecessarily complicated his ability to negotiate disarmament and peace with the Soviet Union.

Eisenhower's search for a nuclear test ban began in his first term.[60] According to Benjamin Greene, the president "entered office horrified at the thought of nuclear war" as a result of watching a top secret film on Operation Ivy and of hearing only nine months later of the Soviet Union's first thermonuclear detonation. [61] In May 1954, the National Security Council debated a testing moratorium which Eisenhower seemed inclined to endorse. The president worried in particular about the size of recent Soviet nuclear tests and about the ability of the Soviet Union to hide future tests from the international community. His primary concern was how a moratorium might contribute to peace and security in the Cold War. He "could perceive no final answer to the problem of nuclear warfare if both sides simply went ahead making bigger and better nuclear weapons." Though he did not want the Soviets to surpass the United States in nuclear arms, he thought it wrong "to take a negative view of this terrible problem." "We must try to find some positive answer" to this deep "despair" caused by looking out at "a future which contained nothing but more and more bombs," the president pleaded. He warned that if the United States continued on "a course which had no future for us" then nuclear testing would only enhance "our capability to destroy."[62] The idea of test cessation of any sort met significant opposition from some of Eisenhower's key advisers including Lewis Strauss and the Joint Chiefs of Staff. But Eisenhower's failure to achieve a test ban in his first term, according to Greene, was the result of "a series of highly complex technical matters beyond [Eisenhower's] realm of understanding."[63]

Between the first failed push toward a moratorium and the presidential election of 1956, the controversy surrounding fallout from nuclear testing grew at a considerable rate. In the United States and around the world, politicians and citizens grew more organized and vocal in their concerns about nuclear fallout. The global fallout controversy can be traced back to Japan on 14 March 1954, the day the Japanese fishing vessel *Lucky Dragon* returned to Yaizu harbor. Two weeks earlier, on 1 March, the Atomic Energy Commission had begun a series of nuclear tests code-named Castle. Bravo, the first shot of the Castle series, unexpectedly released a large amount of radiation upon detonation and generated a significant amount of radioactive fallout. After a gray ash began falling in the immediate area, American naval units stationed in the vicinity evacuated islanders and took precautions to decontaminate their own ships. Eighty-five miles away, however, Japanese fisherman aboard the *Lucky Dragon* soon experienced a light rain accompanied by a white ash almost like snow. The *Lucky Dragon* was dusted with radioactive fallout. Because the boat had inadvertently strayed into the test zone unnoticed by the AEC, the fisherman had not been made aware of the potential danger and they took no steps to decontaminate themselves, their vessel, or their catch. When the crew returned to harbor on 14 March, a majority of the crew presented symptoms of radiation poisoning, and two days later Japanese newspapers reported that the men had been made ill by an atomic test.[64] American newspapers picked up the story, and they looked to the government for more information about the dangers of nuclear fallout. "It is quite clear that this time something must have happened that we have never experienced before," Eisenhower admitted. "Very properly," he continued, "the United States has to take precautions that never occurred to them before."[65]

The Castle-Bravo test and the *Lucky Dragon* incident soon spurred new investigations into fallout. In a meeting of 24 May 1954, Brigadier General Kenneth E. Fields, head of the Atomic Energy Commission's Office of Military Applications, illustrated in graphic detail what would have happened had Bravo been detonated in Washington, D.C. The nation's capital, Philadelphia, and New York would have received lethal amounts of radioactive fallout which would have stretched as far north as Maine.[66] Ralph Lapp, an independent journalist, soon published articles explaining the details of fallout in the *Bulletin of Atomic Scientists* and the *New Republic*. According to Richard Hewlett and Jack Holl, the feeling in Washington was the "sweet taste of success with a sickening reality: mankind had succeeded in producing a weapon that could destroy large areas and threaten life over thousands of square miles."[67] When Lewis Strauss told the White House press corps that the United States' new hydrogen bomb could be built large enough to destroy an entire city, any city, the public debate over nuclear testing accelerated.[68]

In the United States, politicians, scientists, activists, and ordinary citizens began a campaign for less secrecy regarding atomic weapons and a halt to nuclear testing. Around the world, Castle-Bravo and the *Lucky Dragon* incident prompted widespread condemnation. From Jawaharlal Nehru to Albert Schweitzer to Pope Pius XII, world leaders expressed great concern about thermonuclear testing and fallout. Even in Great Britain, the United States' staunch ally in the Cold War, Labour Party leaders in Parliament advised Prime Minister Churchill's government to seek a bilateral test ban with the Soviet Union.[69] The U.S. government's release of an unclassified version of the Operation Ivy film which chronicled the world's first thermonuclear test did not comfort by rather stimulated national and international concern over nuclear testing and fallout.[70]

On 15 February 1955, to meet the growing controversy, the Eisenhower administration released its first official report on Castle-Bravo in particular and fallout in general. The report addressed specifically nuclear fallout and its effects on the human population. The report further described the danger from Strontium-90, a radioactive isotope created by nuclear explosions, but concluded that "the amount of radiostrontium now present in the soil as a result of all nuclear explosions to date would have to be increased many thousand times before any effect on humans would be noticeable."[71] The total exposure of human populations to radioactive products was only a fraction of that which individuals would receive over their lifetimes from normal background radiation.[72] The risk of radioactive fallout was far less than the immediate threat of communism to the security of the free world, the report concluded.

With the public debate increasing in volume, Eisenhower hoped the report would calm the situation. He admitted that the issue of nuclear weapons was "one of the most serious problems facing us today." But the purpose of the Atomic Energy Commission's report was to provide the public "a considerable amount of information on the effects of thermonuclear weapons, and, particularly, the fallout," he continued. "You have to look facts in the face," the president reminded the nation, and "you have to have the stamina to do it without just going hysterical." On the issue of fallout, Eisenhower refused to state clearly if he believed fallout was as dangerous as others had argued. "There could be very serious consequences" downwind of test sites, but "it is also possible for the individual to take care of himself."[73] At that time, in March 1955, Eisenhower seemed genuinely unsure if fallout posed a serious health hazard to human beings in the United States and around the world.

Scientific studies had in part shaped Eisenhower's view of the fallout issue. In December 1955, *The Scientific Monthly* published a study titled "Effects of Nuclear Weapons Testing," which had some impact on Eisenhower. The author, Gordon Dunning, was a medical doctor with the Atomic Energy Commission and his analysis was quite optimistic. He concluded that the radioactivity emitted from nuclear tests was negligible and did not constitute a significant threat to human health. He did note some exceptions, including *Lucky Dragon* sailors who were directly affected by fallout from the Castle-Bravo test. Dunning cited only one death in the case of the *Lucky Dragon* and explained that fatality resulted from hepatitis which he argued was not directly attributable to radiation. Anecdotally, he asserted that the tuna exposed to nuclear fallout on the *Lucky Dragon* would be "considered safe for unlimited consumption."[74] The testing of nuclear weapons did not pose a serious threat to Americans and furthermore, Dunning opined, any associated risks were necessary and acceptable because "the continuation of our nuclear testing program is mandatory to the defense of our country."[75]

Eisenhower seemed to accept this view then and later. "The best scientific information available," Eisenhower later wrote, "indicated that the present level of testing did not imperil the health of humanity, while our latest tests were enabling scientists to learn better methods for reducing fallout."[76] The view that radioactivity from nuclear weapons tests posed no significant biological hazard to humans was further supported by a National Academy of Sciences study of October 1956.[77] "That is the authoritative document by which I act up to this moment," he told the press, "because there has been no change that I know of." The Academy "gave a very full discussion of the whole matter," including a discussion of radiation exposure "from natural sources." From the sun all the way "down even to include phosphorous on the dial of your watch" background radiation existed and fallout contributed only minimally to that slight risk. Indeed, when and where scientists disagreed on this issue, they were either "out of their own field of competence" or participating in "an organized affair."[78] In addition to scientists, politicians also entered the debate. In the 1956 presidential contest, Democrat Adlai Stevenson criticized the president for his failure to enact a test ban treaty. Eisenhower had done his best not to address the fallout controversy in his campaign as he thought that the matter was far too complex for a political campaign. Eisenhower won in 1956 by an even greater margin than in 1952, but Stevenson had succeeded in interjecting fallout into the political debate, a development Eisenhower detested. The president placed his faith in testimony from the Atomic Energy Commission and the National Academy of Sciences, "the nation's foremost scientific body," which contradicted the "misleading statements presented by partisans on the advice of their 'experts.'"[79]

For Eisenhower, the danger of fallout had been exaggerated. "The widespread and growing fear of radioactive fallout from nuclear tests was, according to the best authorities, unreasoning," Eisenhower later explained, "but it was real."[80] Testing itself was not evil, but many "have been brought to believe that it is." Terrifying weapons such as flamethrowers and fire bombs produced great blast and heat after all, but were accepted as tools of war, he reasoned. The danger of radioactivity by contrast was little understood by people and "therefore deeply feared by populations."[81] To correct this problem, Eisenhower felt obliged to respond to public fear about fallout with a new tactic.

Eisenhower believed he could steer the conversation toward his efforts at peace through a test ban. "Everybody seems to think that we're skunks, saber-rattlers and warmongers," he complained in 1954, "we ought not to miss any chance to make clear our peaceful objectives." The president saw the potential for a great public relations coup for the United States. Assuming the maximum possible effectiveness in nuclear weapons had been achieved, "it might give us a tremendous psychological advantage over the enemy if we could propose a moratorium on future tests."[82] Eisenhower "accepted that the abolition of tests would probably hurt us comparatively in a military sense," but believed the national credibility and demonstration of American good served the United States' interest as well. He told the former Manhattan Project scientist and Columbia University professor Isidor Rabi that "our world situation requires that we achieve the political benefits of this action."[83] The peoples of the world seemed greatly more afraid of atomic warfare than "the long list of Russian violations of agreements," Eisenhower argued, and he insisted that the United States take steps which account for and take advantage of that reality.[84] It was "simply intolerable to remain in a position wherein the United States, seeking peace, and giving loyal partnership to our allies, is unable to achieve an advantageous impact on world opinion." To pursue a test ban promised political and psychological rewards far beyond any risk to America's military standing. In addition, as he explained, the pursuit of a test ban offered "some basis for hope for our people and for world opinion."[85]

Test ban negotiations however proved even more difficult than he imagined. The principal problem for the Eisenhower administration in negotiating a test ban treaty with the Soviet Union was that Eisenhower did not trust Soviet leaders to honor any bargain struck by the two sides. Issues of psychological advantage, fallout, disarmament, hope, and peace all motivated Eisenhower to reach an agreement, but the Soviets, Eisenhower believed, did not reciprocate that sincerity. Some of his advisers, including Atomic Energy Commission Chairman Strauss, warned the president about Soviet duplicity, a characteristic the president well understood.[86] "The Soviets had no intention of allowing a true agreement on nuclear testing," Eisenhower told his staff in January 1959, but the United States needed to press the issue to achieve either an agreement or a propaganda advantage.[87]

In order for Eisenhower to have faith in any agreement struck with the Soviet Union, the agreement needed reliable safeguards to guarantee compliance. He was convinced however that modern technology provided an answer to the compliance problem. The twin pillars of compliance verification were monitoring and inspections. Eisenhower insisted that the two parties agree to a system of appropriately situated monitoring stations both in and around the territorial boundaries of the superpowers in order to detect any underground or atmospheric nuclear test. If any doubt arose about a suspected test, the second pillar would become necessary; inspection teams would be sent in to ascertain whether a test had been conducted. Already wary about monitoring stations that would be placed so close to Soviet territory, inspections proved another great hurdle. The Soviets greatly valued the secrecy of their state and worked hard to preserve it. To allow both monitoring stations and on-site inspections threatened that secrecy. To sacrifice that secrecy meant to give away a key advantage the Soviets believed they possessed. Despite these difficulties, Eisenhower continued to press his advisors to find an agreement, "even if the arrangement is not necessarily a perfect one." If the Soviets rejected an unlimited number of inspections per year, for example, the number of manned or unmanned stations would be need to be increased in order to compensate.[88]

As negotiations toward a test ban limped along, Eisenhower became increasingly concerned about America's testing program. In December 1956, he "expressed some doubt as to the advisability" of a series of nuclear tests proposed by the Atomic Energy Commission for the beginning of May 1957.[89] John Foster Dulles later noted that "the President had been appalled by the number of these tests."[90] According to Dulles, the president worried that, because he had said the country was on track to build smaller, clean bombs, large tests struck at the president's credibility. "The main dilemma in conducting tests of this magnitude," the president explained, "is that of planning and carrying out extensive tests on the one hand while professing a readiness to suspend testing in a disarmament program on the other." This conduct "may bring accusations of bad faith," he noted.[91] Although he approved the Hardtack series of 1958, he argued that the clean weapons test of 1958, Operation Pinon, "should be called off."[92]

In late March 1958, Eisenhower heard from British Prime Minister Macmillan about rumors of a possible Soviet testing moratorium, and the president "gave very serious thought to anticipating a possible Soviet move on suspension of testing by a statement of our own." The United States was "being pushed into a rather difficult position from the standpoint of world opinion," he understood, but maintained that the best course of action at that point was to do nothing.[93] He also did not want to announce a moratorium until after the British had completed an important test series of their own. On 31 March 1958, the Soviet Union announced a suspension of nuclear tests. The Soviet moratorium followed a series of tests begun the previous August which sometimes included numerous, multiple-megaton bombs detonated in a single day. In a letter to the new Soviet Chairman Nikita Khrushchev, Eisenhower noted the irony. "It seems peculiar that the Soviet Union, having just concluded a series of tests of unprecedented intensity should now, in bold headlines, say that it will not test again," Eisenhower noted, "but add, in small type, that it may test again if the United States carries out its already long announced and now imminent series of tests." Eisenhower reminded the new chairman that a stoppage of tests was merely a means toward disarmament and requested the new Soviet leader reexamine his government's attitude toward Eisenhower's previous proposals for disarmament. "Surely, the heart of the nuclear problem is not the mere *testing* of weapons," the president reasoned, "but the weapons themselves."[94] Still, the Soviets had beaten Eisenhower to the punch on announcing a test suspension and the president knew it. The Soviet moratorium frustrated Eisenhower personally and wounded him politically. At his press conference of April 2, Eisenhower referred to the "testing thing" dismissed it as simply "a side issue," "a gimmick," and something not be taken seriously.[95]

Eisenhower then took steps to repair the damage done to America's international reputation. In addition to considering seriously a matching American moratorium, Eisenhower instructed Dulles to chair a new committee aimed at revising the administration's disarmament proposals. He also proposed to Khrushchev a disarmament conference in Geneva. At the conference to begin on 1 July, scientists from the United States, Western Europe and the Soviet bloc would join to discuss detection of nuclear tests. If Eisenhower decided to institute his own testing moratorium, he wanted reliable means to verify the Soviet pledge through a conference of experts in Switzerland.[96] Soviet and American scientists at the conference ultimately reached an agreement on four technical methods to detect nuclear tests.[97] On 12 August 1958, Dulles wrote Eisenhower to inform him of the impending agreement and the urgent need for an official administration policy on nuclear testing.[98] According to Eisenhower, "world opinion is shifting, if not toward the Soviets, at least away from the West because of our alleged intransigence about all aspects of nuclear testing and so on." To regain the moral high ground, Eisenhower could not wait out of a fear that the Soviets would argue that America only begrudgingly entered into a moratorium out of guilt when Eisenhower genuinely sought to emphasize American good will and sincere pursuit of disarmament and peace.[99]

On 22 August 1958, Eisenhower announced the United States would halt nuclear testing for one year. He hoped the success of Geneva and the American test suspension might spur other nuclear powers to begin negotiations for a worldwide suspension of nuclear testing and a control system based on the Geneva experts' agreement. His moratorium was to be a key step toward an abolition of tests, control of weapons, and ultimately disarmament. "To facilitate the detailed negotiations," Eisenhower continued, "the United States is prepared, unless testing is resumed by the Soviet Union, to withhold further testing on its part of atomic and hydrogen weapons for a period of one year from the beginning of the negotiations." The United States also pledged to renew the moratorium, assuming satisfactory progress in negotiations on a yearly basis for an indefinite period of time. For now, the moratorium would begin on 31 October 1958. The president genuinely believed the moratorium would lead to further discussions and "more substantial agreements relating to limitation and reduction of fissionable material for weapons and to other essential phases of disarmament."[100]

Eisenhower made this proposal with great hope for the future of the atomic world, and in doing so the president sought to restore worldwide faith in America's peaceful intentions. According to one study, Eisenhower "saw a test ban as necessary in a long-term solution to the danger of nuclear warfare."[101] The United States held a moral obligation, the president believed, to begin the end of the nuclear arms race and to relieve the dread of the overall atomic menace. Testing was an obstacle to progress. As nations continued to test nuclear weapons, their capacity to destroy improved and international tension increased. American tests made hollow Eisenhower's push for disarmament and made the United States appear guilty of poisoning the world's air, soil, and water. The more bombs the United States exploded, the more the world became convinced that the United States was a nation to be feared, not loved, a nation that wanted war, not peace. Eisenhower pursued a nuclear test ban treaty with the Soviet Union and instituted the American testing moratorium because he sought to take concrete steps toward disarmament and because he wanted to demonstrate to his friends and enemies his nation's sincere desire for peace. The pursuit of these broad goals served U.S. national interests, Eisenhower believed, because they announced to the world the United States' firm intention to encourage constructive dialogue, to support basic human morality, and to defend the rights of all citizens to live in peace with their neighbors.

d. Out of the Dark, Into the Light

Eisenhower's central dilemma in the nuclear age was how to preserve the hope of a bright future despite the great fear of a perpetual arms race, nuclear weapons proliferation, and thermonuclear war. The buildup of nuclear weapons and technology as directed by Eisenhower afforded the United States financial, military, and industrial strength. That same growth in strength however generally increased the danger if not the likelihood of nuclear war. Fear followed, and throughout Eisenhower's administration, Americans' deep worry about nuclear war grew. A national poll conducted by the American Institute of Public Opinion in February 1953 showed that 66 percent of Americans believed that the hydrogen bomb would be used against their country if another war began. The percentage steadily grew from 63 percent in April 1954 to 71 percent in May 1957. In May 1958, three out of four Americans believed the hydrogen bomb would be used against the United States in the event of war.[102]

Within this climate of fear, Eisenhower also had to compete with the fearful images of nuclear war in American popular culture. The film *On the Beach* for example, which premiered on 17 December 1959, depicted the end of human civilization after a massive nuclear war. Nevil Shute, the author of the novel upon which the film was based, and the movie's director Stanley Kramer hoped the graphic images of nuclear holocaust would force world leaders to eliminate the threat of nuclear annihilation through whatever means necessary. For Eisenhower, *On the Beach* presented problems. On the one hand,

Eisenhower and his advisors feared the film would be a huge success and convince Americans that the world would be best served by unilateral nuclear disarmament and by joining radical "ban-the-bomb" organizations. On the other hand, the film threatened to erode American moral strength by feeding the overwhelming fear of nuclear war. The depictions of slow death from nuclear fallout might bring a spiritual and emotional depression. To Eisenhower's great dismay, *On the Beach* offered no hope for the future of a nuclear world. The film's main characters wait for the fallout cloud to descend upon the last bastion of human existence in Australia. As the cloud can not be stopped, humanity ends with the closing credits.

Many observers anticipated that *On the Beach* would be a huge success. Large advertisements like those in the *Los Angeles Times* celebrated the film as a "really extraordinary motion picture event."[103] Dr. Robert M. Hutchins of the Fund for the Republic called *On the Beach* "no ordinary film" as it dealt seriously with the "greatest threat hanging over our free society," atomic war, and Dr. Linus Pauling thought it would be remembered for saving the world.

While the book described the war in some detail, the motion picture showed only the results. Viewers are told early on that radioactive fallout from a nuclear exchange is expected to arrive in Australia in five months. Apparently nothing can be done to stop it. The main characters attempt to live out their lives with as much dignity, strength, and pleasure as possible. Produced and directed by Stanley Kramer, the film starred Gregory Peck as Captain Dwight Towers, commander of the American submarine *Sawfish* which is patrolling the South Pacific when the war begins. He and his crew are all that remained of the United States. Ava Gardner plays Moira Davidson, an Australian socialite whose free-wheeling approach to life only compounds her despair in the final days. Fred Astaire portrays the cynical scientist, Julian Osborn, who fulfills his final wish of racing automobiles before his death. Anthony Perkins plays Australian Navy lieutenant Peter Holmes whose primary role is to counteract the overwhelming feeling of dread felt by his wife, Mary, played by Donna Anderson.

In a moment of high drama, the Holmes family hosts a party which quickly deteriorates into a discussion on the cause of the deadly war and the fate of mankind. "We're all doomed, you know. The whole, silly, drunken, pathetic lot of us," Julian laments, "Doomed by the air we're about to breath." "Stop it! I won't have it, Julian" Mary screams. "There is hope. There has to be hope. There's always hope. We just can't go on like this. We can't," she cries.[104] In the meantime, the Australian Navy detects a radio signal which seems to originate in California where, according to data, no one should be alive to send a message. Captain Towers and his crew, along with Osborn and Holmes, volunteer to make the hopeful journey north both to find the source of the signal and to see if the radiation levels have lessened from rain and snow. In San Diego, the crew discovers that the signal was being made by a soda bottle which dangled from a cord and was being raised and lowered by the wind on to a telegraph machine.

After the return of the *Sawfish* to Australia, Australians begin to line up to collect from their government poison pills they could take to avoid an excruciating death from radiation poisoning. Before the end, the characters manage to entertain one another, racing cars, having dinner parties, and relaxing on the beach. But as the time approaches, they become more depressed and hopeless. Osborn sits in his race car in the garage, running the engine and asphyxiating himself in carbon monoxide. Holmes and his wife poison their infant daughter and themselves. Powers enjoys his time with Davidson, but his crew elects to return to the United States to die rather than remain in a foreign land. The *Sawfish* sails for America just as Davidson arrives at the harbor, late and left behind. The final scene shows an empty urban area with garbage blowing in the poisoned wind, and the banner reminding audiences "there is still time . . . brother."[105]

As the premiere of *On the Beach* drew near, the Eisenhower administration prepared for the worst. The Operations Coordinating Board (OCB) of Eisenhower's National Security Council distributed an information packet prepared in early December 1959 by the United States Information Agency (USIA) and the State Department to U.S. missions in cities around the world. The packet provided an official response to questions likely to be raised about the film and instructed personnel how to conduct themselves to achieve the desired result. The USIA and State Department advocated exposing the film's fundamental flaws and then letting the issue die from neglect. "Our attitude should be one of matter-of-fact interest, showing no special concern," the Board recommended, and "We should refrain from public criticism of the film, which would be counter-productive." The administration should be equally careful to "avoid any implications of U.S. government approval." Beyond this, the merits of the film should be discussed only in private and only when necessary.[106]

U.S. officials overseas were instructed to concentrate on what the USIA and State Department saw as the three major issues raised by *On the Beach*. First, viewers might have a "strong emotional experience" and emerge with an urgency to push for nuclear disarmament. In this case, officials should stress that the U.S. government was pursuing this objective and that "real progress is attainable." Second, if "the scientific inaccuracies mislead people and drive them to pressure for ban-the-bomb-type solutions to the nuclear weapons problem," officials should stress two major flaws in the film's scientific data. One, fallout from a war in the northern hemisphere would never reach the southern hemisphere even if the maximum number of nuclear weapons were used. Two, despite the film's portrayal of a civilian population with no options, civil defense measures currently in place would save humans from fallout. The third and final point concerned the human response to disaster conditions and reflected Eisenhower's commitment to the preservation of hope in the nuclear age. "The film grossly misconstrues the basic nature of man," the Board argued. "The resort to mass suicide is not only unnecessary but wholly fatalistic, misinterpreting the vitality of the human spirit," they continued, "It is inconceivable that even in the event of a nuclear war, mankind would not have the strength and ingenuity to take all possible steps toward self-preservation."[107]

Eisenhower's cabinet discussed *On the Beach* in a meeting of 11 December 1959. "In view of the attempts made [by third parties] to get Cabinet members, collectively or individually, to endorse or even sponsor the December 18 Washington premiere, and to attend it," the Operations Coordinating Board thought to provide the appropriate information to Cabinet members. Karl Harr informed the Cabinet that the "unprecedented publicity given to this movie" made its discussion by the Cabinet necessary. He reiterated the contents of the USIA-State instruction sheet. Former Iowa Governor Leo Hoegh of the Office of Civil Defense Mobilization took particular offense at the film's effect of undermining civil defense initiatives. Hoegh found the film "very harmful because it produced a feeling of utter hopelessness."[108]

The problem the film presented for the Eisenhower administration was not the threat of nuclear war but the image of a world without hope. Though the actual war did not appear on the screen, the post-war world was hardly one worth living in; life would soon be over and there was little that any person could do but wait for the end. Eisenhower recognized that any nuclear war would cost a huge number of American lives, but the nation and its people would live for another day. To combat the kind of hopelessness *On the Beach* fostered, Eisenhower had six years earlier considered Operation Candor, a program intended to brief Americans on the survivability of nuclear war, but he had abandoned it because as the ideas proved too morbid for distribution to the American people. When *On the Beach* hit theaters in 1959, Candor had long been extinct, but the threat of nuclear war remained. The Eisenhower administration prepared for the film's release with trepidation, anticipating some public reaction to the film. But no significant public response came. A fear of nuclear war already existed in the United States by 1959. Gallup Polls indicated that civil defense drills and government-sponsored scientific reports on nuclear war had already made Americans aware of perils of the atomic age. Perhaps because Americans resisted looking ahead at a world without hope or perhaps because they had already been contemplating this world for some time, Americans recognized the fallacies of *On the Beach* and were largely unaffected by the film. To the delight of the Eisenhower administration, the movie was not the blockbuster some had anticipated, and it had little measurable effect on America's fears of nuclear war.

On the Beach debuted to mostly negative reviews. Newspapers, popular and scientific magazines, as well as religious publications all condemned the film as too dark, too morbid, and too implausible. "Although possessing unwavering concern for life," film historian Joseph Keyerleber wrote, *On the Beach* "is a film of overwhelming nondistinction."[109] Viewers did not respond to the film the way producer-director Stanley Kramer hoped or the way the Eisenhower administration feared. Kramer meant for the film to be powerful and thought-provoking, and officials in Washington feared it would be powerful and thought-numbing, pushing people either to indulge in hysteria or to join pacifist movements.[110] Robert Hatch, a reviewer for *The Nation*, noted the applause which erupted at the film's end. "That is unusual movie-house behavior," he wrote, "and I wondered what they were applauding. Had they 'enjoyed' the picture or were they glad to be alive?"[111]

The depiction of human nature in the film greatly disturbed many in both popular and religious publications. *Life* commented that the film would prove controversial as critics would shun a film suggesting that "real people would die with so little shouting" and advocating the use of suicide pills.[112] Hatch argued that Kramer's expectations of human behavior in the face of the end of the world were "optimistic to the point of fantasy." When all hope is gone, "men do not go about muttering 'bad show' and preparing for decorous death. They turn horribly mad."[113] *America*, a Catholic publication, thought *On the Beach* suffered "from the inability of human skill and imagination to measure up to its awful theme."[114]

But a writer for *Catholic World* best articulated the general concern over the film's lack of hope. James Schall argued that Kramer had intended to make a film which brought to the world a message of hope that "men will realize the danger of the present situation."[115] Schall quoted Kramer: "There are differences and fears and mistrust in this world and always the sober reminder of the need for realistic thinking. We have tried

Eisenhower delivers his *Atoms for Peace* speech to the General Assembly of the United Nations on 8 December 1953. (Dwight D. Eisenhower Presidential Library)

to be aware of this, and then tried to transcend it by a concept of hope on celluloid – namely, to reach out to the hearts of people everywhere that they might feel compassion – for themselves."[116] Despite Kramer's intent, for Schall the movie offered no hope at all. Man should have demanded of himself that life should not be destroyed on the earth; life should continue and should be peaceful. But Kramer's film did not demonstrate any measure of hope as man accepted death calmly and willingly. Schall expected a film about the hope of humanity, but left the theater disappointed.[117] *On the Beach* depicted the exact image of a hopeless world that the Eisenhower rejected at the beginning of his presidency. Eisenhower opted instead for Atoms for Peace which he imagined would prove uplifting and full of hope in a world with nuclear power.

Eisenhower's single most important initiative aimed at restoring hope for the nuclear age was Atoms for Peace which he announced before the General Assembly of the United Nations in December 1953. "I know that the American people share my deep belief," Eisenhower told the United Nations, "that if a danger exists in the world, it is a danger shared by all – and equally, that if hope exists in the mind of one nation, that hope should be shared by all." The proliferation of atomic weapons from the United States to the Soviet Union and Great Britain suggested that soon other nations might also possess the atomic bomb, the president noted, and the danger of massive surprise attack and subsequent retaliation would not only persist but grow. But, Eisenhower continued, "to pause there would be to confirm the hopeless finality of a belief that two atomic colossi are doomed malevolently to eye each other indefinitely across a trembling world." He rejected the state of perpetual fear. "My country's purpose is to help us move out of the dark chamber of horrors into the light," he continued, "to find a way by which the minds of men, the hopes of men, the souls of men everywhere, can move forward toward peace and happiness and well being."[118]

The president wished to trade fear for hope. "In the capitals and military headquarters of the world; in the hearts of men everywhere, be they governors or governed, may they be the decisions which will lead this world out of fear and into peace," Eisenhower prayed. He imagined that he might be able to redeploy the atomic weapon to the cause of peace, "to help solve the fearful atomic dilemma," and "to find the way by which the miraculous inventiveness of man shall not be dedicated to his death, but consecrated to his life."[119] Eisenhower told his brother Milton only three days after the speech that he believed Atoms for Peace might "bring some hope to replace fear in the world."[120] In his diary Eisenhower wrote that in his Atoms for Peace speech he intended "to make a clear effort to get the Soviet Union working with us in some phase of this whole atomic field that would have only peace and the good of mankind as a goal."[121]

Though Eisenhower offered few specifics in his original Atoms for Peace proposal, the program ultimately included a variety of measures aimed either at a reduction of fissile material available for bombs or the peaceful applications of atomic energy. To accomplish both tasks, he hoped to have all nuclear powers donate fissile material to an international bank held by the International Atomic Energy Agency (IAEA). "The International Atomic Energy Agency would provide a practical meeting place–a common ground of cooperative effort among nations," Eisenhower wrote in a message to Congress in March 1957. Americans had already seen the potential benefit of the peaceful atom, Eisenhower remarked, including "electric power, treatment of disease, and extraordinary service to agriculture, industry and science itself." Other peoples in other nations of the world also saw the "great hope of the atom for the development of their economies and advancement of their welfare," he continued. The president explained that the primary purpose of the IAEA would be to improve the lives of the world's citizens as well as a demonstration "of our fixed and unending determination to open and widen all possible avenues toward a just and enduring world peace."[122]

Atoms for Peace also involved the pursuit of international agreements to help stem the proliferation of nuclear weapons. Eisenhower imagined he could allow individual nations to share the benefits of nuclear power and scientific knowledge without giving away the bomb itself. It was a difficult balancing act. On one hand, Eisenhower needed to convince the world of the United States' sincerity to use atoms for peaceful purposes by providing the neediest nations with nuclear technology in support of electrical power where none had previously been available. On the other hand, if the United States provided too much information and technology, the receiving nation might easily turn Eisenhower's good intentions into weapons of war and increase the number of nuclear-armed nations dramatically in a short period of time. "But there is a great feeling that the atom can and should be used in a variety of peaceful uses," Eisenhower told Lewis Strauss, "and I believe that every country that wants to work toward this end should be encouraged."[123]

Accordingly, the Eisenhower administration negotiated agreements to establish atomic research reactors in foreign countries. Through these "research bilaterals" the United States government provided unclassified information on the design, construction, and operation of atomic reactors. Because the U.S. also promised to provide enriched uranium to participating nations, those nations had to promise to institute safeguards for the protection of that material, to allow American inspections of the facilities, and to return spent nuclear fuel to the United States. The first research bilateral was signed between the U.S. and Turkey. Thirty-seven more agreements were concluded by the end of 1961.[124]

In addition to the bilateral treaties, Eisenhower supervised the negotiations of EURATOM, the European Atomic Energy Community, which was a pact designed to promote the generation of electrical power for European industry.[125] In the midst of a disagreement with the Atomic Energy Commission over the implementation of Atoms for Peace and EURATOM, Eisenhower announced he would make available to foreign nations fissile material under the authority provided by the Atomic Energy Act of 1954. "This action demonstrates the confidence of the United States in the possibilities of developing nuclear power for civilian uses," he stated in February 1956. "It is an earnest of our faith that the atom can be made a powerful instrument for the promotion of world peace," he concluded.[126] According to Hewlett and Holl, Eisenhower put pressure on the AEC to move quickly toward EURATOM because the president believed that a European atomic community "was a prerequisite to a stable Western alliance and world peace."[127]

To sustain America in the Cold War against an atheistic enemy, Eisenhower believed the United States needed to bolster moral strength. He further believed that the nuclear weapon could serve in a variety of ways to build up this moral strength. He sought to convince the world community of the peaceful goals of the United States and the desire to make science and technology work for the benefit of man. Through effort and faith, he made Atoms for Peace a part of the global dialogue and he countered Soviet claims about American militarism. But Atoms for Peace, like his push for disarmament and a nuclear test ban treaty, ultimately served the larger goal of building American strength through nuclear weapons. "The more people in the world that understand that atomic energy and all of the newly developed sciences can be of benefit to them and do not have to be, and should not be, sequestered off in some dark corner to be used merely for destructive purposes," Eisenhower explained in a 1954 press conference, "the greater the moral force will be in favor of general peace, general disarmament, and a better life for all of us."[128] The president struggled to accept the negative aspect of deterrence, the dangers inherent in weapons testing on the natural world and its inhabitants, and the great threat of nuclear weapons proliferation throughout the world. But he also believed that nuclear weapons possessed an innate potential to serve mankind. For Eisenhower, the nuclear weapon may not have been divinely inspired, but the basic nature of the atom had been provided by the Almighty and because it had, the United States could use nuclear technology to support the natural right of man to live in freedom, in peace, and without fear. In the Cold War, the United States needed to occupy the moral high ground in the realm of nuclear energy.

Conclusion

A recognized nuclear intellectual argued in 1957 that "a revolution cannot be mastered until it develops the mode of thinking appropriate to it."[1] Rapid and dramatic advances in nuclear science and technology revolutionized warfare after World War II, and humans struggled to adapt their intellectual paradigms to the new reality. In the twelve years after the world's first atomic explosion, fission had begotten fusion and kilotons of explosive power had become megatons. The primary challenge of the nuclear age which faced Eisenhower, his successors, the citizens of the American republic, and the inhabitants of the world was how to reconcile the desire for security with the risk of catastrophe and how to win a cold war when there was no alternative to peace.

When Eisenhower became president of the United States, he faced this challenge directly, and produced a new mode of thinking for the nuclear revolution. In his efforts to build national strength, he established the basic intellectual framework for presidential understanding and utilization of nuclear weapons in the United States and solidified the practice of using atomic weapons as a force for good in the world. Because the president understood that atomic weapons could not be uninvented, he concluded that the United States government must expand the nation's atomic assets and allow atomic weapons and nuclear technology to serve national security in a variety of ways.

As he simultaneously discouraged other nations from building atomic weapons, Eisenhower emphasized the proper management for nuclear weapons technology to nourish and augment American national strength in the face of Cold War threats. He believed that nuclear weapons contributed to economic, military, industrial, and moral strength of the nation, all of which helped prepare and sustain the United States for the long pull against international communism. "We have learned from bitter and conclusive experience that peace cannot be defended by the weak," he stated, "It demands strength – strength of our armies, strength of our economies and, above all, strength of our spirit."[2] He concluded that cumulative national strength over the long term best served the republic because he believed "that properly balanced strength will promote the probability of avoiding war."[3] Moreover, he concluded that balanced meant strength which grew from four sources: "industrial and economic strength," "necessary military strength," and a "complete devotion to democracy, which means a faith in men as men (essentially religious concept)" accompanied by "moral probity in all dealings."[4] The communist attack on the free world was "so broad in its character that we cannot be complacent in anything, in the realm of the spirit and the intellectual world, the material world, and the economic."[5] For these reasons, Eisenhower championed the role played by nuclear weapons and technology, including both civilian and military uses. The president needed then only to abolish the taboo on the use of nuclear weapons in order to build satisfactory strength to defend U.S. national security.

The president's faith in the nuclear weapon to provide national strength remained virtually unchanged throughout his two terms. The invention of the hydrogen bomb forced Eisenhower to reconsider the proper military function of nuclear weapons, but he successfully adopted a strategy to integrate the new weapons. He quite clearly saw the fiscal and tactical benefits of the fission bomb and he sought to take advantage of those opportunities. The successful test of a fusion bomb on the eve of his election and the shocking Castle-Bravo test of 1954 startled Eisenhower into a new reality. The president understood immediately that the thermonuclear weapon posed new risks and dangers, but he was not dissuaded from using nuclear weapons to achieve his goals. Instead, he devised a new strategic plan for the thermonuclear weapon so he could take full advantage of this new device. In so doing, Eisenhower asserted the right of the United States to pursue nuclear weapons and nuclear technology in the national interest and the responsibility to protect the interests of the free world by denying that right to others. It was a burden Eisenhower willingly bore as did all who have followed him as president of the United States.

At times like these, Eisenhower believed that the United States was fortunate to possess the nuclear weapon. He concluded that the American republic was not as prepared as totalitarian states to manage a long, sustained conflict against a powerful enemy, that the United States' democratic traditions put the nation at a disadvantage in a global Cold War, and that the nuclear weapon could provide some relief. The nuclear weapon was a scientific and technological springboard which could propel the nation ahead of the enemy in a contest in which failure meant the total destruction of the American way of life. Despite the possible horrors of thermonuclear war, Eisenhower transformed this weapon of mass destruction into an instrument of national destiny, to be employed by the republic to advance the cause of liberty, equality, justice, and peace.

During his final press conference in 1961, Eisenhower was asked what was his most "heartbreaking failure" of his eight years in office. "The big disappointment I felt is one not of a mere incident," Eisenhower explained, "it was the fact that we could not in these 8 years get to the place where we could say it now looks as if permanent peace with justice is really in sight." He explained his regret "that we haven't done better in getting a more constructive and positive indication that real disarmament is around the corner."[6] He made a similar point in his farewell message when he regretfully noted that "disarmament, with honor and confidence, is a continuing imperative." "I confess that I lay down my official responsibilities in this field with a definite sense of disappointment," he admitted.[7] His last, best push toward a test ban treaty with the Soviet Union and disarmament died after the downing of a U-2 spy plane over Soviet territory and the resulting collapse of the Paris Peace Conference in 1959.

Beyond these two tangible failures, Eisenhower also expressed concern in the last days of administration about what exactly he had built in the pursuit of nuclear strength. In his often-quoted farewell address to the nation, he warned about the danger of misplaced power in the form of a military-industrial complex. The president also warned the nation in that speech about the dangerous possibility that "public policy could itself become the captive of a scientific-technological elite." In the midst of gathering nuclear resources to build national strength for the long pull against communism, Eisenhower had simultaneously and unwittingly knocked out of balance the delicate equilibrium of American life between the power of the state and the rights of the individual, between the need for freedom and the desire for security. He remarked that any imbalance between these powerful forces risked an erosion of what he called "the supreme goals of our free society."[8] In the end, his warning seemed to be as much an admission of responsibility for helping to create this new danger as anything else.

At the end of his presidency in 1961, Eisenhower could count many accomplishments in the realm of nuclear weapons and power. First, he had built a sizable nuclear arsenal. When he left office, America's stockpile totaled 18,638 nuclear weapons which could yield 20,491 megatons of explosive power. From 1953 levels, this represented an increase of more than 2,000 percent in the number of weapons and 400 percent increase in total explosive yield. At the end of 2002, the United States possessed just under 9,000 nuclear weapons, less than half the total 18,000 weapons at the end of 1960, but more than ten times the 800 weapons held by the United States at the beginning of the Eisenhower administration.[9] Though the American stockpile has been reduced in the years since the end of the Cold War, the number of nuclear warheads has not dropped below the pre-Eisenhower level. In addition, Eisenhower advanced and introduced new systems designed to deliver nuclear weapons accurately to targets around the world. These systems included the B-52 intercontinental jet bomber, the Jupiter, Thor, and Polaris intermediate range ballistic missiles, and the liquid-fueled Atlas intercontinental ballistic missile. The solid-fueled Minuteman ICBM was also under development at the end of his presidency. The three nuclear power plants which were operating or scheduled to begin operating in the United States in the early 1960s grew to a total of 66 by 2005 and the number of reactors exceeded 104 decades after Eisenhower. The Atomic Energy Commission morphed into the Department of Energy and the Nuclear Regulatory Commission in the 1970s, but the basic functions of initiation, coordination, and regulation of atomic energy projects continued to be housed in the federal government. Indeed, the bulk of Eisenhower's nuclear establishment survived and continued to grow throughout his term, his life, and the twentieth century.

Dwight Eisenhower died on 28 March 1969 at Walter Reed Army Hospital in Washington, D.C. Five days later on 2 April, he was interred near his childhood home on the grounds of the Eisenhower Center in Abilene, Kansas. He last resided in Kansas in 1911, before the Great War, before the Bolshevik Revolution in Russia, and even before science fiction writer H.G. Wells had introduced the idea of an atomic bomb in his book *The Last War.* Then only twenty years old, Eisenhower could never have imagined the great responsibilities he would hold, the challenges he would face, or the power he would wield in his long career in service to the United States of America. As military officer and public servant, Eisenhower struggled through two great global conflicts, World War II and the Cold War. In one contest, he occupied the highest military post, and, in the other, the highest political office. In neither contest could he afford to fail. In World War II, he commanded armies the size and strength of which the world had never seen. In the Cold War, he led the United States through the hour of maximum danger when communist military strength and aggression made Americans more fearful than any other time in their national history.

Despite the claims of the early orthodox scholars that Eisenhower was aloof and unintelligent, it is clear that Eisenhower was the primary intellectual architect of the nation's nuclear policy from 1953 to 1961. The president's thinking about the tactical value of atomic weapons, the consequences of nuclear war, and the desirability of fallout shelters, for example, drove him to implement policies such as the New Look and massive retaliation. His thinking on the costs and benefits of civilian nuclear energy and the threat of nuclear proliferation led him to launch Atoms for Peace. In addition, because he believed he could negotiate peace only from a position of great national strength, he continued to build more and better nuclear weapons, while simultaneously lobbying for disarmament. The common theme that unified Eisenhower's disparate array of ideas and programs for nuclear weapons was the pursuit of national strength. He valued and utilized as much as possible nuclear weapons in pursuit of his national goals. Perhaps more than any other president, he made nuclear weapons abundant in the United States and indispensable to national security and as a result fully integrated those weapons in national life. This study also supports the conclusions of those scholars who have argued that Eisenhower's successes and failures as president were his own and that the president's two terms were marked as much by failure as by success. Despite the fact that he largely conceived of and sincerely believed in the initiatives of his administration in the realm of nuclear weapons, he met significant failures. For example, although he instituted policies to limit military spending through the use of nuclear weapons, the president failed to rein in defense spending over the long term. He did manage to balance the budget, but spending on national defense including nuclear weapons continued to grow through the end of his presidency. In addition, as others have documented, the threat of massive retaliation deterred large-scale conflict between the United States and the Soviet Union but did not prevent communist agitation in places such as Vietnam and Cuba. Civilian nuclear power proved to be more complicated, expensive, and risky than the president imagined and private electric power from nuclear reactions never became the boon for industrial energy he hoped it would be. He failed to negotiate a nuclear test ban treaty with the Soviet Union and made no significant progress toward disarmament. Even worse, Atoms for Peace may have contributed to the proliferation of nuclear weapons. Eisenhower did export fissile material to energy-deprived nations under Atoms for Peace, but the proliferation of nuclear weapons continued ultimately to France, China, India, Pakistan, Israel, and North Korea. In the case of a nuclear test ban treaty, Eisenhower's failures were the result of his inability to gain the support of the Congress or create a consensus among his key advisors. The unwillingness of the Soviet Union to compromise ruined his chances for real disarmament, and the inability of scientists to deliver a clean nuclear weapon fatally wounded Plowshare. These were failures of implementation not necessarily of intellect.

In his effort to build national strength with nuclear weapons, he made the bomb a permanent fixture of the American military arsenal, the national political scene, and the cultural landscape. But Eisenhower did not view this entrenchment as a negative development. He believed that, if the United States used the weapon as an instrument to advance sincere national goals, then the nuclear weapon, like all weapons, could be a force for good. He embedded deep in the national conscience the premise upon which future nuclear policy would be made: only the United States of America had the scientific knowledge, the liberal political tradition, the social stability, and the moral values necessary to use nuclear weapons in the best interests of humanity. As the Cold War progressed and Eisenhower continued to find ways to put the atom to work in service of the republic, he institutionalized the nuclear bomb in American government and society. He allowed the nuclear weapon to become an indispensable part of the American political system and he encouraged the search for as many possible uses for the bomb as could be found. As described, he eventually found ways for the bomb to serve

Eisenhower's funeral services at the Washington National Cathedral on 31 March 1969. (Richard Nixon Library)

the nation's economic, military, industrial, and moral interests. Eisenhower imagined he could provide help to the poor, power to the weak, sustenance to the starved, and hope to the discouraged with the proper use of the nuclear weapon.

In the end, Eisenhower looked for and found a comfortable and permanent place in the American conscience for this weapon of mass destruction and every single American chief executive since 1961 followed his lead. Even John F. Kennedy, Eisenhower's successor who campaigned to "get America moving again," found little cause or opportunity to alter significantly the direction in nuclear policy established by Eisenhower. Although the Kennedy administration popularized the notion of using a flexible nuclear response to international crises, this concept was hardly new. Kennedy contrasted flexible response with the rigidity of Eisenhower's New Look and argued that Eisenhower endangered the nation both with unacceptable weakness and unnecessary risk. But in the years between the administrations of Eisenhower and Nixon, the two Democratic presidents, Kennedy and Johnson, took advantage of and retained what Eisenhower had built. Because of Eisenhower, those presidents could choose between tactical atomic war or general thermonuclear war if necessary, encourage the use of atomic energy for electrical power, rely upon an undeniable nuclear deterrent to manage crises, steer the world away from nuclear proliferation, and continue to lead the free world toward peace. By laboring to abolish the taboo on the full use of atomic and thermonuclear weapons in both civilian and military applications, Eisenhower hoped that the United States would not have to choose between defeat or bankruptcy, fear or war, security or liberty, or righteousness or peace in its struggle with international communism.

Notes

Introduction

1 "Memorandum to Lewis Strauss from Robert Cutler," 21 October 1953, Papers of Lewis S. Strauss, Atomic Energy Commission Series, Box 8, Atoms for Peace, 1949-1954, Herbert Hoover Presidential Library, West Branch, Iowa, hereinafter Hoover Library, 1.

2 Joseph Carroll, *House of War: The Pentagon and the Disastrous Rise of American Power* (Boston: Houghton Mifflin, 2007), 209. Carroll borrowed this phrase from Neil Rosendorf, "John Foster Dulles' Nuclear Schizophrenia," in John Lewis Gaddis, Philip H. Gordon, Ernest R. May, and Jonathan Rosenberg, eds., *Cold War Statesmen Confront the Bomb: Nuclear Diplomacy Since 1945* (Oxford: Oxford University Press, 1999), 63.

3 Dwight D. Eisenhower, *Public Papers of the Presidents of the United States: Dwight D. Eisenhower, 1953-1960*, vol. 1 (Washington, D.C.: GPO, 1960), 820, 822.

4 Prentice C. Dean, *Energy History Chronology from World War II to the Present* (Washington, D.C.: Department of Energy, 1982).

5 In this book, the term "atomic" refers to fission weapons fueled by uranium or plutonium which typically yield explosions in the kiloton range or smaller. The term "thermonuclear" refers to fusion weapons fueled by hydrogen which yield explosions measured from the high kilotons to the megaton range. These fusion weapons will also be referred to as hydrogen bombs. The term "nuclear" shall refer generally to all weapons fueled by fission or fusion reactions.

6 "Estimated U.S. and Soviet/Russian Nuclear Stockpiles, 1945-1994," *Bulletin of Atomic Scientists* (November/December 1994): 58-9.

7 "Minutes of Meeting," 23 June 1954, Papers of Dwight D. Eisenhower as President, 1953-1961 (Ann Whitman File), NSC Series, Box 5, 203rd Meeting, Dwight D. Eisenhower Presidential Library, Abilene, Kansas, hereinafter DDE Library, 2.

8 Robert J. Donovan, *Eisenhower: The Inside Story* (New York: Harper, 1956), 330-1.

9 For an opposing view, see Richard H. Immerman, "Confessions of an Eisenhower Revisionist: An Agonizing Reappraisal," *Diplomatic History* 14, no. 3 (1990): 325.

10 Robert Griffith, ed., *Ike's Letters to a Friend, 1941-1958* (Lawrence, KS: University of Kansas Press, 1984), 36.

11 Henry DeWolf Smyth, *Atomic Energy for Military Purposes: The Official Report on the Development of the Atomic Bomb under the Auspices of the United States Government, 1940-1945* (Princeton: Princeton University Press, 1945); Bernard Brodie, ed., *The Absolute Weapon: Atomic Power and World Order* (New York: Harcourt, Brace and Company, 1946).

Chapter 1

1 Stephen Ambrose, *Eisenhower: Soldier and President* (New York: Simon and Schuster, 1990), 573.

2 Arthur M. Schlesinger, Jr., "Rating the Presidents: Washington to Clinton," *Political Science Quarterly* 112, no. 2, (1997): 183. See also William J. Ridings, Jr. and Stuart B. McIver, *Rating the Presidents: From the Great and Honorable to the Dishonest and Incompetent* (New York: Citadel Press, 1997).

3 Stephen G. Rabe, "Eisenhower Revisionism: A Decade of Scholarship," *Diplomatic History* 17 (Winter 1995): 98.

4 Pre-presidential biographies of Eisenhower include Francis Trevelyan Miller, *Eisenhower, Man and Soldier* (Philadelphia: The John C. Winston Company, 1944); Alden Hatch, *General Ike: A Biography of Dwight D. Eisenhower* (Chicago: Consolidated Book, 1944); Delos Wheeler Lovelace, *General "Ike" Eisenhower* (New York, Thomas Y. Crowell Company, 1944); Helen Nicolay, *Born to Command: The Story of General Eisenhower* (New York: D. Appleton-Century Company, Inc., 1945); Kenneth S. Davis, *Soldier of Democracy: A Biography of Dwight Eisenhower* (Garden City, NY: Doubleday and Company, Inc., 1945).

5 Miller, *Eisenhower, Man and Soldier*, 1.

6 Personal accounts from the war and post war period include Harry C. Butcher, *My Three Years with Eisenhower: The Personal Diary of Captain Harry C. Butcher, USNR, Naval Aide to General Eisenhower, 1942 to 1945* (New York: Simon and Schuster, 1946); Michael James McKeogh, *Sgt. Mickey and General Ike* (New York: G.P. Putnam's Sons, 1946); Walter Bedell Smith, *Eisenhower's Six Great Decisions: Europe, 1944-1945* (New York, Longmans, Green, 1956).

7 Thomas Robson Hay, review of *Soldier of Democracy: A Biography of Dwight Eisenhower*, by Kenneth S. Davis, *The Mississippi Valley Historical Review* 34 (September 1947): 325.

8 John Gunther, *Eisenhower, The Man and The Symbol* (New York, Harper, 1952), 132.

9 Allan Taylor, *What Eisenhower Thinks* (New York: Thomas Y. Crowell Company, 1952), i, 180.

10 Kevin McCann, *Man from Abilene* (Garden City, NY: Doubleday, 1952), 13, 18.

11 Robert J. Donovan, *Eisenhower: The Inside Story* (New York: Harper, 1956). See also Merriman A. Smith, *Meet Mister Eisenhower* (New York, Harper, 1955).

12 John Merlo Pusey, *Eisenhower, the President* (New York: MacMillan, 1956), 293.

13 Marty Snyder, *My Friend Ike* (New York, F. Fell, 1956), 237.

14 Arthur Schlesinger, Jr., "Ike Age Revisited" *Reviews in American History* 11, no. 1 (1983): 2.

15 Richard Rovere, *Affairs of State: The Eisenhower Years* (New York: Farrar, Straus, and Cudahy, 1956); Schlesinger, "Ike Age," 1-11. See Marquis Childs, *Eisenhower, Captive Hero: A Critical Study of the General and the President* (New York: Harcourt Brace, 1958).

16 Schlesinger, "Ike Age Revisited," 11; See Emmet John Hughes, *The Ordeal of Power: A Political Memoir of the Eisenhower Years* (New York: Atheneum, 1963); Arthur Larson, *Eisenhower: The President Nobody Know* (London: Leslie Frewin Publishers Limited, 1968); Sherman Adams, *Firsthand Report: The Story of the Eisenhower Administration* (New York: Harper & Brothers, 1961).

17 William V. Shannon, "Eisenhower as President: A Critical Appraisal of the Record," *Commentary* 26 (November 1958): 390.

18 Vincent P. De Santis, "Eisenhower Revisionism," *The Review of Politics* 38, no. 2 (1976): 190-207; Richard H. Immerman, "Confessions of an Eisenhower Revisionist: An Agonizing Reappraisal," *Diplomatic History* 14, no. 3 (1990): 319-42; Gary Reichard, "Eisenhower as President: The Changing View," *South Atlantic Quarterly* 77 (Summer 1979): 265-81; Mary S. McAuliffe, "Eisenhower, the President," *The Journal of American History* 68, no. 3 (1981): 625-32; Robert J. McMahon, "Eisenhower and Third World Nationalism: A Critique of the Revisionists," *Political Science Quarterly* 101, no. 3 (1986): 453-73; Anthony James Joes, "Eisenhower Revisionism and American Politics," in *Dwight D. Eisenhower: Soldier, President, Statesman*, ed., Joann P. Krieg (New York: Greenwood, 1987): 283-96; Robert Burk, "Eisenhower Revisionism Revisited: Reflections on the Eisenhower Scholarship," *Historian* 50 (February 1988): 196-209.

19 See Edwin A. Roberts, Jr., "Thoughts on the Man from Abilene," *National Observer*, 14 December 1974.

20 Richard H. Rovere, "Eisenhower Revisited – A Political Genius? A Brilliant Man?" *New York Times Magazine*, 7 February 1971, 14 quoted in de Santis, "Eisenhower Revisionism," 198.

21 Schlesinger, "Rating the Presidents," 182.

22 Revisionist accounts by journalists include Arthur Krock, "Impressions of the President – and the Man," *New York Times Magazine*, 23 June 1957, 5, 34-39; Edwin A. Roberts, Jr., "Thoughts on the Man from Abilene," *National Observer*, 14 December 1974; Murray Kempton, "The Underestimation of Dwight D. Eisenhower," *Esquire*, September 1967, 108-109, 156; Richard Rhodes, "Ike: Artist in Iron," *Harper's Magazine*, July 1970, 70-77; Robert L. Branyan, "Eisenhower the Politician," *American Chronicle*, 1 January 1972, 43-47. Scholarly accounts include Thomas A. Bailey, *Presidential Greatness: The Image and the Man from George Washington to the Present* (New York: Appleton-Century,1966); Garry Wills, *Nixon Agonistes: The Crisis of the Self-Made Man* (Boston: Houghton Mifflin, 1970); William J. O'Neill, *Coming Apart: An Informal History of America in the 1960s* (Chicago: Quadrangle, 1971); Barton J. Bernstein, "Foreign Policy in the Eisenhower Administration," *Foreign Service Journal* 50 (May 1973): 17-20, 29-30, 38. Later revisionist works include Blanche Wiesen Cook, *Dwight D. Eisenhower: Antimilitarist in White House* (St. Charles, MO: Forum Press, 1974); Peter Lyon, *Eisenhower: Portrait of a Hero* (Boston: Little Brown, 1974); Charles C. Alexander, *Holding the Line: the Eisenhower Era, 1952-1961* (Bloomington, IN: Indiana University Press, 1975); Gary W. Reichard, *The Reaffirmation of Republicanism: Eisenhower and the Eighty-Third Congress* (Knoxville: University of Tennessee Press, 1975); Blanche Wiesen Cook, *The Declassified Eisenhower: A Divided Legacy* (Garden City, NY: Doubleday, 1981); Stephen G. Rabe, *Eisenhower and Latin America: The Foreign Policy of Anticommunism* (Chapel Hill: The University of Carolina Press, 1988); Stephen Ambrose, *Eisenhower: Soldier and President* (New York: Simon and Schuster, 1990).

23 Fred I. Greenstein, "Eisenhower as an Activist President: A Look at New Evidence," *Political Science Quarterly* 94, no. 4 (1979-1980): 575-99; Fred Greenstein, *The Hidden-Hand Presidency: Eisenhower as Leader* (Baltimore: Johns Hopkins University Press, 1994), xiii.

24 Greenstein, *The Hidden-Hand Presidency*, xiii.

25 Greenstein, "Eisenhower as an Activist President," 577.

26 Greenstein, *The Hidden-Hand Presidency*, 212, 227.

27 Herbert Parmet, *Eisenhower and the American Crusades* (New York: MacMillan, 1972); Robert Divine, *Eisenhower and the Cold War* (New York: Oxford University Press, 1981).

28 Parmet, *Eisenhower and the American Crusades*, 573, 578.

29 Divine, *Eisenhower and the Cold War*, 154.

30 Richard G. Hewlett and Jack M. Holl, *Atoms for Peace and War, 1953-1961: Eisenhower and the Atomic Energy Commission*, with a foreword by Richard S. Kirkendall and an essay on sources by Roger M. Anders (Berkeley: University of California Press, 1989) xi. On declassification of documents, see page 661.

31 Richard H. Immerman, "Confessions of an Eisenhower Revisionist: An Agonizing Reappraisal," *Diplomatic History* 14, no. 3 (1990): 325; For a revisionist analysis of Eisenhower as systematic thinker, see Robert Griffith, "Dwight D. Eisenhower and the Corporate Commonwealth," *American Historical Review* 87, no. 1 (1982): 87-122.

32 Chester J. Pach and Elmo Richardson, *The Presidency of Dwight D. Eisenhower* Revised Edition (Lawrence: University of Kansas Press, 1991), xiii.

33 Günter Bischof and Stephen E. Ambrose, eds., *Eisenhower: A Centenary Assessment* (Baton Rouge, LA: Louisiana State University Press, 1995), 7-13.

34 Ibid., 239.

35 Robert J. McMahon, "Eisenhower and Third World Nationalism: A Critique of the Revisionists," *Political Science Quarterly* 101, no. 3 (1986): 457. For other post revisionist accounts of Eisenhower's foreign policy in the Third World, see Madelein G. Kalb, *The Congo Cables: The Cold War in Africa –*

from Eisenhower to Kennedy (New York: Macmillan, 1982); Steven L. Speigel, *The Other Arab-Israeli Conflict: Making America's Middle East Policy from Truman to Reagan* (Chicago: University of Chicago Press, 1985); Stephen G. Rabe, *Eisenhower and Latin America: The Foreign Policy of Anticommunism* (Chapel Hill: The University of Carolina Press, 1988).

36 Divine, *Eisenhower and the Cold War.*

37 David L. Anderson, *Trapped by Success: The Eisenhower Administration and Vietnam, 1953-1961* (New York: Columbia University Press, 1991), xiii-xiv.

38 Rosemary Foot, "Nuclear Coercion and the Ending of the Korean Conflict," *International Security* 13, no. 3 (1988-1989): 92-112; Rosemary Foot, "The Eisenhower Administration's Fear of Empowering the Chinese," *Political Science Quarterly* 111, no. 3 (1996): 505-21.

39 Gordon H. Chang, "To the Nuclear Brink: Eisenhower, Dulles, and the Quemoy-Matsu Crisis," *International Security* 12, no. 4 (1988): 96-123; For evidence on Eisenhower's misunderstanding Chinese actions, see Gordon H. Chang and He Di, "The Absence of War in the U.S.-China Confrontation over Quemoy and Matsu in 1954-1955: Contingency, Luck, Deterrence?" *The American Historical Review* 98, no. 5 (1993): 1500-24.

40 H. W. Brands Jr., "The Age of Vulnerability: Eisenhower and the National Insecurity State," *The American Historical Review* 94, no. 4 (1989): 989. See also David Alan Rosenberg, "The Origins of Overkill: Nuclear Weapons and American Strategy, 1945-1960," *International Security* 7, no. 4 (1983): 3-71.

41 H. W. Brands Jr.,"Testing Massive Retaliation: Credibility and Crisis Management in the Taiwan Strait," *International Security* 12, no. 4 (1988): 124-51.

42 Jeremi Suri, "America's Search for a Technological Solution to the Arms Race: The Surprise Attack Conference of 1958 and a Challenge for 'Eisenhower Revisionists,'" *Diplomatic History* 21, no. 3 (1997): 451.

43 Martha Smith-Norris, "The Eisenhower Administration and the Nuclear Test Ban Talks, 1958-1960: Another Challenge to 'Revisionism,'" *Diplomatic History* 27, no. 4 (2003): 503-41.

44 Benjamin P. Greene, "Eisenhower, Science and the Nuclear Test Ban Debate, 1953-56," *The Journal of Strategic Studies* 26, no. 4 (2003): 157.

45 Rovere, *Affairs of State*, 17.

46 Merle Miller, *Plain Speaking: An Oral Biography of Harry S. Truman* (New York: Berkley Publishing Corporation, 1973), 344-5.

47 Adams, *Firsthand Report*, 20.

48 John McCone, 26 July 1976, OH-396, Oral Histories, DDE Library, 45-6, 3.

49 Adams, *Firsthand Report*, 72-3. According to biographer Geoffrey Perret , Eisenhower routinely read much longer memorandums, but preferred that they be as short as possible. Eisenhower would ask for more detail if desired. The president often read long budget reports which could reach over one hundred pages. See Geoffrey Perret, *Eisenhower* (Holbrook, MA: Adams Media Corporation, 1999), 435.

50 Hughes, *The Ordeal of Power*, 98.

51 Herbert Brownell, with John P. Burke, *Advising Ike: The Memoirs of Attorney General Herbert Brownell*, with a foreword by John Chancellor (Lawrence, KS: University of Kansas Press, 1993), 288, 290, 302.

52 Arthur Larson, *Eisenhower: The President Nobody Knew* (London: Leslie Frewin Publishers Limited, 1968), 20.

53 Adams, *Firsthand Report*, 14-15.

54 Brownell, *Advising Ike*, 288-9.

55 Larson, *The President Nobody Knew*, 185-87.

56 Andrew J. Goodpaster Jr., 10 April 1982, OH-877, Oral Histories, DDE Library, 14. This quotation is Kennan's as told to Goodpaster.
57 Brownell, *Advising Ike*, 288.
58 James R. Killian, *Sputnik, Scientists, and Eisenhower: A Memoir of the First Special Assistant to the President for Science and Technology* (Cambridge, MA: MIT Press, 1977), 219-21.
59 Adams, *Firsthand Report*, 72-3.
60 Michael Beschloss, *MAYDAY: Eisenhower, Khrushchev, and the U-2 Affair* (New York: Harper & Row, 1986), 49.
61 David Lilienthal, *Journals of David Lilienthal, Vol. II, The Atomic Energy Years, 1945-1950* (New York: Harper and Row, 1964), 375 quoted in Piers Brendon, *Ike: His Life and Times* (New York: Harper & Row, 1986), 11.
62 Brendon, *Ike: His Life and Times*, 11, 4-5.
63 De Santis, "Eisenhower Revisionism," 195.
64 John Keegan, "Eisenhower and the American Dream," The Dwight D. Eisenhower Lectures in War and Peace: A Biennial Series, no. 2, (Manhattan, KS, 1988).
65 Zachary Shands Davis, "Eisenhower's Worldview and Nuclear Strategy" (Ph.D. diss., University of Virginia, 1989), 45.
66 Shannon, "Eisenhower as President, 392.
67 Dwight D. Eisenhower, *The White House Years: Mandate for Change, 1953-1956* (Garden City, NY: Doubleday, 1963), 227, 426.
68 "Letter to John S. D. Eisenhower, 19 January 1962," Papers of Dwight D. Eisenhower, Post Presidential Series, 62 Principal File, Box 47, Chrono File January 1962, DDE Library, 1.
69 "Minutes of Meeting," 12 January 1958, Papers of Dwight D. Eisenhower as President, 1953-1961 (Ann Whitman File), NSC Series, Box 7, 272nd Meeting, DDE Library, 18.
70 "Letter to C. D. Jackson," 26 March 1958, Papers of C. D. Jackson, 1931-1967, Box 50, Eisenhower, Dwight D. – Correspondence, 1958, DDE Library, 2.
71 "Letter to Chynoweth," 20 July 1954, Papers of Dwight D. Eisenhower as President, 1953-1961 (Ann Whitman File), Names Series, Box 5, Chynoweth, Brig. Gen., B. G., DDE Library, 2.
72 Quoted in Adams, *Firsthand Report*, 99-100.
73 "Letter to C. D. Jackson," 21 October 1957, Papers of C. D. Jackson, 1931-1967, Box 50, Eisenhower, Dwight D. – Correspondence, 1957, DDE Library, 1.
74 Robert W. Griffith, ed., *Ike's Letters to a Friend, 1941-1958* (Lawrence, KS: University of Kansas Press, 1984), 47.
75 George H. Quester, "Was Eisenhower a Genius?" *International Security* 4, no. 2 (1979): 169, 172.
76 Immerman, "Confessions of an Eisenhower Revisionist," 342.
77 Griffith,"Dwight D. Eisenhower and the Corporate Commonwealth," 88.
78 Leslie R. Groves, *Now It Can Be Told: The Story of the Manhattan Project* (New York: De Capo Press, 1975), 188.
79 Ibid., 200-1.
80 Eisenhower, *Crusade in Europe*, 229-30.
81 "Letter to George Catlett Marshall," 11 May 1944, Louis Galambos, ed., *The Papers of Dwight David Eisenhower: The War Years*, vol. III, (Baltimore: The Johns Hopkins University Press, 1970), 1859-60.
82 Groves, *Now It Can Be Told*, 185-98, 207-23.
83 Quoted in Ibid., 208.
84 Groves, *Now It Can Be Told*, 234.

85 Gar Alperovitz, *Atomic Diplomacy: Hiroshima and Potsdam*, revised edition, (New York: Penguin, 1985).
86 Barton Bernstein, "Ike and Hiroshima: Did He Oppose It?" *Journal of Strategic Studies* 10 (September 1987): 377-89.
87 Dwight D. Eisenhower, *Crusade in Europe* (Garden City, NY: Doubleday, 1948), 443. See Alperovitz, *Atomic Diplomacy*, 353.
88 Dwight D. Eisenhower, *The White House Years: Mandate for Change, 1953-1956* (Garden City, NY: Doubleday, 1963), 312-3.
89 Alperovitz, *Atomic Diplomacy*, 352-8.
90 Bernstein, "Did He Oppose It?," 377-89.
91 Barton Bernstein, "Eclipsed by Hiroshima and Nagasaki: Early Thinking About Tactical Nuclear Weapons," *International Security* 15, no. 4 (1991): 150.
92 Barton Bernstein, "Truman and the A-Bomb: Targeting Noncombatants, Using the Bomb, and His Defending the 'Decision,'" *The Journal of Military History* 62, no. 3 (1998): 561.
93 Gar Alperovitz, Robert L. Messer, and Barton J. Bernstein, "Marshall, Truman, and the Decision to Drop the Bomb," *International Security* 16, no. 3 (1991-92): 211.

Chapter 2

1 Richard H. Rovere, *Affairs of State: The Eisenhower Years* (New York: Farrar, Straus and Cudahy, 1956), 7.
2 "Diary Entry," 27 January 1949, Louis Galambos, ed., *The Papers of Dwight David Eisenhower: Columbia University*, vol. X, (Baltimore: The Johns Hopkins University Press, 1978), 449.
3 A. E. Holmans, "The Eisenhower Administration and the Recession, 1953-1955," *Oxford Economic Papers* 10, no. 1 (1958): 34.
4 Ann Mari May, "President Eisenhower, Economic Policy, and the 1960 Presidential Election," *The Journal of Economic History* 50, no. 2 (1990): 424.
5 Quoted in Steve Neal, *Harry and Ike: The Partnership that Remade the Postwar World* (New York: Scriber, 2001), 244.
6 May, "President Eisenhower, Economic Policy, and the 1960 Presidential Election," 417.
7 Robert H. Ferrell, ed., *The Eisenhower Diaries* (New York: W.W. Norton and Company, 1981), 140, 136.
8 Robert W. Griffith, ed., *Ike's Letters to a Friend, 1941-1958* (Lawrence, KS: University of Kansas Press, 1984), 55.
9 Melvyn P. Leffler, *A Preponderance of Power: National Security, the Truman Administration, and the Cold War* (Stanford, CA: Stanford University Press, 1992), 271.
10 "Diary Entry," 19 February 1949, Louis Galambos, ed., *The Papers of Dwight David Eisenhower: Columbia University*, vol. X, (Baltimore: The Johns Hopkins University Press, 1978), 497.
11 "Memorandum to Joints Chiefs of Staff," 2 April 1946, Louis Galambos, ed., *The Papers of Dwight David Eisenhower: The Chief of Staff*, vol. VII (Baltimore: The Johns Hopkins University Press, 1978), 976-7.
12 "Forrestal to Truman," 9 November 1948 quoted in Louis Galambos, ed., *The Papers of Dwight David Eisenhower: Columbia University*, vol. X, (Baltimore: The Johns Hopkins University Press, 1978), 284, note 3.
13 Quoted in Louis Galambos, ed., *The Papers of Dwight David Eisenhower: Columbia University*, vol. X, (Baltimore: The Johns Hopkins University Press, 1978), 367, note 2.

14 "Diary Entry," 13 December 1948, Louis Galambos, ed., *The Papers of Dwight David Eisenhower: Columbia University*, vol. X, (Baltimore: The Johns Hopkins University Press, 1978), 365-6. Emphasis in original.

15 "Diary Entry," 27 January 1949, Louis Galambos, ed., *The Papers of Dwight David Eisenhower: Columbia University*, vol. 10, (Baltimore: The Johns Hopkins University Press, 1978), 448.

16 The national security budget for fiscal years 1946/47, 1947/48, and 1948/49 were $14.368 billion, $11.771 billion, and $12.908 billion respectively. See U.S. Bureau of the Census, *Historical Statistics of the United States: Colonial Times to 1957* (Washington, D.C.: GPO, 1960), 719 quoted in "Diary Entry," April 1949, Note 2, Louis Galambos, ed., *The Papers of Dwight David Eisenhower: Columbia University*, vol. X, (Baltimore: The Johns Hopkins University Press, 1978), 551.

17 "Diary Entry," April 1949, Louis Galambos, ed., *The Papers of Dwight David Eisenhower: Columbia University*, vol. X, (Baltimore: The Johns Hopkins University Press, 1978), 551.

18 Dwight D. Eisenhower, *The White House Years: Waging Peace, 1956-1961* (Garden City, NY: Doubleday, 1963), 225.

19 "Letter to Forrestal," 21 December 1948, Louis Galambos, ed., *The Papers of Dwight David Eisenhower: Columbia University*, vol. X, (Baltimore: The Johns Hopkins University Press, 1978), 379-80.

20 "Diary Entry," 8 January 1949, Louis Galambos, ed., *The Papers of Dwight David Eisenhower: Columbia University*, vol. X, (Baltimore: The Johns Hopkins University Press, 1978), 402.

21 Dwight Eisenhower, *The White House Years: Mandate for Change, 1953-1956* (Garden City, NY: Doubleday, 1963), 132.

22 "Diary Entry," 9 February 1949, Louis Galambos, ed., *The Papers of Dwight David Eisenhower: Columbia University*, vol. X, (Baltimore: The Johns Hopkins University Press, 1978), 483.

23 "Diary Entry," 19 February 1949, Louis Galambos, ed., *The Papers of Dwight David Eisenhower: Columbia University*, vol. X, (Baltimore: The Johns Hopkins University Press, 1978), 497.

24 "Memorandum for Bradley, Denfeld and Vandenberg," 28 February 1949, Louis Galambos, ed., *The Papers of Dwight David Eisenhower: Columbia University*, vol. X, (Baltimore: The Johns Hopkins University Press, 1978), 515.

25 "Diary Entry," 19 February 1949, Louis Galambos, ed., *The Papers of Dwight David Eisenhower: Columbia University*, vol. X, (Baltimore: The Johns Hopkins University Press, 1978), 497.

26 Dwight D. Eisenhower, *At Ease: Stories I Tell to Friends* (Garden City, NY: Doubleday, 1967), 355. The final military budget for fiscal year 1950/51 was $13.1 billion.

27 Walter LaFeber, *America, Russia, and the Cold War, 1945-2006*, 10th ed. (Boston: McGraw Hill, 2007), 91-8.

28 Ernest R. May, ed., *American Cold War Strategy: Interpreting NSC 68* The Bedford Series in History and Culture (Boston: Bedford/St. Martin's, 1993), 80-1.

29 Ferrell, *The Eisenhower Diaries*, 175-6.

30 Leffler, *A Preponderance of Power*, 371-3.

31 Ferrell, *The Eisenhower Diaries*, 181.

32 Leffler, *A Preponderance of Power*, 371.

33 Ferrell, *The Eisenhower Diaries*, 181.

34 Eisenhower, *Mandate for Change*, 132.

35 Andrew P. N. Erdmann, "'War No Longer Has Any Logic Whatever': Dwight D. Eisenhower and the Thermonuclear Revolution" in John Gaddis, John Lewis, Philip H. Gordon, Ernest R. May, and Jonathan Rosenberg, eds., *Cold War Statesmen Confront the Bomb: Nuclear Diplomacy Since 1945* (Oxford: Oxford University Press, 1999), 91.

36 Ferrell, The Eisenhower Diaries, 137-9.

37 William V. Shannon, "Eisenhower as President: A Critical Appraisal of the Record," *Commentary* 26 (November 1958), 397.

38 Shannon, "Eisenhower as President," 395.

39 "Diary Entry," 14 January 1949, Louis Galambos, ed., *The Papers of Dwight David Eisenhower: Columbia University*, vol. X, (Baltimore: The Johns Hopkins University Press, 1978), 430.

40 Ferrell, *The Eisenhower Diaries*, 209, 212.

41 Ibid., 209-10.

42 Ibid., 210-213.

43 Ibid., 209.

44 Ibid., 213.

45 "Minutes of Meeting," 28 January 1958, Papers of Dwight D. Eisenhower as President, 1953-1961 (Ann Whitman File), NSC Series, Box 7, 272nd Meeting, DDE Library, 7.

46 "Minutes of Meeting," 30 October 1958, Papers of Dwight D. Eisenhower as President, 1953-1961 (Ann Whitman File), NSC Series, Box 10, Folder "384th Meeting," DDE Library, 6

47 "Minutes of Meeting," 1 May 1958, Papers of Dwight D. Eisenhower as President, 1953-1961 (Ann Whitman File), NSC Series, Box 10, Folder "364th Meeting," DDE Library, 10.

48 "Memorandum to the Secretary of State," 20 May 1959, Papers of Dwight D. Eisenhower as President, 1953-1961 (Ann Whitman File), DDE Diary Series, Box 3, Folder 8 – 9/53 (2), DDE Library, 2.

49 Eisenhower, *Mandate for Change*, 180.

50 Ross Gregory and Richard Balkin, eds., *Cold War America, 1946-1991* (New York: Facts on File, Inc., 2003), 254, 273.

51 "Estimated U.S. and Soviet/Russian Nuclear Stockpiles, 1945-1994," *Bulletin of Atomic Scientists* (November/December 1994): 58-9.

52 "Memorandum to Joint Chiefs of Staff," 17 December 1945, Louis Galambos, ed., *The Papers of Dwight David Eisenhower: Chief of Staff*, vol. VII, (Baltimore: The Johns Hopkins University Press, 1978), 639-40.

53 "Memorandum to the Joint Chiefs of Staff," 3 December 1945, Louis Galambos, ed., *The Papers of Dwight David Eisenhower: Chief of Staff*, vol. VII, (Baltimore: The Johns Hopkins University Press, 1978), 575.

54 "Memorandum to the Joint Chiefs of Staff," 16 January 1946, Louis Galambos, ed., *The Papers of Dwight David Eisenhower: Chief of Staff*, vol. VII, (Baltimore: The Johns Hopkins University Press, 1978), 760.

55 Edward H. Judge and John W. Langdon, eds., *The Cold War: A History through Documents* (Upper Saddle River, New Jersey: Prentice Hall, 1999), 21-2.

56 "Letter to Bernard Mannes Baruch," 14 June 1946, Louis Galambos, ed., *The Papers of Dwight David Eisenhower: Chief of Staff*, vol. VII, (Baltimore: The Johns Hopkins University Press, 1978), 1125-6. Emphasis in original.

57 "Letter to Dorothy Thompson," 25 June 1946, Louis Galambos, ed., *The Papers of Dwight David Eisenhower: Chief of Staff*, vol. VII, (Baltimore: The Johns Hopkins University Press, 1978), 1149. Emphasis in original.

58 "Letter to Bernard Mannes Baruch,"14 June 1946, Louis Galambos, ed., *The Papers of Dwight David Eisenhower: Chief of Staff*, vol. VII, (Baltimore: The Johns Hopkins University Press, 1978), 1126.

59 *New York Times*, 12 March 1950.

60 "Letter to Regis J. Colasanti," 21 March 1950, Louis Galambos, ed., *The Papers of Dwight David Eisenhower: Columbia University*, vol. XI, (Baltimore: The Johns Hopkins University Press, 1978), 1019.

61 *New York Times*, 12 March 1950.

62 "Diary Entry," 18 October 1951, Louis Galambos, ed., *The Papers of Dwight David Eisenhower: NATO and the Campaign of 1952*, vol. XII, (Baltimore: The Johns Hopkins University Press, 1978), 650-1. Emphasis in original.

63 Quoted in Robert R. Bowie and Richard Immerman, *Waging Peace: How Eisenhower Shaped an Enduring Cold War Strategy* (New York: Oxford University Press, 1998), 14.

64 Andrew J. Goodpaster Jr., 10 April 1982, OH-877, Oral Histories, DDE Library, 2.

65 Melvyn Leffler, *The Specter of Communism: The United States and the Origins of the Cold War, 1917-1953* (New York: Hill and Wang, 1994), 103-4.

66 Stephen E. Ambrose, *Eisenhower: Soldier and President* (New York: Simon and Schuster, 1990), 285.

67 "Letter to Charles Erwin Wilson," 1 July 1953, Louis Galambos, ed., *The Papers of Dwight David Eisenhower: The Middle Way*, vol. XIV, (Baltimore: The Johns Hopkins University Press, 1978), 355.

68 "Memorandum of Discussion at the 134th Meeting of the National Security Council, Wednesday, February 25, 1953, *Foreign Relations of the United States, 1952-1954*, vol. 2, National Security Affairs (Washington, D.C.: GPO, 1984), 11-2.

69 Eisenhower, *Public Papers of the Presidents*, vol. 1, 17.

70 Ibid., 19.

71 Chester J. Pach and Elmo Richardson, *The Presidency of Dwight D. Eisenhower* Revised Edition (Lawrence, KS: University of Kansas Press, 1991), 53.

72 Eisenhower, *Mandate for Change*, 131.

73 Eisenhower, *Public Papers of the Presidents*, vol. 1, 182.

74 NSC 162/2, 30 October 1953, Papers of Dwight D. Eisenhower as President, 1953-1961 (Ann Whitman File), NSC Series, Policy Papers Subseries, Box 6, NSC 162/2, DDE Library, 5.

75 Ibid., 6, 14-5.

76 Ibid., 19.

77 Pach and Richardson, *The Presidency of Dwight D. Eisenhower*, 53.

78 NSC 162/2, 30 October 1953, Papers of Dwight D. Eisenhower as President, 1953-1961 (Ann Whitman File), NSC Series, Policy Papers Subseries, Box 6, NSC 162/2, DDE Library, 7-8.

79 Ibid., 22.

80 Henry Kissinger, "Strategy and Organization," *Foreign Affairs* 35, no. 3 (1957): 379-94.

81 Maxwell Taylor, *The Uncertain Trumpet* (New York: Harper and Brothers, Publishers, 1959), 17-8.

82 "Memorandum to Acting Secretary of State Christian Herter," 31 July 1957, Papers of Dwight D. Eisenhower as President, 1953-1961 (Ann Whitman File), Diary Series, Box 25, July 1957 DDE Dictation, DDE Library, 1.

83 "Minutes of Meeting," 12 January 1958, Papers of Dwight D. Eisenhower as President, 1953-1961 (Ann Whitman File), NSC Series, Box 7, 272nd Meeting, DDE Library, 7.

84 Sherman Adams, *Firsthand Report: The Story of the Eisenhower Administration* (New York: Harper & Brothers, 1961), 155.

85 "Memorandum of Conversation" 23 May 1962, Papers of Dwight D. Eisenhower, Post Presidential, 1961-1969, Augusta-Reed Series, Box 2, Memorandum of Conf, 1961-63 (2), DDE Library, 1.

86 Eisenhower, *Mandate for Change*, 180.

Chapter 3

1 "Diary Entry," 30 June 1950, Louis Galambos, ed., *The Papers of Dwight David Eisenhower: Columbia University*, vol. XI, (Baltimore: The Johns Hopkins University Press, 1978), 1190. Emphasis in original.

2 Dwight Eisenhower, *The White House Years: Mandate for Change, 1953-1956* (Garden City, NY: Doubleday, 1963), 178.

3 Ibid., 178-80.

4 Richard H. Immerman, "Confessions of an Eisenhower Revisionist: An Agonizing Reappraisal," *Diplomatic History* 14, no. 3 (1990): 340.

5 Roger Dingman, "Atomic Diplomacy during the Korean War," *International Security* 13, no. 3 (1988-1989): 50-91.

6 Andrew J. Goodpaster Jr., 10 April 1982, OH-877, Oral Histories, DDE Library, 23.

7 Mark Bender, "Watershed at Leavenworth: Dwight D. Eisenhower at the Command and General Staff School," Command and General Staff College, Combined Arms Research Library, 1990 [on-line]; available from http://www.cgsc.army.mil/ carl/resources/csi/bender/ bender.asp; Internet; accessed 14 May 2008.

8 Dwight D. Eisenhower, *At Ease: Stories I Tell to Friends* (Garden City, NY: Doubleday, 1967), 187.

9 "Letter to Miss Tamborelle" 2 March 1966, Papers of Dwight D. Eisenhower as President, 1953-1961, Post Presidential Convenience, Box 1, DDE "Personals," DDE Library, 1.

10 Dwight D. Eisenhower, *Public Papers of the Presidents of the United States*: Dwight D. Eisenhower, vol. 1 (Washington, D.C.: GPO, 1960), 109.

11 Eisenhower, *Mandate for Change*, 171.

12 Robert W. Griffith, ed., *Ike's Letters to a Friend, 1941-1958* (Lawrence, KS: University of Kansas Press, 1984), 109.

13 "Memorandum to Lewis Strauss from Robert Cutler," 5 December 1953, Papers of Lewis L. Strauss, 1917-1974, Atomic Energy Commission Series, Box 8, Atoms for Peace, 1949-1954, Hoover Library, 1.

14 "Memorandum for the File," 5 December 1953, Papers of Lewis L. Strauss, 1917-1974, Atomic Energy Commission Series, Box 260, Eisenhower, Dwight D., 1953, Oct-Dec, Hoover Library, 2.

15 "Memorandum of Meeting," 24 May 1956, Papers of Dwight D. Eisenhower as President, 1953-1961 (Ann Whitman File), DDE Diary Series, Box 5, May '56 Goodpaster, DDE Library, 2.

16 "Minutes of Meeting," 6 May 1953, Papers of Dwight D. Eisenhower as President, 1953-1961 (Ann Whitman File), NSC, Box 4, 143rd Meeting, DDE Library, 11.

17 Eisenhower, *Mandate for Change*, 181.

18 Chester Bowles, *Ambassador's Report* (New York: Harper, 1954), 242 quoted in Edward Friedman, "Nuclear Blackmail and the End of the Korean War," *Modern China* 1, no. 1 (1975): 80.

19 Goodpaster Jr., 10 April 1982, OH-877, DDE Library, 8, 23-4.

20 Ibid., 24.

21 "Minutes of Meeting, 11 February 1953, Papers of Dwight D. Eisenhower as President, 1953-1961 (Ann Whitman File), NSC, Box 4, 131st Meeting, DDE Library, 3.

22 "Diary Entry," 16 March 1955, Diary Entries, Box 1a, Hagerty Diary March 1955, James C. Hagerty Papers, Press Secretary to the President, 1953-61, DDE Library, 2.

23 "Minutes of Meeting," 28 April 1953, Papers of Dwight D. Eisenhower as President, 1953-1961 (Ann Whitman File), NSC, Box 4, 141st Meeting, DDE Library, 1.

24 Eisenhower, *Public Papers*, vol. 1, 16-7.

25 Eisenhower, *Mandate for Change*, 123.

26 Ibid., 248.

27 Ibid.

28 "Memorandum for the File," 5 December 1953, Papers of Lewis L. Strauss, 1917-1974, Atomic Energy Commission Series, Box 260, Eisenhower, Dwight D., 1953, Oct-Dec, Hoover Library, 2.

29 "Memorandum from Gordon Arneson from Under Secretary of State Walter B. Smith, 12 March 1953, Top Secret," Record Group 59, Department of State Records, Decimal Files, 1950-1954, 711,5611, various dates, 1.

30 "Minutes of Meeting," 11 February 1953, Papers of Dwight D. Eisenhower as President, 1953-1961 (Ann Whitman File), NSC, Box 4, 131st Meeting, Meeting, DDE Library, 3.

31 Eisenhower, *Mandate for Change*, 248.

32 Ibid., 172, 95.

33 "Memorandum of Conference with the President," 24 May 1956, Papers of Dwight D. Eisenhower as President, 1953-1961 (Ann Whitman File), DDE Diary Series, Box 15, May '56 Goodpaster, DDE Library, 2.

34 "Memorandum for the File," 5 December 1953, The Papers of Lewis L. Strauss, 1917-1974, Atomic Energy Commission Series, Box 260, Eisenhower, Dwight D., 1953, Oct-Dec, Hoover Library, 2.

35 "Minutes of Meeting," 20 May 1953, Papers of Dwight D. Eisenhower as President, 1953-1961 (Ann Whitman File), NSC Series, Box 4, 145th Meeting, DDE Library, 8.

36 Eisenhower, *Waging Peace*, 295.

37 "Minutes of Meeting," 11 February 1953, Papers of Dwight D. Eisenhower as President, 1953-1961 (Ann Whitman File), NSC Series, Box 4, 131st Meeting, DDE Library, 3.

38 "Minutes of Meeting," 13 May 1953, Papers of Dwight D. Eisenhower as President, 1953-1961 (Ann Whitman File), NSC Series, Box 4, 144th Meeting, DDE Library, 3.

39 Griffith, ed., *Ike's Letters to a Friend*, 36.

40 "Minutes of Meeting," 11 February 1953, Papers of Dwight D. Eisenhower as President, 1953-1961 (Ann Whitman File), NSC Series, Box 4, 131st Meeting, DDE Library, 3.

41 "Minutes of Meeting," 13 May 1953, Papers of Dwight D. Eisenhower as President, 1953-1961 (Ann Whitman File), NSC Series, Box 4, 144th Meeting, DDE Library, 11.

42 "Minutes of Meeting," 20 May 1953, Papers of Dwight D. Eisenhower as President, 1953-1961 (Ann Whitman File), NSC Series, Box 4, 145th Meeting, DDE Library, 8.

43 "Minutes of Meeting," 11 February 1953, Papers of Dwight D. Eisenhower as President, 1953-1961 (Ann Whitman File), NSC Series, Box 4, 131st Meeting, DDE Library, 3.

44 "Minutes of Meeting," 13 May 1953, Papers of Dwight D. Eisenhower as President, 1953-1961 (Ann Whitman File), NSC Series, Box 4, 144th Meeting, DDE Library, 11.

45 Sherman Adams, *Firsthand Report: The Story of the Eisenhower Administration* (New York: Harper & Brothers, 1961), 49. Scholars disagree over whether threats from the Eisenhower administration of atomic war shortened the Korean War. See Edward Friedman, "Nuclear Blackmail and the End of the Korean War," *Modern China* 1, no. 1 (1975): 75-91; Daniel Calingaert, "Nuclear Weapons and the Korean War," *Journal of Strategic Studies* 11, no. 2 (1988): 177-202; Rosemary Foot, "Nuclear Coercion and the Ending of the Korean Conflict," *International Security* 13, no. 3 (1988-1989): 92-112; Roger Dingman, "Atomic Diplomacy during the Korean War," *International Security* 13, no. 3 (1988-1989): 50-91; Meena Bose, "Winning Peace By Threatening Nuclear War: The Foreign Policy of Eisenhower and Dulles," *Presidential Studies Quarterly* 29, no. 4 (1999): 946-48.

46 Robert Divine, *Eisenhower and the Cold War* (New York: Oxford University Press, 1981).

47 David Alan Rosenberg, "The Origins of Overkill: Nuclear Weapons and American Strategy, 1945-1960," *International Security* 7, no. 4 (1983): 27.

48 Eisenhower, *Waging Peace*, 615.

49 Melvyn P. Leffler, *A Preponderance of Power: National Security, the Truman Administration, and the Cold War* (Stanford, CA: Stanford University Press, 1992), 511.

50 Edward H. Judge and John W. Langdon, *The Cold War: A History through Documents* (Upper Saddle River, NJ: Prentice Hall, 1999), 74-5.

51 Samuel F. Wells, Jr., "The Origins of Massive Retaliation," *Political Science Quarterly* 96, no. 1 (1981): 44.

52 "Statement of Policy by the National Security Council," 30 October 1953, *Foreign Relations of the United States, 1952-1954, vol. 2, National Security Affairs* (Washington, D.C.: United States GPO, 1984), 590.

53 Eisenhower, *Public Papers,* vol. 2, 58.

54 Campbell Craig, "The Thermonuclear Revolution and American Postwar Realism" (Ph.D. Diss., Ohio University, 1995), 155-6.

55 Ibid., 160-1.

56 "Minutes of Meeting," 12 January 1956, Papers of Dwight D. Eisenhower as President, 1953-1961 (Ann Whitman File), NSC Series, Box 7, 272nd Meeting, DDE Library, 8-9.

57 Ibid., 6.

58 "Minutes of Meeting," 28 January 1954, Papers of Dwight D. Eisenhower as President, 1953-1961 (Ann Whitman File), NSC Series, Box 5, 182nd Meeting, DDE Library, 8.

59 Ibid.

60 "Memorandum of Conference with the President," 4 March 1959, Papers of Dwight D. Eisenhower as President, 1953-1961 (Ann Whitman File), DDE Diary Series, Box 39, Staff Notes March 1-15, 1959, 1959 (2), DDE Library, 3.

61 "Minutes of Meeting," 11 July 1957, Papers of Dwight D. Eisenhower as President, 1953-1961 (Ann Whitman File), NSC Series, Box 9, 330th Meeting, DDE Library, 1.

62 "Minutes of Meeting," 12 January 1958, Papers of Dwight D. Eisenhower as President, 1953-1961 (Ann Whitman File), NSC Series, Box 7, 272nd Meeting, DDE Library, 8.

63 "Minutes of Meeting," 18 December 1958, Papers of Dwight D. Eisenhower as President, 1953-1961 (Ann Whitman File), NSC Series, Box 10, 391st Meeting, DDE Library, 2.

64 "Minutes of Meeting," 11 July 1957, Papers of Dwight D. Eisenhower as President, 1953-1961 (Ann Whitman File), NSC Series, Box 9, 330th Meeting, DDE Library, 5-6.

65 "Minutes of Meeting," 18 December 1958, Papers of Dwight D. Eisenhower as President, 1953-1961 (Ann Whitman File), NSC Series, Box 10, 391st Meeting, DDE Library, 2.

66 "The Human Effects of Nuclear Weapons Development," Papers of Dwight D. Eisenhower as President, 1953-1961 (Ann Whitman File), Administration Series, Box 4, Folder 1 AEC, 1955-56, DDE Library, 3.

67 "Minutes of Meeting," 7 February 1957, Papers of Dwight D. Eisenhower as President, 1953-1961 (Ann Whitman File), NSC, Box 8, 312th Meeting, DDE Library, 2-6.

68 "Survival of Population Following a Massive Nuclear Exchange," White House Office, Office of Special Assistant for National Security Affairs, Records 1952-1961, NSC Policy Series, Policy Paper Subseries, Box 24, NSC 5807/1 Shelter Program (5), DDE Library, 2.

69 "Diary Entry," 23 January 1956, Papers of Dwight D. Eisenhower as President, 1953-1961 (Ann Whitman File), Diary Series, Box 12, Jan 56, January 23, 1956, DDE Library, 2.

70 L. Douglas Keeney, *The Doomsday Scenario: The Official Doomsday Scenario Written by the United States Government During the Cold War,* foreword by Stephen I. Schwartz (St. Paul, MN: MBI Publishing Company, 2002).

71 "Minutes of Meeting," 17 June 1955, Papers of Dwight D. Eisenhower as President, 1953-1961 (Ann Whitman File), Name Series, Box 6, Civil Defense Drills (Cdr. Beach) November 1, 1954 (2), DDE Library, 2.

72 "Minutes of Meeting," 11 July 1957, Papers of Dwight D. Eisenhower as President, 1953-1961 (Ann Whitman File), NSC Series, Box 9, 330th Meeting, DDE Library, 2-3.

73 "Minutes of Meeting," 17 June 1955, Papers of Dwight D. Eisenhower as President, 1953-1961 (Ann Whitman File), Name Series, Box 6, Civil Defense Drill's (Cdr. Beach) November 1, 1954 (2), DDE Library, 5.

74 "Minutes of Meeting," 22 December 1960, Papers of Dwight D. Eisenhower as President, 1953-1961 (Ann Whitman File), NSC Series, Box 12, 471st Meeting, DDE Library, 11.

75 "Memorandum of Conversation between Eisenhower and Senator Bridges," 21 May 1957, Papers of Dwight D. Eisenhower as President, 1953-1961 (Ann Whitman File), Ann C. Whitman Diaries Series, Box 8, April 1956 (1), DDE Library, 5.

76 "Minutes of Meeting," 17 June 1955, Papers of Dwight D. Eisenhower as President, 1953-1961 (Ann Whitman File), Name Series, Box 6, Civil Defense Drills (Cdr. Beach) November 1, 1954 (2), DDE Library, 1.

77 "Minutes of Meeting," 25 March 1954, Papers of Dwight D. Eisenhower as President, 1953-1961 (Ann Whitman File), NSC Series, Box 5, 190th Meeting, DDE Library, 9.

78 "Minutes of Meeting," 17 June 1955, Papers of Dwight D. Eisenhower as President, 1953-1961 (Ann Whitman File), Name Series, Box 6, Civil Defense Drills (Cdr. Beach) November 1, 1954 (2), DDE Library, 1.

79 "Minutes of Meeting," 11 July 1957, Papers of Dwight D. Eisenhower as President, 1953-1961 (Ann Whitman File), NSC, Series Box 9, 330th Meeting, DDE Library, 2.

80 "Memorandum of Conversation between Eisenhower and Senator Bridges," 21 May 1957, Papers of Dwight D. Eisenhower as President, 1953-1961 (Ann Whitman File), Ann C. Whitman Diaries Series, Box 8, April 1956 (1), DDE Library, 5.

81 "Minutes of Meeting," 22 December 1960, Papers of Dwight D. Eisenhower as President, 1953-1961 (Ann Whitman File), NSC Series, Box 12, 471st Meeting, DDE Library, 11.

82 Ibid.

83 "Minutes of Meeting," 27 March 1958, Papers of Dwight D. Eisenhower as President, 1953-1961 (Ann Whitman File), NSC Series, Box 10, 360th Meeting, DDE Library, 6.

84 "Letter from Eisenhower to Jackson," Undated, CD Jackson Papers, Box 50, Eisenhower, Dwight D. Correspondence, 1956, DDE Library, 1.

85 Andrew J. Goodpaster Jr., 16 January 1978, OH-378, Oral Histories, DDE Library, 83, 100.

86 Eisenhower, *Mandate for Change*, 214.

87 "Minutes of Meeting," 16 January 1958, Papers of Dwight D. Eisenhower as President, 1953-1961 (Ann Whitman File), NSC Series, Box 9, 351st Meeting, DDE Library, 12.

88 Andrew J. Goodpaster Jr., 16 January 1978, OH-378, Oral Histories, DDE Library, 100; "Memorandum of Conference with the President," 4 March 1959, Papers of Dwight D. Eisenhower as President, 1953-1961 (Ann Whitman File), DDE Diary Series, Box 39, Staff Notes March 1-15, 1959, 1959 (2), DDE Library, 4.

89 Andrew J. Goodpaster Jr., 16 January 1978, OH-378, Oral Histories, DDE Library, 30.

90 Eisenhower, *Public Papers*, vol. 4, 713.

91 Adams, *Firsthand Report*, 413.

92 "Minutes of Meeting," 20 November 1958, Papers of Dwight D. Eisenhower as President, 1953-1961 (Ann Whitman File), NSC Series, Box 10, 387th Meeting, DDE Library, 5.

93 "Minutes of Meeting," 11 July 1957, Papers of Dwight D. Eisenhower as President, 1953-1961 (Ann Whitman File), NSC Series, Box 9, 330th Meeting, DDE Library, 5-6.

94 Richard G. Hewlett and Jack M. Holl, *Atoms for Peace and War, 1953-1961: Eisenhower and the Atomic Energy Commission*, with a foreword by Richard S. Kirkendall and an essay on sources by Roger M. Anders (Berkeley: University of California Press, 1989), 149.

95 "Letter to Henry Luce," 6 July 1960, Papers of Dwight D. Eisenhower as President, 1953-1961 (Ann Whitman File), Name Series, Box 21, Luce, Harry (1), DDE Library, 1. Emphasis in original.

96 "Minutes of Meeting," 18 March 1953, Papers of Dwight D. Eisenhower as President, 1953-1961 (Ann Whitman File), NSC Series, Box 4, 137th Meeting, DDE Library, 7-8.

97 "Minutes of Meeting," 17 June 1955, Papers of Dwight D. Eisenhower as President, 1953-1961 (Ann Whitman File), Name Series, Box 6, Civil Defense Drills (Cdr. Beach) November 1, 1954 (2), DDE Library, 2.

98 "Minutes of Meeting," 28 January 1954, Papers of Dwight D. Eisenhower as President, 1953-1961 (Ann Whitman File), NSC Series, Box 5, 182nd Meeting, DDE Library, 4.

99 "Memorandum of Conversation," 15 July 1961, Post Presidential--August Reed Series, Box 2, Memorandum of Conf, 1961-63 (1), DDE Library, 8.

100 "Minutes of Meeting," 16 January 1958, Papers of Dwight D. Eisenhower as President, 1953-1961 (Ann Whitman File), NSC Series, Box 9, 351st Meeting, DDE Library, 9.

101 "Minutes of Meeting," 11 December 1958, Papers of Dwight D. Eisenhower as President, 1953-1961 (Ann Whitman File), NSC Series, Box 10, 390th Meeting, DDE Library, 3.

102 Ibid., 2-3.

103 "Minutes of Meeting," 27 March 1958, Papers of Dwight D. Eisenhower as President, 1953-1961 (Ann Whitman File), NSC Series, Box 10, 360th Meeting, DDE Library, 6-7.

104 "Memorandum of Conversation," 15 July 1961, Post Presidential--August Reed Series, Box 2, Memorandum of Conf, 1961-63 (1), DDE Library, 8.

105 Ibid.

106 "Letter to Freeman Gosden" 25 September 1961, Dwight D. Eisenhower Post Presidential Series, Special Name SubSeries, Box 4, Gosden, Freeman, 1961, DDE Library, 1-2.

107 "The Human Effects of Nuclear Weapons Development," 21 November 1956, Papers of Dwight D. Eisenhower as President, 1953-1961 (Ann Whitman File), Administration Series, Box 4, Folder 1, Atomic Energy Commission 1955-56, DDE Library, 3, 11, 12.

108 David L. Snead, *The Gaither Committee, Eisenhower, and the Cold War* (Columbus: Ohio State University Press, 1999), 2. See also "Deterrence and Survival in the Nuclear Age," 2, 152-3.

109 Quoted in Snead, *The Gaither Committee, Eisenhower, and the Cold War*, 2.

110 Chester J. Pach and Elmo Richardson, *The Presidency of Dwight D. Eisenhower*, revised edition (Lawrence: University of Kansas Press, 1991), 172-3.

111 "Minutes of Meeting," 27 March 1958, Papers of Dwight D. Eisenhower as President, 1953-1961 (Ann Whitman File), NSC, Box 10, 360th Meeting, DDE Library, 6-7.

112 Chen Jian, *Mao's China and the Cold War* (Chapel Hill, NC: The University of North Carolina Press, 2001), 167-9.

113 Eisenhower, *Public Papers*, vol. 3, 236.

114 "Letter to Martin Withington Clement," 9 January 1952, Louis Galambos, ed., *The Papers of Dwight David Eisenhower: NATO and the Campaign of 1952*, vol. XIII, (Baltimore: The Johns Hopkins University Press, 1978), 867.

115 Eisenhower, *Public Papers*, vol. 3, 186.

116 "Letter to Henry Robinson Luce," 24 January 1955, Louis Galambos, ed., *The Papers of Dwight David Eisenhower: The Presidency: The Middle Way*, vol. XVI, (Baltimore: The Johns Hopkins University Press, 1978), 1520.

117 Eisenhower, *Mandate for Change*, 464.

118 "Minutes of Meeting," 8 January 1954, Papers of Dwight D. Eisenhower as President, 1953-1961 (Ann Whitman File), NSC Series, Box 5, 179th Meeting, DDE Library, 8.

119 Eisenhower, *Mandate for Change*, 464.
120 Ibid.
121 Pach and Richardson, *The Presidency of Dwight D. Eisenhower*, 100-1.
122 Eisenhower, *Public Papers*, vol. 3, 208-9.
123 Ibid, 209.
124 Ibid., 210.
125 Ibid., 225-6.
126 Eisenhower, *Mandate for Change*, 608.
127 "Letter to Winston Spencer Churchill," 18 February 1955, Louis Galambos, ed., *The Papers of Dwight David Eisenhower: The Presidency: The Middle Way*, vol. XVI, (Baltimore: The Johns Hopkins University Press, 1978), 1576.
128 Eisenhower, *Mandate for Change*, 476-77.
129 Eisenhower, *Public Papers*, vol. 3, 332, 357-8.
130 See "Letter to Alfred Maximillian Gruenther," 1 February 1955, Louis Galambos, ed., *The Papers of Dwight David Eisenhower: The Presidency: The Middle Way*, vol. XVI, (Baltimore: The Johns Hopkins University Press, 1978), 1537 and "Letter to Winston Spencer Churchill," 10 February 1955, Louis Galambos, ed., *The Papers of Dwight David Eisenhower: The Presidency: The Middle Way*, vol. XVI, (Baltimore: The Johns Hopkins University Press, 1978), 1563.
131 "Letter to Winston Spencer Churchill," 10 February 1955, Louis Galambos, ed., *The Papers of Dwight David Eisenhower: The Presidency: The Middle Way*, vol. XVI, (Baltimore: The Johns Hopkins University Press, 1978), 1564. Emphasis in original.
132 Eisenhower, *Public Papers*, vol. 3, 358.
133 Quoted in Eisenhower, *Mandate for Change*, 480.
134 Eisenhower, *Mandate for Change*, 459, 467.
135 Goodpaster Jr., April 10, 1982, OH-877, DDE Library, 6.
136 Eisenhower, *Mandate for Change*, 477.
137 Goodpaster Jr., April 10, 1982, OH-877, DDE Library, 6.
138 "Minutes of Meeting," 8 January 1954, Papers of Dwight D. Eisenhower as President, 1953-1961 (Ann Whitman File), NSC, Box 5, 179th Meeting, DDE Library, 7.

Chapter 4

1 Dwight D. Eisenhower, *Public Papers of the President of the United States*, vol. 3 (Washington, D.C.: GPO, 1959), 594-95, 598.
2 "Interim Report by the Ad Hoc Committee of the NSC Planning Board on Armaments and American Policy," *Foreign Relations of the United States, 1952-1954*, vol. 2, National Security Affairs (Washington, D.C.: GPO, 1984), 1153.
3 Paul Boyer, *By the Bomb's Early Light: American Thought and Culture at the Dawn of the Atomic Age* (Chapel Hill: University of North Carolina Press, 1994), 32.
4 Ibid., 109-10, 32.
5 Ibid.
6 Eisenhower, *Public Papers*, vol. 3, 773.
7 Eisenhower, *Public Papers*, vol. 1, 635.
8 Vincent C. Jones, *United States Army in World War II: Manhattan, the Army and the Atomic Bomb* (Washington, D.C.: Center of Military History, 1985), ix.
9 Richard G. Hewlett and Oscar Anderson, *The New World, 1939-1946, Vol. I, A History of the U.S. Atomic Energy Commission* (University Park: Pennsylvania State University Press, 1962), 428-31.

10 Philip L. Cantelon, Richard G. Hewlett, and Robert C. Williams, eds., *The American Atom: A Documentary History of Nuclear Policies from the Discovery of Fission to the Present* 2nd ed. (Philadelphia: University of Pennsylvania Press, 1984), 69.

11 Ibid., 70.

12 Ibid., 77-78.

13 "Letter to Robert Porter Patterson," 4 June 1946, Louis Galambos, ed., *The Papers of Dwight David Eisenhower: Chief of Staff,* vol. VII, (Baltimore: The Johns Hopkins University Press, 1978), 1101.

14 Quoted in Ibid., note 2.

15 "Letter to Robert Porter Patterson," 4 June 1946, Louis Galambos, ed., *The Papers of Dwight David Eisenhower: Chief of Staff,* vol. VII, (Baltimore: The Johns Hopkins University Press, 1978), 1101.

16 Eisenhower, *Public Papers*, vol. 1, 182. Emphasis in original.

17 Ibid.

18 Ibid., 185.

19 Ibid., 187. Emphasis in original.

20 Eisenhower, *Public Papers*, vol. 2, 261.

21 Ibid., 789-90.

22 Richard G. Hewlett and Jack M. Holl, *Atoms for Peace and War, 1953-1961: Eisenhower and the Atomic Energy Commission*, with a foreword by Richard S. Kirkendall and an essay on sources by Roger M. Anders (Berkeley: University of California Press, 1989), 33.

23 Eisenhower, *Public Papers*, vol. 1., 177.

24 Hewlett and Holl, *Atoms for Peace and War*, 184.

25 Eisenhower, *Public Papers*, vol. 1, 820-21.

26 Eisenhower, *Public Papers*, vol. 2, 262-9.

27 Lewis L. Strauss, *Men and Decisions* (Garden City, NJ: Doubleday, 1962), 313.

28 Eisenhower, *Public Papers*, vol. 2, 267-68.

29 Dwight D. Eisenhower *The White House Years: Mandate for Change, 1953-1956* (Garden City, NY: Doubleday, 1963), 294.

30 Eisenhower, *Mandate for Change*, 294.

31 Hewlett and Holl, *Atoms for Peace and War*, 120.

32 United States Nuclear Regulatory Commission, *Nuclear Regulatory Legislation, 107th Congress, 1st Session*, NUREG 0980 Vol. 1, No. 6 (Washington, D.C.: 2002), 9-10.

33 Ibid., 28.

34 Eisenhower, *Public Papers*, vol. 2, 777.

35 John Baylis, "Exchanging Nuclear Secrets: Laying the Foundation of the Anglo-American Nuclear Relationship," *Diplomatic History* 25, no. 1 (2001): 33-61

36 Ibid., 36.

37 Eisenhower, *Public Papers*, vol. 2, 777.

38 Ibid., 262.

39 Hewlett and Holl, *Atoms for Peace and War*, 195.

40 Ibid., 197.

41 Ibid., 201.

42 Eisenhower, *Public Papers*, vol. 2, 840-41.

43 Hewlett and Holl, *Atoms for Peace and War*, 227-28.

44 Prentice C. Dean, *Energy History Chronology from World War II to the Present* (Washington, D.C.: Department of Energy, 1982), 23.

45 Hewlett and Holl, *Atoms for Peace and War*, Table 3, 511-12.

46 "Eight Years of Progress in Atomic Energy," 3 January 1961, John A. McCone Papers, 1958-1961, Box 1, Com 1 – 1 – Chairman's Reading File, October Thru January 20, 1961 [GT File], DDE Library, 12-13.
47 Hewlett and Holl, *Atoms for Peace and War*, 199.
48 Eisenhower, *Public Papers*, vol. 5, 807.
49 Ibid., 794, 808, 790.
50 Ibid., 798-9.
51 Ibid., 794-9.
52 Eisenhower, *Public Papers*, vol. 7, 405-406.
53 Eisenhower, *Public Papers*, vol. 6, 2, 7.
54 Ibid, 7.
55 Ibid., 12.
56 Eisenhower, *Public Papers*, vol. 5, 814.
57 Eisenhower, *Public Papers*, vol. 6, 12.
58 Richard Vernon Damms, "Scientists and Statesmen: President Eisenhower's Science Advisers and National Security Policy, 1953-1961" (Ph.D. diss., The Ohio State University, 1993); Richard V. Damms, "James Killian, the Technological Capabilities Panel, and the Emergence of President Eisenhower's 'Scientific-Technological Elite.'" *Diplomatic History* 24, no. 1 (2000): 57-78; Zuoyue Wang, "American Science and the Cold War: The Rise of the United States President's Science Advisory Committee" (Ph.D. diss., University of California, Santa Barbara, 1994).
59 "Memorandum of Conference with the President," 4 May 1955, Papers of Dwight D. Eisenhower as President, 1953-1961 (Ann Whitman File), Administration Series, Box 4, AEC 1955-56 (7), DDE Library, 1.
60 "Diary Entry," 6 February 1956, Papers of Dwight D. Eisenhower as President, 1953-1961 (Ann Whitman File), Ann C. Whitman Diary Series, Box 8, February 1956, February 6, 1956, DDE Library, 1.
61 Eisenhower, *Public Papers*, vol. 3, 553-4.
62 Adams, *Firsthand Report*, 416.
63 "Memorandum of Discussion at the 244th Meeting of the National Security Council, April 7, 1955," *Foreign Relations of the United States, 1955-1957, Regulation of Armaments; Atomic Energy*, (Washington, D.C.: GPO, 1990), 66.
64 "Republican Party Platform for 1956," The American Presidency Project, University of California at Santa Barbara, [on-line]; available at http://www.presidency.ucsb.edu/platforms.php ; accessed February 6, 2007.
65 Peter Goodchild, *Edward Teller: The Real Dr. Strangelove* (Cambridge, MA: Harvard University Press, 2004), 284.
66 Goodchild, *The Real Dr. Strangelove*, 285.
67 Katherine Magraw, "Teller and the 'Clean Bomb' Episode," *Bulletin of Atomic Scientists* 44, no. 4 (1988): 32, 34.
68 Ibid., 32.
69 Quoted in Ibid. Magraw referred to but did not cite the following: "Memorandum of Conversation with the President, White House, Washington, 24 June 1957, *Foreign Relations of the United States, 1955-1957, Regulation of Armaments; Atomic Energy* (Washington, D.C.: GPO, 1984), 638-40.
70 Quoted in Magraw, "Teller and the 'Clean Bomb' Episode," 32.
71 "Memorandum of Conversation with the President, White House, Washington, June 24, 1957, *Foreign Relations of the United States, 1955-1957, Regulation of Armaments; Atomic Energy* (Washington, D.C.: GPO, 1984), 639.

72 Ibid.
73 Strauss, *Men and Decisions*, 419.
74 Quoted in Magraw, "Teller and the 'Clean Bomb' Episode," 32.
75 Eisenhower, *Public Papers*, vol. 5, 498.
76 Ibid., 499.
77 Ibid., 519.
78 Scott Kirsch, *Proving Grounds: Project Plowshare and the Unrealized Dream of Nuclear Earthmoving* (New Brunswick, NJ: Rutgers University Press, 2005), 33.
79 George B. Kistiakowsky, *A Scientist at the White House: The Private Diary of President Eisenhower's Special Assistant for Science and Technology*, introduction by Charles S. Maier (Cambridge, MA: Harvard University Press, 1976), 365.
80 Goodchild, *The Real Dr. Strangelove*, 285.
81 Kirsch, *Proving Grounds*, 38.
82 Strauss, *Men and Decisions*, 421.
83 Goodchild, *The Real Dr. Strangelove*, 285.
84 Strauss, *Men and Decisions*, 421-25.
85 Hewlett and Holl, *Atoms for Peace and War*, 529.
86 Ibid., 528-30.
87 Strauss, *Men and Decisions*, 420.
88 "Meeting with the President," 12 July 1958, President's Science Advisory Committee Records, 1957-1961, Administrative, Box 3, Meeting with the President, July 12, 1958, DDE Library, 1.
89 "Minutes of Meeting," 16 October 1958, Papers of Dwight D. Eisenhower as President, 1953-1961 (Ann Whitman File), NSC, Box 10, 383rd Meeting, DDE Library, 2.
90 Goodchild, *The Real Dr. Strangelove*, 285.
91 Kistiakowsky, *A Scientist at the White House*, 365. Kistiakowsky mistakenly wrote of a canal through Mexico. The bulk of the evidence suggests all proposed Plowshare-related canals ran through the narrowest part of the Central American isthmus, either through Panama or Colombia.
92 Gerald W. Johnson, "Plowshare at the Crossroads," *Bulletin of Atomic Scientists* 26, no. 6 (1970): 84.
93 Kirsch, *Proving Grounds*, 41.
94 Edward Teller and Allen Brown, *The Legacy of Hiroshima* (Garden City, NY: Doubleday and Company Inc., 1962), 84 quoted in Scott Kirsch and Don Mitchell, "Earth-Moving as the 'Measure of Man': Edward Teller, Geographical Engineering, and the Matter of Progress," *Social Text* 54 (Spring 1998): 106.
95 Kirsch and Mitchell, "Earth-Moving as the 'Measure of Man,'" 106. Emphasis in original.
96 Hewlett and Holl, *Atoms for Peace and War*, 529.
97 Kirsch, *Proving Grounds*, 43, 47.
98 Quoted in Ibid., 48.
99 Quoted in Goodchild, *The Real Dr. Strangelove*, 285.
100 "Memorandum for the File," 2 March 1959, John A. McCone Papers, 1958-1961, Box 5, McCone Sealed File Number 5 (2), DDE Library, 3.
101 Eisenhower, *Public Papers*, vol. 2, 267, 269.

Chapter 5

1 "Text of Eisenhower Speech," *New York Times*, 23 December 1952, 16.
2 Richard H. Immerman, "Confessions of an Eisenhower Revisionist: An Agonizing Reappraisal," *Diplomatic History* 14, no. 3 (1990): 335.

3 Dwight D. Eisenhower, *Public Papers of the Presidents of the United States*, vol. 1 (Washington, D.C.: GPO, 1960), 774.

4 Eisenhower, *Public Papers*, vol. 5, 798-9.

5 "Letter to Bela Kornitzer," 17 March 1955, Papers of Dwight D. Eisenhower as President, 1953-1961 (Ann Whitman File), Ann C. Whitman Diary, Box 4, March 1955 (4), DDE Library, 5.

6 "Letter to Nancy Bierce," 4 April 1960, Papers of Dwight D. Eisenhower as President, 1953-1961 (Ann Whitman File), DDE Diary Series, Box 49, Folder "DDE Dictation April 1960," DDE Library, 1-2. Eisenhower paraphrased the following: "When a strong man armed keepeth his palace, his goods are in peace. But when a stronger than he shall come upon him and overcome him, he taketh from him all his armour wherein he trusted, and divideth his spoils." Luke 11:21-22, *Holy Bible*, King James Version.

7 "Text of Eisenhower Speech," *New York Times*, 23 December 1952, 16.

8 Robert Griffith, ed., *Ike's Letters to a Friend, 1941-1958* (Lawrence, KS: University of Kansas Press, 1984), 168.

9 Richard V. Pierard and Robert D. Linder, *Civil Religion and the Presidency* (Grand Rapids, Michigan: Academie Books, 1988), 184, 192.

10 Dwight D. Eisenhower, *Crusade in Europe* (Garden City, NY: Doubleday, 1948).

11 Pierard and Linder, *Civil Religion and the Presidency*, 194.

12 "Letter to Clifford Roberts," 29 July 1952, Papers of Dwight D. Eisenhower as President, 1953-1961 (Ann Whitman File), Name Series, Box 27, Roberts Clifford 1952-53 (2), DDE Library, 2.

13 *New York Times*, 23 December 1952, 16 quoted in Pierard and Linder, *Civil Religion and the Presidency*, 184.

14 For discussions about the nature, sources, and forms of civil religion see Robert N. Bellah, "Civil Religion in America," *Daedalus* 96 (Winter 1967): 1-21; For specific focus on American presidents and civil religion, see Pierard and Linder, *Civil Religion and the Presidency*.

15 Robert N. Bellah, "Civil Religion in America," *Daedalus* 96 (Winter 1967): 1-21.

16 *New York Times*, 18 February 1955, 28, quoted in Pierard and Linder, *Civil Religion and the Presidency*, 205.

17 Quoted in Pierard and Linder, *Civil Religion and the Presidency*, 202.

18 Pierard and Linder, *Civil Religion and the Presidency*, 199.

19 Historian Jack Holl argues that Eisenhower was a deeply religious man who used prayer to strengthen his sense of universal brotherhood. The United States was a religious place, a chosen place, and Eisenhower saw it as his responsibility to save the nation from the Cold War and nuclear annihilation through a return to basic religious values. See Jack Holl, "Dwight D. Eisenhower: Exegetical President in the Nuclear Age," 2002. TMs (photocopy).

20 Eisenhower, *Public Papers*, vol. 6, 454-5.

21 Eisenhower, *Public Papers*, vol. 2, 947.

22 Dwight D. Eisenhower, *The White House Years: Waging Peace, 1956-1961* (Garden City, NY: Doubleday, 1963), 368.

23 Eisenhower, *Public Papers*, vol. 2, 562.

24 Eisenhower, *Public Papers*, vol. 1, 75.

25 "Memorandum of Conversation with Joint Chiefs of Staff," 24 May 1956, Papers of Dwight D. Eisenhower as President, 1953-1961 (Ann Whitman File), Diary Series, Box 15, May '56 Goodpaster, DDE Library, 2.

26 Eisenhower, *Public Papers*, vol. 6, 454.

27 Eisenhower, *Waging Peace*, 483.

28 Andrew J. Goodpaster Jr., 10 April 1982, OH-877, Oral Histories, DDE Library, 31-2.

29 "AEC Memo for the Record," 20 August 1958, Papers of Lewis L. Strauss, 1917-1974, Atomic Energy Commission Series, Box 69, Eisenhower, Dwight D., 1957, August-December, Hoover Library, 3.
30 "Letter to Chairman of the Foreign Relations Committee," Post Presidential Papers of Dwight D. Eisenhower, 1963 Principal File, Box 65, Test Ban Treaty (1), DDE Library, 2.
31 "Letter to C.D. Jackson," 31 December 1953, Box 29, Atoms for Peace – Evolution (2), Papers of C.D. Jackson, DDE Library, 1-2.
32 Eisenhower, *Waging Peace*, 483.
33 Ibid., 467.
34 Goodpaster Jr., 16 January 1978, OH-378, DDE Library, 106.
35 "Memorandum for the Files," 10 March 1960, John A. McCone Papers, 1958-1961, Box 5, McCone Sealed File Number 5 (1), DDE Library, 1.
36 Eisenhower, *Public Papers*, vol. 3, 375.
37 Ibid., 376.
38 Sherman Adams, *Firsthand Report: The Story of the Eisenhower Administration* (New York: Harper & Brothers, 1961), 317-8.
39 Eisenhower, *Public Papers*, vol. 3, 344.
40 C.D. Jackson, "Chronology – – Candor-Wheaties," 30 September 1954, Box 29, Atoms for Peace Folder 1, Papers of C.D. Jackson, DDE Library, 1.
41 John Lear, "Ike and the Peaceful Atom," *The Reporter*, 12 January 1956, 11.
42 "Draft Presidential Speech on Atomic Energy," 16 June 1953, Dwight D. Eisenhower Records as President, White House Central Files, 1953-1961, Confidential File, Box 13, Folder 18, DDE Library, 1.
43 "Draft Presidential Speech on Atomic Energy," 22 June 1953, Dwight D. Eisenhower Records as President, White House Central Files, 1953-1961, Confidential File, Box 13, Folder 16, DDE Library, 1.
44 Eisenhower, *Waging Peace*, 52.
45 Ibid., 254.
46 Eisenhower, *Public Papers*, vol. 3, 716.
47 "Letter to Nikolai Aleksandrovich Bulganin," 11 October 1955, Louis Galambos, ed., *The Papers of Dwight David Eisenhower: The Presidency: The Middle Way*, vol. XVI, (Baltimore: The Johns Hopkins University Press, 1978), 1866.
48 Eisenhower, *Public Papers*, vol. 3, 713-4.
49 "Diary Entry," 8 February 1956, Louis Galambos, ed., *The Papers of Dwight David Eisenhower: The Presidency: The Middle Way*, vol. XVI, (Baltimore: The Johns Hopkins University Press, 1978), 2009-10.
50 "Minutes of Meeting, 18 February 1960, Papers of Dwight D. Eisenhower as President, 1953-1961 (Ann Whitman File), NSC, Box 12, Special Meeting of NSC, DDE Library, 4.
51 "Harold Stassen to Dwight Eisenhower," 26 January 1957 quoted in Louis Galambos, ed., *The Papers of Dwight David Eisenhower: The Presidency: Keeping the Peace*, vol. XVIII, (Baltimore: The Johns Hopkins University Press, 1978), 15, note 2.
52 "Letter to Harold Edward Stassen," 28 January 1957, Louis Galambos, ed., *The Papers of Dwight David Eisenhower: The Presidency: Keeping the Peace*, vol. XVIII, (Baltimore: The Johns Hopkins University Press, 1978), 14.
53 "Letter to Harold Macmillan," 16 June 1957, Louis Galambos, ed., *The Papers of Dwight David Eisenhower: The Presidency: Keeping the Peace*, vol. XVIII, (Baltimore: The Johns Hopkins University Press, 1978), 265.

54 "US Position on First Phase of Disarmament," 11 June 1957, *Foreign Relations of the United States, 1955-1957, Regulation of Armaments; Atomic Energy, vol. 20* (Washington, D.C.: United States Government Printing Office, 1984), 620-4.
55 "Letter to Nikita Sergeyevich Khrushchev," 8 April 1958, Louis Galambos, ed., *The Papers of Dwight David Eisenhower: The Presidency: Keeping the Peace*, vol. XIX, (Baltimore: The Johns Hopkins University Press, 1978), 819.
56 Eisenhower, *Waging Peace*, 467-8.
57 Goodpaster Jr., 10 April 1982, OH-877, DDE Library, 32.
58 Eisenhower, *Waging Peace*, 467.
59 "Diary Entry," 10 January 1956, Louis Galambos, ed., *The Papers of Dwight David Eisenhower: The Presidency: The Middle Way*, vol. XVI, (Baltimore: The Johns Hopkins University Press, 1978), 1947.
60 Benjamin P. Greene, "Eisenhower, Science and the Nuclear Test Ban Debate, 1953-56," *The Journal of Strategic Studies* 26, no. 4 (2003): 156-85.
61 Ibid.,159.
62 "Memorandum of the Discussion at the 199th Meeting of the National Security Council," 27 May 1954, *Foreign Relations of the United States, 1952-1954, National Security Affairs, Vol. 2* (Washington, D.C.: United States Government Printing Office, 1984), 1455.
63 Greene, "Eisenhower, Science and the Nuclear Test Ban Debate," 180.
64 Robert A. Divine, *Blowing on the Wind: The Nuclear Test Ban Debate, 1954-1960* (New York: Oxford University Press, 1978), 3-5, 7.
65 Eisenhower, *Public Papers*, vol. 2, 346.
66 Hewlett and Holl, *Atoms for Peace and War*, 181-2.
67 Ibid., 181.
68 Divine, *Blowing on the Wind*, 13.
69 Ibid., 21.
70 Ibid., 24. See also Greene, "Eisenhower, Science and the Nuclear Test Ban Debate," 156-85.
71 "A Report by the United States Atomic Energy Commission on the Effects of High-Yield Nuclear Explosions," 15 February 1955 quoted in Divine, *Blowing on the Wind*, 39.
72 Divine, *Blowing on the Wind*, 39.
73 Eisenhower, *Public Papers*, vol. 3, 332-3.
74 Gordon M. Dunning, "Effects of Nuclear Weapons Testing," *The Scientific Monthly* 81, no. 6 (1955): 268.
75 Ibid., 265.
76 Eisenhower, *Waging Peace*, 18.
77 Carolyn Kopp, "The Origins of the American Scientific Debate over Fallout Hazards," *Social Studies of Science* 9, no. 4 (1979): 413.
78 Eisenhower, *Public Papers*, vol. 5, 429.
79 Ibid., 475.
80 Eisenhower, *Waging Peace*, 474.
81 "Memorandum of Meeting with President," 24 March 1958, Papers of Dwight D. Eisenhower as President, 1953-1961 (Ann Whitman File), Diary Series, Box 31, Staff Notes March 1958 (1), DDE Library, 4.
82 "Minutes of Meeting," 6 May 1954, Papers of Dwight D. Eisenhower as President, 1953-1961 (Ann Whitman File), NSC Series, Box 5, 195th Meeting, DDE Library, 12-13.

83 "Memorandum of Meeting with President," 18 August 1958, Papers of Dwight D. Eisenhower as President, 1953-1961 (Ann Whitman File), Diary Series, Box 33, Aug 58 Staff Notes (1), DDE Library, 1.

84 "Minutes of Meeting," 6 May 1954, Papers of Dwight D. Eisenhower as President, 1953-1961 (Ann Whitman File), NSC Series, Box 5, 195th Meeting, DDE Library, 14.

85 "Memorandum of Meeting with President," 24 March 1958, Papers of Dwight D. Eisenhower as President, 1953-1961 (Ann Whitman File), Diary Series, Box 31, Staff Notes March 1958 (1), DDE Library, 3-4.

86 "Diary Entry," 18 February 1960, Papers of Dwight D. Eisenhower as President, 1953-1961 (Ann Whitman File), Diary Series, Box 27 DDE Diary Oct 1957, DDE Library, 1.

87 "Memorandum of Conversation with the President," 12 January 1959, Papers of Dwight D. Eisenhower as President, 1953-1961 (Ann Whitman File), Diary Series, Box 38, Staff Notes – January 1959 (2), DDE Library, 2.

88 "Memorandum of Conversation," 5 May 1959, John A. McCone Papers, 1958-1961, Box 5, McCone Sealed File Number 3, DDE Library, 2.

89 "Memorandum of Conversation with the President," 26 December 1956, The Papers of John Foster Dulles, White House Memo Series, Box 4, Meetings with the President Aug. Thru Dec. 1956 (1), DDE Library, 1.

90 "Memorandum of Conversation with the President," 3 August 1957, The Papers of John Foster Dulles, White House Memo Series, Box 5, Meetings with the President – 1957 (4), DDE Library, 2.

91 Memorandum of Conference with the President," 9 August 1957, *Foreign Relations of the United States, 1955-1957, Regulation of Armaments; Atomic Energy, vol. 20*, (Washington, D.C.: United States Government Printing Office, 1990), 700.

92 Hewlett and Holl, *Atoms for Peace and War*, 456; "Memorandum for the Files," 24 July 1958, Papers of Lewis L. Strauss, 1917-1974, Atomic Energy Commission Series, Box 26E, Eisenhower, Dwight D., 1958, July-December, Hoover Library, 1.

93 "Letter to Harold Macmillan," 28 March 1958, Louis Galambos, ed., *The Papers of Dwight David Eisenhower: Keeping the Peace*, vol. XIX (Baltimore: The Johns Hopkins University Press, 2001), 805.

94 "Letter to Nikita Sergeyevich Khrushchev," 8 April 1958, Louis Galambos, ed., *The Papers of Dwight David Eisenhower: Keeping the Peace*, vol. XIX (Baltimore: The Johns Hopkins University Press, 2001), 819. Emphasis in original.

95 Eisenhower, *Public Papers*, vol. 6, 262.

96 Hewlett and Holl, *Atoms for Peace and War*, 486-7.

97 Divine, *Blowing on the Wind*, 225.

98 "Letter to Harold Macmillan," 19 August 1958, Louis Galambos, ed., *The Papers of Dwight David Eisenhower: Keeping the Peace*, vol. XIX (Baltimore: The Johns Hopkins University Press, 2001), 1058-59, Note 1.

99 "Letter to Harold Macmillan," 20 August 1958, Louis Galambos, ed., *The Papers of Dwight David Eisenhower: Keeping the Peace*, vol. XIX (Baltimore: The Johns Hopkins University Press, 2001), 1060-1.

100 Eisenhower, *Public Papers*, vol. 6, 635-6.

101 Hewlett and Holl, *Atoms for Peace and War*, 275.

102 Hazel Gaudet Erskine, "The Polls: Atomic Weapons and Nuclear Energy," *The Public Opinion Quarterly* 27, no. 2 (1963): 157.

103 Philip K. Scheuer, "Chilling 'On the Beach' Premiers in 18 Nations," *Los Angeles Times*, 18 December 1959, part 1, pg. 2.

104 *On the Beach*, prod. and dir. Stanley Kramer, 134 min., Metro-Goldwyn-Mayer Studios, 1959, DVD.

105 Ibid. See Jay Robert Nash and Stanley Ralph Ross, "On the Beach," *The Motion Picture Guide*, vol. 6, *N–R, 1927-1983* (Chicago: Cinebooks, Inc., 1986), 2247-8; Frances Taylor Patterson, "On the Beach," *Films in Review* 11 (January 1960): 36-9.

106 "'On the Beach' – Joint USIA-State Information Guidance for Missions Abroad," 7 December 1959, Papers of Dwight D. Eisenhower as President, 1953-1961 (Ann Whitman File), Cabinet Series, Box 15, DDE Library, 1.

107 Ibid.

108 "Cabinet Agenda for Friday, December 11," 10 December 1959, Papers of Dwight D. Eisenhower as President, 1953-1961 (Ann Whitman File), Cabinet Series, Box 15, DDE Library, 1.

109 Joseph Keyerleber, "On the Beach" in Jack G. Shaheen, ed., *Nuclear War Films* (Carbondale, IL: Southern Illinois University Press, 1978), 31.

110 Donald Spoto, *Stanley Kramer: Film Maker* (New York: G.P. Putnam's Sons, 1978), 212; "Memorandum for the Vice President," 10 December 1959, Papers of Dwight D. Eisenhower as President, 1953-1961 (Ann Whitman File), Cabinet Series, Box 15, DDE Library, 1.

111 Robert Hatch, Untitled, review of *On the Beach* (UA movie) *The Nation*, 2 January 1960, 20.

112 "Dire Drama on the Death of the World," review of *On the Beach* (UA movie) *Life*, 30 November 1959, 93.

113 Hatch, Review of *On the Beach*, 20.

114 Untitled, review of *On the Beach* (UA movie), *America* 102, December 19-26, 381.

115 James V. Schall, S.J., "'On the Beach': the Limits of Mortality," review of *On the Beach* (UA movie) *Catholic World* 191 (May 1960), 82.

116 "Program for the Washington Premiere of On the Beach,"quoted in Schall, "'On the Beach': the Limits of Mortality," 82.

117 Schall, "'On the Beach': the Limits of Mortality," 82.

118 Eisenhower, *Public Papers*, vol. 1, 814-7.

119 Ibid., 822.

120 "Eisenhower to Milton," 11 December 1953, Papers of Dwight D. Eisenhower as President, 1953-1961 (Ann Whitman File), Name Series, 12, Eisenhower, Milton 1952 thru 1953 (2), DDE Library, 1.

121 Ferrell, ed., *The Eisenhower Diaries*, 261.

122 Eisenhower, *Public Papers*, vol. 5, 207-8.

123 "Letter to Strauss from Eisenhower," 23 February 1965, Papers of Lewis L. Strauss, 1917-1974, Atomic Energy Commission Series, Box 26E, Eisenhower, Dwight D., 1959-1961, Hoover Library, 1.

124 Hewlett and Holl, *Atoms for Peace and War*, 236.

125 Ibid., 320.

126 Eisenhower, *Public Papers*, vol. 4, 259.

127 Hewlett and Holl, *Atoms for Peace and War*, 321.

128 Eisenhower, *Public Papers*, vol. 2, 551.

Conclusion

1 Henry Kissinger, *Nuclear Weapons and Foreign Policy*, with a foreword by Gordon Dean (New York: Harper and Brothers, 1957), xi.

2 Eisenhower, *Public Papers*, vol. 1, 161.

3 Robert H. Ferrell, ed., *The Eisenhower Diaries* (New York: W.W. Norton and Company, 1981), 213.

4 Ibid., 137.

5 Eisenhower, *Public Papers*, vol. 2, 548.

6 Eisenhower, *Public Papers*, vol. 8, 1043-4.

7 Ibid., 1039.

8 Eisenhower, *Public Papers*, vol. 8, 1039.

9 "Estimated U.S. and Soviet/Russian Nuclear Stockpiles, 1945-1994," *Bulletin of Atomic Scientists* (November/December 1994), 58-9; National Resources Defense Council, "Table of Nuclear Warheads," [on-line]; available at http://www.nrdc.org/ nuclear/nudb/datab9.asp; accessed 22 August 2007.

Bibliography

PRIMARY SOURCES

Manuscript Sources

1. The Dwight D. Eisenhower Presidential Library, Abilene, Kansas
    a. Eisenhower, Dwight D.: Papers as President (Ann Whitman File), 1953-1961
    b. Eisenhower, Dwight D.: Papers, Pre-Presidential, 1916-1952
    c. Eisenhower, Dwight D.: Papers, Post-Presidential, 1961-69
    d. Eisenhower, Dwight D.: Records as President (White House Central Files), 1953-61
    e. Dulles, John Foster: Papers, 1951-59
    f. Hagerty, James: Papers, 1953-61
    g. Jackson, C.D.: Papers, 1931-67
    h. McCone, John A.: Papers, 1958-61
    i. U.S. President's Science Advisory Committee: Records
    j. White House Office, Office of the Special Assistant for National Security Affairs (Robert Cutler, Dillon Anderson, and Gordon Gray): Records, 1952-61
    k. White House Office, Office of the Staff Secretary Records of Paul T. Carroll, Andrew J. Goodpaster, L. Arthur Minnich, and Christopher H. Russell, 1952-61
2. The Herbert Hoover Presidential library, West Branch, Iowa
    i. The Papers of Lewis L. Strauss, 1917-1974
    ii. Atomic Energy Commission Series
    iii. Articles and Speech Series
    iv. Name and Subject Series I
    v. Name and Subject Series II

Books

Adams, Sherman. *Firsthand Report: The Story of the Eisenhower Administration*. New York: Harper & Brothers, 1961.

Branyan, Robert L. *The Eisenhower Administration, 1953-1961: A Documentary History*. New York: Random House, 1971.

Brodie, Bernard, ed. *The Absolute Weapon: Atomic Power and World Order*. New York: Harcourt, Brace and Company, 1946.

Brodie, Bernard. *Strategy in the Missile Age*. Princeton, NJ: Princeton University Press, 1959.

Brownell, Herbert with John P. Burke. *Advising Ike: The Memoirs of Attorney General Herbert Brownell*. Foreword by John Chancellor. Lawrence, KS: University of Kansas Press, 1993.

Butcher, Harry C. *My Three years with Eisenhower: The Personal Diary of Captain Harry C. Butcher, USNR, Naval Aide to General Eisenhower, 1942 to 1945*. New York: Simon and Schuster, 1946.

Eisenhower, Dwight D. *Crusade in Europe*. Garden City, NY: Doubleday, 1948.
________. *Peace with Justice: Selected Addresses of Dwight D. Eisenhower*. Foreword by Grayson Kirk. New York: Colombia University Press, 1961.
________. *The White House Years: Mandate for Change, 1953-1956*. Garden City, NY: Doubleday, 1963.
________. *The White House Years: Waging Peace, 1956-1961*. Garden City, NY: Doubleday, 1963.
________. *At Ease: Stories I Tell to Friends*. Garden City, NY: Doubleday, 1967.
________. *In Review: Pictures I've Kept, A Concise Pictorial Autobiography*. New York: Doubleday and Company, Inc., 1969.
________. *Letters to Mamie*. Edited and with commentary by John S. D. Eisenhower. Garden City, NY: Doubleday, 1978.
________. *The Papers of Dwight D. Eisenhower*. Edited by Alfred D. Chandler. Vols. 1-21. Baltimore: Johns Hopkins University Press, 1970-2001.
Eisenhower, John S. D. *Strictly Personal: A Memoir*. New York: Doubleday and Company, Inc., 1974.
________. *General Ike: A Personal Reminiscence*. New York: Simon and Schuster, 2003.
Eisenhower, Milton S. *The President Is Calling*. New York: Doubleday and Company, Inc., 1974.
Ferrell, Robert H., ed. *Off the Record: The Private Papers of Harry S. Truman*. New York: Harper and Row, 1980.
________. *The Autobiography of Harry S. Truman*. Boulder, CO: Colorado Associated University Press, 1980.
________. *The Eisenhower Diaries*. New York: W.W. Norton and Company, 1981.
Griffith, Robert ed. *Ike's Letters to a Friend, 1941-1958*. Lawrence, KS: University of Kansas Press, 1984.
Groves, Leslie R. *Now It Can Be Told: The Story of the Manhattan Project*. New York: Harper & Row, Publishers, 1962.
Hagerty, James C. and Robert Ferrell, eds. *The Diary of James C. Hagerty: Eisenhower in Mid-Course, 1954-1955*. Bloomington: Indiana University Press, 1983.
Holt, Daniel and James Leyerzapf. *Eisenhower: The Prewar Diaries and Selected Papers, 1905-1941*. Baltimore: Johns Hopkins University Press, 1998.
Hughes, Emmet John. *The Ordeal of Power: A Political Memoir of the Eisenhower Years*. New York: Atheneum, 1963.
Jameson, Henry B. *My Friend Ike*. [Special Collections, Kansas State University]
Kahn, Herman. *On Thermonuclear War*. Princeton, NJ: Princeton University Press, 1960.
Keeney, L. Douglas. *The Doomsday Scenario: The Official Doomsday Scenario Written By The United States Government During the Cold War*. Foreword by Stephen I. Schwartz. St. Paul, MN: MBI Publishing Company, 2002.
Killian, James Rhyne. *Sputnik, Scientists, and Eisenhower: A Memoir of the First Special Assistant to the President for Science and Technology*. Cambridge, MA: MIT Press, 1977.
Kissinger, Henry. *Nuclear Weapons and Foreign Policy*. Foreword by Gordon Dean. New York: Harper and Brothers, 1957.

Kistiakowsky, George B. *A Scientist at the White House: The Private Diary of President Eisenhower's Special Assistant for Science and Technology.* Introduction by Charles S. Maier. Cambridge, MA: Harvard University Press, 1976.

Larson, Arthur. *Eisenhower: The President Nobody Know.* London: Leslie Frewin Publishers Limited, 1968.

McKeogh, Michael James and Richard Lockridge. *Sgt. Mickey and General Ike.* New York: G.P. Putnam's Sons, 1946.

Morrow, E. Frederic. *Black Man in the White House: A Diary of the Eisenhower Years By the Administrative Officer for Special Projects, the White House, 1955-1961.* New York: Coward–McCann, Inc., 1963.

Hobbs, Joseph Patrick, ed. *Dear General: Eisenhower's Wartime Letters to Marshall.* Baltimore: Johns Hopkins University Press, 1971.

Morgan, Kay Summersby. *Past Forgetting: My Love Affair with Dwight D. Eisenhower.* New York: Simon and Schuster, 1976.

Rostow, W.W. *Europe After Stalin: Eisenhower's Three Decisions of March 11, 1953.* Austin: University of Texas Press, 1982.

Slater, Ellis D. *The Ike I Knew.* Ellis D. Slater Trust, 1980.

Smith, Walter Bedell. *Eisenhower's Six Great Decisions: Europe, 1944-1945.* New York: Longmans, Greens, 1956.

Smyth, Henry DeWolf. *Atomic Energy for Military Purposes: The Official Report on the Development of the Atomic Bomb under the Auspices of the United States Government, 1940-1945.* Princeton: Princeton University Press, 1945.

Snyder, Marty. *My Friend Ike.* New York: F. Fell, 1956.

Stassen, Harold and Marshall Houts. *Eisenhower: Turning the World Toward Peace.* St. Paul, MN: Merrill/Magnus Publishing Corporation, 1990.

Strauss, Lewis L. *Men and Decisions.* Garden City, NJ: Doubleday, 1962.

Taylor, Allan. *What Eisenhower Thinks.* New York: Crowell, 1952.

Taylor, Maxwell. *The Uncertain Trumpet.* New York: Harper and Brothers, Publishers, 1959.

Thompson, Kenneth W., ed. *The Eisenhower Presidency: Eleven Intimate Perspectives of Dwight D. Eisenhower.* Lanham, MD: University Press of America, 1984.

Williams, Robert C. And Philip L. Cantelon, eds. *The American Atom: A Documentary History of Nuclear Policies from the Discovery of Fission to the Present, 1939-1984.* Philadelphia: University of Pennsylvania Press, 1984.

U.S. Department of State. *Foreign Relations of the United States, 1955-1957 Vol. 20 Regulation of Armaments; Atomic Energy.* Washington, D.C.: United States Government Printing Office, 1990.

U.S. President. *Public Papers of the Presidents of the United States* (Washington, D.C.: Office of the Federal Register, National Archives and Records Service, 1953-), Dwight D. Eisenhower.

SECONDARY SOURCES

Articles

Alperovitz, Gar, Robert L. Messer, and Barton J. Bernstein. "Marshall, Truman, and the Decision to Drop the Bomb" *International Security* 16, No. 3 (Winter 1991-92): 204-221.

Alperovitz, Gar and Kai Bird. "A Theory of Cold War Dynamics: U.S. Policy, Germany, and the Bomb" *The History Teacher* 29, No. 3 (May 1996): 281-300.

Ambrose, Stephen E. "Eisenhower and the Intelligence Community in World War II." *Journal of Contemporary History* 16, No. 1 (January 1981): 153-166.

Bacevich, A. J. "The Paradox of Professionalism: Eisenhower, Ridgway, and the Challenge to Civilian Control, 1953-1955." *Journal of Military History* 61, No. 2 (1997): 303-333.

Bailey, Martin J. "Deterrence, Assured Destruction, and Defense." *Orbis* Vol. 16, no. 3 (1972): 682-695.

Barnaby, Frank. "Armaments and Disarmament." *Bulletin of Atomic Scientists* 32, no. 6 (1976): 25-32

Baum, Keith W. "Two's Company, Three's A Crowd: The Eisenhower Administration, France, and Nuclear Weapons." *Presidential Studies Quarterly* 20, No. 2 (1990): 315-328.

Baylis, John. "Exchanging Nuclear Secrets: Laying the Foundation of the Anglo-American Nuclear Relationship" *Diplomatic History* 25, No. 1 (Winter 2001): 33-61.

Bender, Mark. "Watershed at Leavenworth: Dwight D. Eisenhower at the Command and General Staff School," Command and General Staff College, Combined Arms Research Library, 1990. Available from http://www.cgsc.army.mil/carl/ resources/csi/bender/bender.asp. Accessed May 14, 2008.

Bernstein, Barton J. "The Quest for Security: American Foreign Policy and International Control of Atomic Energy, 1942-1946" *The Journal of American History* 60, No. 4 (March 1974): 1003-1044.

________. "The Uneasy Alliance: Roosevelt, Churchill, and the Atomic Bomb, 1940-1945" *The Western Political Quarterly* 29, No. 2 (June 1976): 202-230.

________. "The Challenges and Dangers of Nuclear Weapons: Foreign Policy and Strategy, 1941-1978." *Maryland History* 9 (Spring 1978): 73-99.

________. "Ike and Hiroshima: Did He Oppose It?" *Journal of Strategic Studies* 10 (September 1987): 377-89.

________. "Crossing the Rubicon: A Missed Opportunity to Stop the H-Bomb?" *International Security* 14, No. 2 (Autumn 1989): 132-160.

________. "Eclipsed by Hiroshima and Nagasaki: Early Thinking About Tactical Nuclear Weapons" *International Security* 15, No 4 (Spring 1991): 149-173.

________. "Truman and the A-Bomb: Targeting Noncombatants, Using the Bomb, and His Defending the 'Decision'" *The Journal of Military History* 62, No. 3 (July 1998): 547-570.

Betts, Richard K. "A Nuclear Golden Age? The Balance before Parity." *International Security* 11, No. 3 (Winter 1986-1987): 3-32.

Bhatia, Shyam. "Beyond Proliferation: Political Fears and Scientific Hopes in the Nuclear Debate." *Round Table* [Great Britain] 268 (1977): 325-36.

Blanchard, William H. "National Myth, National Character, and National Policy: A Psychological Study of the U-2 Incident." *Journal of Conflict Resolution* 6, no. 2 (1962): 143-8.

Blechman, Barry M. and Robert Powell. "What in the Name of God Is Strategic Superiority?" *Political Science Quarterly* 97, No. 4 (Winter 1982-1983): 589-602.

Bose, Meena. "Winning Peace By Threatening Nuclear War: The Foreign Policy of Eisenhower and Dulles." *Presidential Studies Quarterly*, 29, No. 4 (1999): 946-948.

Brands Jr., H.W. "A Cold War Foreign Legion? The Eisenhower Administration and the Volunteer Freedom Corps." *Military Affairs* 52, No. 1 (January 1988): 7-11.

________. "The Age of Vulnerability: Eisenhower and the National Insecurity State." *The American Historical Review* 94, no. 4 (1989): 963-989.

________. "Testing Massive Retaliation: Credibility and Crisis Management in the Taiwan Strait." *International Security* 12, No. 4 (Spring 1988): 124-151.

Calingaert, Daniel. "Nuclear Weapons and the Korean War." *Journal of Strategic Studies* 11, No. 2 (1988): 177-202.

Chang, Gordon H. "To the Nuclear Brink: Eisenhower, Dulles, and the Quemoy-Matsu Crisis." *International Security* 12, No. 4 (Spring 1988): 96-123.

Chang, Gordon H. and He Di. "The Absence of War in the U.S.-China Confrontation over Quemoy and Matsu in 1954-1955: Contingency, Luck, Deterrence?" *The American Historical Review* 98, No. 5 (December 1993): 1500-1524.

Collins, Edward M. "Clausewitz and Democracy's Modern Wars" *Military Affairs* 19, No. 1 (Spring 1955): 15-20.

Cook, Blanche Wiesen. "First Comes the Lie: C.D. Jackson and Political Warfare." *Radical History Review* 31 (1984): 42-70.

Cottrell, Alvin J. "The Eisenhower Era in Asia." *Current History* 57:336 (1969): 84-87, 117-118.

Crossman, R. H. S. "The Man in the Vicuna Coat." *New Statesman* [Great Britain] 63 (January 1962): 92-3.

Damms, Richard V. "James Killian, the Technological Capabilities Panel, and the Emergence of President Eisenhower's 'Scientific-Technological Elite.'" *Diplomatic History* 24, No. 1 (Winter 2000): 57-78.

Deighton, Anne. "Constructing a Cold War Peace." *Diplomatic History* 25, No. 1 (2001): 141-146.

De Santis, Vincent P. "Eisenhower Revisionism" *The Review of Politics* 38, No. 2 (April 1976): 190-207.

Dingman, Roger. "Atomic Diplomacy during the Korean War." *International Security* 13, No. 3 (Winter 1988-1989): 50-91.

Dishman, Robert B. "How It All Began: The Eisenhower Pre-Convention Campaign in New Hampshire, 1952." *The New England Quarterly* 26, No. 1 (March 1953): 3-26.

Divine, Robert A. "Eisenhower, Dulles, and the Nuclear Test Ban Issue: Memorandum of a White House Conference, 24 March 1958." *Diplomatic History* 2, No. 3 (1978): 321-330.

Duncan, Francis. "Atomic Energy and Anglo-American Relations, 1946-54." *Orbis* 12 (Winter 1969): 1188-1203.

Dunning, Gordon M. "Effects of Nuclear Weapons Testing" *The Scientific Monthly* 81, No. 6 (December 1955): 265-270.

Erskine, Hazel Gaudet. "The Polls: Atomic Weapons and Nuclear Energy." *Public Opinion Quarterly* 27, no. 2 (1963): 155-90.

Falk, Stanley L. "The National Security Council under Truman, Eisenhower, and Kennedy." *Political Science Quarterly* 79, No. 3 (September 1964): 403-434.

Fallows, James. "The Military-Industrial Complex." *Foreign Policy* No. 133 (November – December 2002): 46-48.

Foot, Rosemary. "Nuclear Coercion and the Ending of the Korean Conflict." *International Security* 13, No. 3 (Winter 1988-1989): 92-112.

________. "The Eisenhower Administration's Fear of Empowering the Chinese." *Political Science Quarterly* 111, No. 3 (Autumn 1996): 505-521.

Fraser, Cary. "Crossing the Color Line in Little Rock: The Eisenhower Administration and the Dilemma of Race for U.S. Foreign Policy" *Diplomatic History* 24, No. 2 (Spring 2000): 233-264.

Freedman, Lawrence. "The First Two Generations of Nuclear Strategists." In *Makers of Modern Strategy*, ed Peter Paret, 735-778, Princeton: Princeton University Press, 1986.

Friedberg, Aaron L. "Why Didn't the United States become a Garrison State?" *International Security* 16, No. 4 (Spring 1992): 109-142.

Friedman, Edward. "Nuclear Blackmail and the End of the Korean War" *Modern China* 1, No. 1 (January 1975): 75-91.

Golden, William T. "President's Science Advisory Committee Revisited." *Science, Technology, and Human Values* 1, No. 2 (Spring 1986): 5-19.

Graham, Thomas W. "The Pattern and Importance of Public Knowledge in the Nuclear Age." *The Journal of Conflict Resolution* 32, No. 2 (June 1988): 319-334.

Gray, Colin S. "'Gap' Prediction and America's Defense: Arms Race Behavior in the Eisenhower Years." *Orbis* 16 (Spring 1972): 257-74.

Greene, Benjamin P. "Eisenhower, Science and the Nuclear Test Ban Debate, 1953-56." *The Journal of Strategic Studies* 26, No. 4 (December 2003): 156-185.

Greenstein, Fred I. "Eisenhower as an Activist President: A Look at New Evidence." *Political Science Quarterly*, 94, No. 4 (Winter 1979-1980): 575-599.

Greenstein, Fred I. and Richard H. Immerman. "What Did Eisenhower Tell Kennedy about Indochina? The Politics of Misperception." *The Journal of American History* 79, No. 2 (September 1992): 568-587.

________. "Effective National Security Advising: Recovering the Eisenhower Legacy." *Political Science Quarterly* 115, no. 3 (2000): 335-345.

Griffith, Robert. "Why They Like Ike." *Reviews in American History* 7, No. 4 (December 1979): 577-583.

________. "Dwight D. Eisenhower and the Corporate Commonwealth" *American Historical Review*, 87, No. 1 (Feb., 1982) , pp. 87-122.

Haight, David. "The Papers of C.D. Jackson: A Glimpse at President Eisenhower's Psychological Warfare Expert." *Manuscripts* 28, no. 1 (1976): 27-37.

Halperin, Morton. "The President and the Military." Foreign Affairs 52, no. 2 (1972): 310-324.

Hart, John. "Eisenhower and the Swelling of the Presidency." *Polity* 24, No. 4 (Summer 1992): 673-691.

Herring, George and Richard H. Immerman. "Eisenhower, Dulles, and Dienbienphu: 'The Day We Didn't Go To War' Revisited.' *The Journal of American History* 71, No. 2 (September 1984): 343-363.

Hoag, Malcolm W. "What New Look In Defense?" *World Politics* 22, Issue 1 (October 1969): 1-28.

Holl, Jack. "Eisenhower's Peaceful Atomic Diplomacy: Atoms for Peace and the Western Alliance." *Materials and Society* 7, Nos. 3/4 (1983): 365-378.

Holmans, A. E. "The Eisenhower Administration and the Recession, 1953-55." *Oxford Economic Papers*, New Series, 10, No. 1 (February 1958): 34-54.

Holsti, Ole R. "The Domestic and Foreign Policy Beliefs of American Leaders." *The Journal of Conflict Resolution* 32, No. 2 (June 1988): 248-294.

Howard, Michael E. "On Fighting a Nuclear War" *International Security* 5, No. 4 (Spring 1981): 3-17.

Huston, James A. "The Eisenhower Era" *Current History* 57:335 (July 1969): 24-30, 53.

Hyman, Herbert H. and Paul B. Sheatsley. "The Political Appeal of President Eisenhower." *Public Opinion Quarterly* 17, No. 4 (Winter 1953-1954): 443-460.

Ilké, Fred. C. "The Nether World of Nuclear Megatonnage." *Bulletin of Atomic Scientists* 31, no. 1 (1975): 20-25.

Immerman, Richard H. "Confessions of an Eisenhower Revisionist: An Agonizing Reappraisal" *Diplomatic History* 14, No. 3 (1990): 319-342.

Johnston, Andrew M. "Mr. Slessor Goes to Washington: The Influence of the British Global Strategy Paper on the Eisenhower New Look." *Diplomatic History* 22, No. 3 (Summer 1998): 361-398.

Keegan, John. "Eisenhower and the American Dream." The Dwight D. Eisenhower Lectures in War and Peace: A Biennial Series. No. 2. Manhattan, KS, 1988.

King, Jr., James E. "Nuclear Plenty and Limited Wars" *Foreign Affairs* 35, No. 2 (January 1957): 238-256.

Kinnard, Douglas. "President Eisenhower and the Defense Budget." *The Journal of Politics* 39, No. 3 (August 1977): 596-623.

Kissinger, Henry A. "Strategy and Organization" *Foreign Affairs* 35, No. 3 (April 1957): 379-394.

Kohut, Thomas A. "Psychohistory as History." *The American Historical Review* 91, No. 2 (April 1986): 336-354.

Larson, Deborah Welch. "The Psychology of Nuclear Statecraft." *Diplomatic History* 15, No. 3 (1991): 449-454.

Lehman, Kenneth. "Revolutions and Attributions: Making Sense of Eisenhower Administration Policies in Bolivia and Guatemala." *Diplomatic History* 21, No. 2 (Spring 1997): 185-213.

Lewy, Guenter. "Superior Orders, Nuclear Warfare, and the Dictates of Conscience: the Dilemma of Military Obedience in the Atomic Age." *The American Political Science Review* 55, No. 1 (March 1961): 3-23.

Libby, W. F. "*Radioactive Fallout*" Proceedings of the National Academy of Sciences of the United States of America 44, No. 8 (August 15, 1958): 800-820.

MacIsaac, David. "Eisenhower: A Reputation in Transition." *Air University Review* (September-October 1982): Online

McAuliffe, Mary S. "Eisenhower, the President." *The Journal of American History* 68, No. 3 (December 1981): 625-632.

McDougall, Walter A. "The Cold War Excursion of Science" *Diplomatic History* 24, No. 1 (Winter 2000): 117-127.

Maddock, Shane. "The Fourth Country Problem: Eisenhower's Nuclear Nonproliferation Policy." *Presidential Studies Quarterly* 28, No. 3 (1998): 553-572.

May, Ann Mari. "President Eisenhower, Economic Policy, and the 1960 Presidential Election." *The Journal of Economic History* 50, No. 2 (1990): 417-427.

Makhijani, Arjun. "Nuclear Targeting: The First 60 Years." *Bulletin of Atomic Scientists* 59, No 3 (May/June 2003): 60-65.

Marchio, James D. "Risking General War in Pursuit of Limited Objectives: U.S. Military Contingency Planning for Poland in the Wake of the 1956 Hungarian Uprising." *The Journal of Military History* 66, No. 3 (July 2002): 783-812.

McMahon, Robert J. "Eisenhower and Third World Nationalism: A Critique of the Revisionists" *Political Science Quarterly* 101, No. 3 (1986): 453-473.

Medhurst, Martin J. "Eisenhower's 'Atoms for Peace' Speech: A Case Study in the Strategic Use of Language." *Communication Monographs* 54, no. 2 (1987): 204-220.

________. "Eisenhower and the Crusade for Freedom: The Rhetorical Origins of a Cold War Campaign." *Presidential Studies Quarterly* 27, no. 4 (1997): 646-661.

________. "Atoms for Peace and Nuclear Hegemony: The Rhetorical Structure of a Cold War Campaign." *Armed Forces and Society* 23, No. 4 (1997): 571-593.

Metz, Steven. "Eisenhower and the Planning of American Grand Strategy." *Journal of Strategic Studies* 14, No. 1 (1991): 49-71.

Moskos Jr., Charles C. "The Concept of the Military-Industrial Complex: Radical Critique or Liberal Bogey?" *Social Problems* 21, No. 4 (April 1974): 498-512.

Mrozek, Donald J. "A New Look at 'Balanced Forces': Defense Continuities From Truman to Eisenhower" *Military Affairs* 38, No. 4 (December 1974): 145-151.

Oakes, Guy. "The Cold War Conception of Nuclear Reality: Mobilizing the American Imagination for Nuclear War in the 1950s." *International Journal of Politics, Culture, and Society* 6, no. 4 (1992): 339-363.

Osgood, Kenneth A. "Form before Substance: Eisenhower's Commitment to Psychological Warfare and Negotiations with the Enemy." *Diplomatic History* 24, no. 3 (2000): 405-433.

Quester, George H. "Was Eisenhower a Genius?" *International Security* 4, No. 2 (Autumn 1979): 159-179.

Pharo, Per F. I. "Revising Eisenhower Revisionism." *The Society for the History of American Foreign Relations Newsletter* 30, no 4. (1999): 18-22.

Pickett, William B. "The Eisenhower Solarium Notes." *Society for Historians of American Foreign Relations Newsletter* 16, No. 2 (1985): 1-10.

Plischke, Elmer. "Eisenhower's 'Correspondence Diplomacy' with Kremlin–Case Study in Summit Diplomatics." *The Journal of Politics* Vol. 30, No. 1 (February 1968): 137-159.

Pogue, Forrest C. "Why Eisenhower's Forces Stopped at the Elbe" *World Politics* 4, No. 3 (April 1952): 356-368.

Quester, George H. "Was Eisenhower A Genius." *International Security* 4, No. 2 (Autumn 1979): 159-179.

Rabe, Stephen G. "Eisenhower Revisionism: A Decade of Scholarship" *Diplomatic History* 17 (Winter 1995): 97-115.

Reardon, Steven L. "Reassessing the Gaither Report's Role." *Diplomatic History* 25, no. 1 (2001): 153-157.

Roman, Peter J. "Eisenhower and Ballistic Missiles Arms Control, 1957-1960: A Missed Opportunity?" *Journal of Strategic Studies* 19, No. 3 (1996): 365-380.

Rosenberg, David Alan. "American Atomic Strategy and the Hydrogen Bomb." *The Journal of American History* 66, No. 1 (June 1979): 72-87.

________. "'A Smoking Radiating Ruin at the End of Two Hours:' Documents on American Plans for Nuclear War with the Soviet Union, 1954-1955" *International Security* 6, No. 3 (Winter 1981-82): 3-38.

________. "The Origins of Overkill: Nuclear Weapons and American Strategy, 1945-1960." *International Security* 7, No. 4 (Spring 1983): 3-71.

Rosi, Eugene. "Mass and Attentive Opinion on Nuclear Weapons Tests and Fallout, 1954-1963." *Public Opinion Quarterly* 29 (Summer 1965): 280-297.

Rushkoff, Bennett C. "Eisenhower, Dulles and the Quemoy-Matsu Crisis, 1954-1955." *Political Science Quarterly* 96, No. 3 (Autumn 1981): 465-480.

Salaff, Stephen. "The Lucky Dragon." *Bulletin of Atomic Scientists* 34, no. 5 (1978): 21-3.

Saunders, Richard M. "Military Force in the Foreign Policy of the Eisenhower Presidency." *Political Science Quarterly* 100, No. 1 (Spring 1985): 97-116.

Schlesinger Jr., Arthur M. "The Ike Age Revisited" *Reviews in American History* 11, No. 1 (March 1983): 1-11.

________. "Rating the Presidents: Washington to Clinton" *Political Science Quarterly* 112, No. 2 (Summer 1997): 179-190.

Sherwin, Martin J. "The Atomic Bomb and the Origins of the Cold War: U.S. Atomic-Energy Policy and diplomacy, 1941-1945." *The American Historical Review* 78, No. 4 (October 1973): 945-968.

________. "Hiroshima as Politics and History." *The Journal of American History* 82, No. 3 (December 1995): 1085-1093.

Siracusa, Joseph M. "Nuclear Diplomacy, the Arms Race and Arms Control: From Truman to Reagan. *Australian Journal of Politics and History* 29, No. 2 (1983): 308-317.

Smith-Norris, Martha. "The Eisenhower Administration and the Nuclear Test Ban Talks, 1958-1960: Another Challenge to 'Revisionism'" *Diplomatic History* 27, No. 4 (September 2003): 503-541.

Smyth, Henry DeWolf. "Nuclear Power and Foreign Policy" *Foreign Affairs* 35, No. 1 (October 1956): 1-16.

Soapes, Thomas F. "A Cold Warrior Seeks Peace: Eisenhower's Strategy for Nuclear Disarmament." *Diplomatic History* 4 (Winter 1980): 57-71.

Suri, Jeremi. "America's Search for a Technological Solution to the Arms Race: The Surprise Attack Conference of 1958 and a Challenge for 'Eisenhower Revisionists.'" *Diplomatic History* 21, No. 3 (1997): 417-451.

Tal, David. "Eisenhower's Disarmament Dilemma: From Chance For Peace to Open Skies Proposal." *Diplomacy and Statecraft* 12, No. 2 (2001): 175-196.

Trachtenberg, Marc. "Strategic Thought in America, 1952-1966. *Political Science Quarterly*, 104, No. 2 (Summer 1989): 301-334.

________. "A 'Wasting Asset': American Strategy and the Shifting Nuclear Balance, 1949-1954." *International Security* 13, No. 3 (Winter 1988-1989): 5-49.

Vandercook, Wm. F. "Making the Very Best of the Very Worst: The 'Human Effects of Nuclear Weapons' Report of 1956." *International Security* 11, No. 1 (1986): 184-195.

Walker, J. Samuel. "Nuclear Power and Nonproliferation: The Controversy over Nuclear Exports, 1974-1980." *Diplomatic History* 25, No. 2 (Spring 2001): 215-249.

Watz, Kenneth N. "Nuclear Myths and Political Realities." *American Political Science Review* 84, No. 3 (1990): 731-745.

Wells, Jr., Samuel F. "The Origins of Massive Retaliation." *Political Science Quarterly* 96, No. 1 (Spring 1981): 31-52.

Books

Aldous, Richard. *MacMillan, Eisenhower and the Cold War.* Four Courts Press, 2005.

Alexander, Charles C. *Holding the Line: The Eisenhower Era, 1952-1961.* Bloomington, IN: Indiana University Press, 1975.

Aliano, Richard A. *American Defense Policy from Eisenhower to Kennedy: The Politics of Changing Military Requirements, 1957-1961.* Athens, OH: Ohio University Press, 1975.

Allen, Craig. *Eisenhower and the Mass Media: Peace, Prosperity, and Prime-time TV.* Chapel Hill: University of North Carolina Press, 1993.

Alperovitz, Gar. *Atomic Diplomacy: Hiroshima and Potsdam*, revised edition, New York: Penguin, 1985.

Ambrose, Stephen E. *The Supreme Commander: The War Years of General Dwight D. Eisenhower.* Garden City, NY: Doubleday, 1970.

_________. *Ike's Spies: Eisenhower and the Espionage Establishment.* Garden City, NY: Doubleday, 1981.

_________. *Eisenhower: Soldier and President.* New York: Simon and Schuster, 1990.

Anderson, David L. *Trapped by Success: The Eisenhower Administration and Vietnam, 1953-1961.* New York: Columbia University Press, 1991.

Arnold, James R. *The First Domino: Eisenhower, the Military, and America's Intervention in Vietnam.* New York: William Morrow and Company, Inc., 1991.

Ball, Howard. *Justice Downwind: America's Atomic Testing Program in the 1950's.* New York: Oxford University Press, 1986.

Barber, James David. *The Presidential Character: Predicting Performance in the White House*, 4th ed. Upper Saddle River, NJ: Prentice Hall, 1992.

Bell, Daniel, ed. *The Radical Right: The New American Right, Expanded and Updated.* Garden City, New York: Doubleday and Company, Inc., 1963.

Beschloss, Michael. *MAYDAY: Eisenhower, Khrushchev, and the U-2 Affair.* New York: Harper & Row, 1986.

Billings-Yun, Melanie. *Decision Against War. Eisenhower and Dien Bien Phu 1954.* New York: Columbia University Press, 1988.

Bischof, Günter and Stephen E. Ambrose. *Eisenhower: A Centenary Assessment.* Baton Rouge, LA: Louisiana State University Press, 1995.

Bobbitt, Philip, Lawrence Freedman, and Gregory F. Treverton. *U.S. Nuclear Strategy: A Reader.* Washington Square, New York: New York University Press, 1989.

Bohanan, Robert D. *Dwight D. Eisenhower: A Selected Bibliography of Periodical and Dissertation Literature.* Washington: National Archives and Records Services, General Services Administration, 1981.

Bowie, Robert R. And Richard Immerman. *Waging Peace: How Eisenhower Shaped an Enduring Cold War Strategy.* New York: Oxford University Press, 1998.

Boyer, Paul. *By the Bomb's Early Light: American Thought and Culture at the Dawn of the Atomic Age.* With a New Preface by the author. Chapel Hill: University of North Carolina Press, 1985, 1994.

Boyle, Peter. *Eisenhower.* New York: Pearson Longman, 2005.

Boyle, Peter, ed. *The Churchill-Eisenhower Correspondence, 1953-1955.* Chapel Hill, NC: University of North Carolina Press, 1990.

________. *The Eden-Eisenhower Correspondence, 1955-1957.* Chapel Hill: University of North Carolina Press, 2005.

Brands, H.W. *Cold Warriors: Eisenhower's Generation and American Foreign Policy.* New York: Columbia University Press, 1988.

Brendon, Piers. *Ike: His Life and Times.* New York: Harper & Row, 1986.

Bundy, McGeorge. *Danger and Survival: Choices about the Bomb in the First Fifty Years.* New York: Random House, 1988.

Burk, Robert. *Dwight D. Eisenhower: Hero and Politician.* Boston: Twayne Publishers, 1986.

Burke, John P. *How Presidents Test Reality: Decision on Vietnam, 1954 and 1965.* New York: Russell Sage Foundation, 1989.

Chernus, Ira. *Eisenhower's Atoms for Peace.* College Station: Texas A & M University Press, 2002.

________. *General Eisenhower, Ideology and Discourse.* East Lansing: Michigan State University Press, 2002.

Childs, Marquis. *Eisenhower, Captive Hero: A Critical Study of the General and the President.* New York: Harcourt, Brace and Company, 1958.

Clarfield, Gerard H. *Security with Solvency: Dwight D. Eisenhower and the Shaping of the American Military Establishment.* Westport, CN: Praeger, 1999.

Clausewitz, Carl Von. *On War.* Indexed Edition. Edited and Translated by Michael Howard and Peter Paret. With Introductory Essays by Peter Paret, Michael Howard, and Bernard Brodie. With a Commentary by Bernard Brodie. Princeton, NJ: Princeton University Press, 1984.

Cook, Blanche Wiesen. *Dwight D. Eisenhower: Antimilitarist in White House.* St. Charles, MO: Forum Press, 1974.

________. *The Declassified Eisenhower: A Divided Legacy.* Garden City, NY: Doubleday, 1981.

Craig, Campbell. *Destroying the Village: Eisenhower and the Thermonuclear War.* New York: Columbia University Press, 1998.

D'Este, Carlo. *Eisenhower: A Soldier's Life.* New York: Henry Holt & Company, 2002.

Dallek, Robert. *Hail to the Chief: The Making and Unmaking of Presidents.* New York: Hyperion, 1996.

Damms, Richard. *The Eisenhower Presidency, 1953-1961.* Seminar Studies in History Series. London: Pearson Education Limited, 2002.

Dary, David. *Dwight David Eisenhower's Two Letters in Abilene that Changed the Course of the World.* Lawrence, KS: Sunflower Press, 1972.

Davis, Kenneth S. *Soldier of Democracy: A Biography of Dwight Eisenhower.* Garden City, NY: Doubleday and Company, Inc., 1945.

Divine, Robert A. *Blowing on the Wind: The Nuclear Test Ban Debate, 1954-1960.* New York: Oxford University Press, 1978.

________. *Eisenhower and the Cold War.* New York: Oxford University Press, 1981.

Donovan, Robert J. *Eisenhower: The Inside Story.* New York: Harper and Brothers, Publishers, 1956.

________. *Confidential Secretary: Ann Whitman's Twenty Years with Eisenhower and Rockefeller.* New York: Dutton, 1988.

Eisenhower, David. *Eisenhower at War, 1943-1945.* New York: Random House, 1986.

Ewald, William Bragg. *Eisenhower the President: The Crucial Days, 1951-1960.* Englewood Cliggs, NJ: Prentice Hall, 1981.

Freedman, Lawrence. *The Evolution of Nuclear Strategy.* 2nd ed. London: MacMillan, 1989.

Fuller, John G. *The Day We Bombed Utah: America's Most Lethal Secret.* New York: New American Library, 1984.

Gaddis, John Lewis, Philip H. Gordon, Ernest R. May, and Jonathan Rosenberg, eds. *Cold War Statesmen Confront the Bomb: Nuclear Diplomacy Since 1945.* Oxford: Oxford University Press, 1999.

Gallagher, Thomas. *Assault in Norway: Sabotaging the Nazi Nuclear Bomb.* First Lyons Press Printing. Guilford, CN: The Lyons Press, 2002.

Geelhoed, E. Bruce and Anthony O. Edwards. *Eisenhower, MacMillan, and Allied Unity, 1957-1961.* New York: Palgrave MacMillan, 2003.

________. *The Macmillan-Eisenhower Correspondence, 1957-1969.* New York: Palgrave MacMillan, 2003.

Graham, Billy. *Just As I Am: The Autobiography of Billy Graham.* New York: HarperCollins, 1997.

Greenstein, Fred. *The Hidden-Hand Presidency: Eisenhower as Leader.* Baltimore: Johns Hopkins University Press, 1982.

Gunther, John. *Eisenhower: The Man and the Symbol.* New York: Harper and Brothers, Publishers, 1952.

Halberstam, David. *The Fifties.* New York: Villard Books, 1993.

Hatch, Alden. *General Ike: A Biography of Dwight D. Eisenhower.* New York: Holt, 1952.

Hewlett, Richard G. and Francis Duncan. *Atomic Shield, 1947-1952, Vol. II of A History of the U.S. Atomic Energy Commission.* University Park: Pennsylvania State University Press, 1969).

Hewlett, Richard G. and Jack M. Holl. *Atoms for Peace and War, 1953-1961: Eisenhower and the Atomic Energy Commission.* With a Foreword by Richard S. Kirkendall and an Essay on Sources by Roger M. Anders. Berkeley: University of California Press, 1989.

Holbo, Paul S. and Robert W. Sellen. *The Eisenhower Era: The Age of Consensus.* Hinsdale, IL: The Dryden Press, 1974.

Holl, Jack M. *Argonne National Laboratory, 1946-96*. With the assistance of Richard G. Hewlett and Ruth R. Harris. Foreword by Alan Schriesheim. Urbana: University of Illinois Press, 1997.
Holland, Matthew. F. *Eisenhower Between The Wars: The Making of a General and Statesman*. Westport, CN: Praeger, 2001.
Jameson, Henry B. *My Friend Ike*. Kansas State University Special Collections. 1986.
Jian, Chen. *Mao's China and the Cold War*. Chapel Hill, N.C.: University of North Carolina Press, 2001.
Jones, Vincent. *United States Army in World War II: Manhattan, the Army and the Atomic Bomb*. Washington, D.C.: Center of Military History, 1985.
Keegan, John. *Eisenhower and the American Dream*. Manhattan, KS: Department of History, Kansas State University, 1988.
Kerr, Thomas J. *Civil Defense in the U.S.: Bandaid for a Holocaust?* Boulder, CO: Westview Press, 1983.
Kinnard, Douglas. *President Eisenhower and Strategy Management: A Study in Defense Politics*. Lexington: University Press of Kentucky, 1977.
Kluckhohn, Frank L. and Donald Ackerman. *The Real Eisenhower*. New York: Columbia Heights Press, 1969.
Krebs, Ronald R. *Dueling Visions: U.S. Strategy toward Eastern Europe Under Eisenhower*. College Station, TX: Texas A & M University Press, 2001.
LaFeber, Walter. *America, Russia, and the Cold War, 1945-2006*, 10th ed. Boston: McGraw Hill, 2007.
Larson, Arthur. *Eisenhower: The President Nobody Knew*. New York: Popular Library, 1968.
Lasby, Clarence. *Eisenhower's Heart Attack: How Ike Beat Heart Disease and Held on to the Presidency*. Lawrence: University of Kansas Press, 1997.
Lee, R. Alton. *Dwight D. Eisenhower: Soldier and Statesman*. Chicago: Nelson-Hall, 1981.
Leffler, Melvyn P. *A Preponderance of Power: National Security, the Truman Administration, and the Cold War*. Stanford, CA: Stanford University Press, 1992.
Lester, David. *Ike and Mamie: The Story of the General and his Lady*. New York: Putnam, 1981.
Leuchentenburg, William E. *In the Shadow of FDR: From Harry Truman to George W. Bush*. 3rd ed. Revised and Updated. Ithaca, NY: Cornell University Press, 2001.
Levine, Michael L. and Eleanora W. Schoeneaum, eds. *The Eisenhower Years*. New York: Facts on File, Inc., 1977.
Lovelace, Delos Wheeler. *General "Ike" Eisenhower*. New York: Thomas Y. Crowell Company, 1944.
Lyon, Peter. *Eisenhower: Portrait of a Hero*. Boston: Little, Brown and Company, 1974.
McCann, Kevin. *Man from Abilene*. Garden City, NY: Doubleday, 1952.
McEnaney, Laura. *Civil Defense Begins at Home: Militarization Meets Everyday Life in the Fifties*. Princeton, NJ: Princeton University Press, 2000.
McKeever, Porter. *Adlai Stevenson: His Life and Legacy*. New York: Quill, 1989.
Mayer, Michael S., ed. *The Eisenhower Presidency and the 1950s*. Boston: Houghton Mifflin, 1998.

Medhurst, Martin. *Dwight D. Eisenhower: Strategic Communicator.* With a foreword by Bernard K. Duffy. Westport, CN: Greenwood Press, 1993.

Melanson, Richard A. and David Mayers. *Reevaluating Eisenhower: American Foreign Policy in the 1950s.* Urbana: University of Illinois Press, 1987.

Miller, Francis Trevelyan. *Eisenhower: Man and Soldier.* Philadelphia: The John C. Winston Company, 1944.

Miller, Merle. *Ike the Soldier: As They Knew Him.* New York: G.P. Putnam and Sons, 1987.

Miller, Richard L. *Under the Cloud: The Decades of Nuclear Testing.* New York: The Free Press, 1986.

Morin, Relman. *Dwight D. Eisenhower: A Gauge of Greatness.* New York: Simon and Schuster, 1969.

Neal, Steve. *Harry and Ike: The Partnership that Remade the Postwar World.* New York: Scriber, 2001.

Nevins, Arthur S. *Gettysburg's Five Star Farmer.* New York: Carlton Press, 1977.

Nicolay, Helen. *Born to Command: The Story of General Eisenhower.* New York: Appleton-Century Company, Incorporated, 1945.

Offner, Arnold A. *Another Such Victory: President Truman and the Cold War, 1945-1953.* Stanford, CA: Stanford University Press, 2002.

Osgood, Kenneth A. *Eisenhower's Secret Propaganda Battle at Home and Abroad.* Lawrence: University of Kansas Press, 2006.

Pach, Chester J. and Elmo Richardson. *The Presidency of Dwight D. Eisenhower.* Revised Edition. Lawrence: University of Kansas Press, 1991.

Palmer, Norman and William V. Levy. *Five Star Golf.* New York: Duell, Sloan, and Pearce, 1964.

Parmet, Herbert. *Eisenhower and the American Crusades.* New York: MacMillan, 1972.

Parry-Giles, Shawn J. *The Rhetorical Presidency, Propaganda, and the Cold War, 1945-1955.* Westport, CN: Praeger, 2002.

Peeters, Paul. *Massive Retaliation: The Policy and Its Critics.* Chicago, IL: Henry Regnery Company, 1959.

Perret, Geoffrey. *Eisenhower.* Holbrook, MA: Adams Media Corporation, 1999.

Pickett, William B. *Eisenhower Decides to Run: Presidential Politics and Cold War Strategy.* Chicago: Ivan R. Dee, 2000.

Pierard, Richard V. and Robert D. Linder. *Civil Religion and the Presidency.* Grand Rapids, Michigan: Academie Books, 1988.

Pinkley, Virgil with James F. Scheer. *Eisenhower Declassified.* Old Tappan, NJ: Fleming H. Revell Company, 1979.

Pruden, Caroline. *Conditional Partners: Eisenhower, the United Nations, and the Search for a Permanent Peace.* Baton Rouge: Louisiana State University Press, 1998.

Pusey, Merlo John. *Eisenhower, the President.* New York: The MacMillan Company, 1956.

Rabe, Stephen G. *Eisenhower and Latin America: The Foreign Policy of Anticommunism.* Chapel Hill: The University of Carolina Press, 1988.

Reichard, Gary W. *The Reaffirmation of Republicanism: Eisenhower and the Eighty-third Congress.* Knoxville: University of Tennessee Press, 1975.

Relman, Morin. *Dwight D. Eisenhower: A Gauge of Greatness.* Associated Press, 1969.

Rhodes, Richard. *The Making of the Atomic Bomb*. New York: Touchstone, 1986.
Roman, Peter J. *Eisenhower and the Missile Gap*. Ithaca, NY: Cornell University Press, 1995.
Rossiter, Clinton. *The American Presidency*. New York: Harcourt Brace, 1956.
Rostow, W. W. *Open Skies: Eisenhower's Proposal of July 21, 1955*. Austin, TX: University of Texas Press, 1982.
Rovere, Richard H. *Affairs of State: The Eisenhower Years*. New York: Farrar, Straus and Cudahy, 1956.
Rubenzer, Steven J. and Thomas R. Faschingbauer. *Personality, Character, and Leadership: Psychologists Assess the Presidents*. Washington, D.C.: Brassey's Inc, 2005.
Rusoli, Edward and Candace Rusoli. *Dwight D. Eisenhower: General, President, and Cook*. Allentown, PA: Benedettini Books, 1990.
Schwartz, Stephen et. al. *Atomic Audit: The Cost and Consequences of Nuclear Weapons Since 1945*. Washington: Brookings Institution, 1998.
Sloan, John W. *Eisenhower and the Management of Prosperity*. Lawrence, KS: University of Kansas Press, 1991.
Smith, A. Merriman. *Meet Mister Eisenhower*. New York: Harper, 1955.
________. *A President's Odyssey*. New York: Harper, 1961.
Snead, David L. *The Gaither Committee, Eisenhower and the Cold War*. Columbus: Ohio State University Press, 1999.
Stapleton, Margaret L. *The Truman and Eisenhower Years, 1945-1960*. Metuchen, NJ: The Scarecrow Press, Inc., 1973.
Statler, Kathryn C. and Andrew L. Johns, eds. *The Eisenhower Administration, the Third World, and the Globalization of the Cold War*. Rowman & Littlefield Publishers, Inc.,2006.
Steiner, Barry. *Bernard Brodie and the Foundations of American Nuclear Strategy*. Lawrence: University of Kansas Press, 1991.
Tananbaum, Duane. *The Bricker Amendment Controversy: A Test of Eisenhower's Political Leadership*. Ithaca, NY: Cornell University Press,1988.
Taubman, Philip. *Secret Empire: Eisenhower, the CIA, and the Hidden Story of America's Space Espionage*. New York: Simon and Schuster, 2003.
Thompson, Kenneth W., ed. *The Eisenhower Presidency: Eleven Intimate Perspectives of Dwight D. Eisenhower*. Portraits of American Presidents Series, Vol III. Boston: University Press of America, 1984.
Titus, A. Constandina. *Bombs in the Backyard: Atomic Testing and American Politics*. Reno: University of Nevada Press, 1986.
Tudda, Chris. *Truth Is Our Weapon: The Rhetorical Diplomacy of Dwight D. Eisenhower and John Foster Dulles*. Baton Rouge, LA: Louisiana State University Press, 2006.
Twigge, Stephen and Len Scott. *Planning Armageddon: Britain, the United States, and the Command of Western Nuclear Forces, 1945-1964*. Amsterdam: Harwood Academic Publishers, 2000.
Vexler, Robert I. *Dwight D. Eisenhower, 1890-1969: Chronology-Documents-Bibliographical Aids*. Dobbs Ferry, New York: Oceana Publications, Inc., 1970.
Wagner, Steven. *Eisenhower Republicanism: Pursuing the Middle Way*. Illinois: Northern Illinois Press, 2006.

Warshaw, Shirley Anne. *Reexamining the Eisenhower Presidency.* Foreword by Louis Galambos. Westport, CN: Greenwood Press, 1993.
Weart, Spencer R. *Nuclear Fear: A History of Images.* Cambridge, MA: Harvard University Press, 1988.
Williamson, Daniel C. *Separate Agendas: Churchill, Eisenhower, and Anglo-American Relations, 1953-1955.* Rowman & Littlefield Publishers, Inc., 2006.
Wilson, Robert A., ed. *Character Above All: Ten Presidents from FDR to George Bush.* New York: Simon and Schuster, 1995.
Wohlstetter, Albert, et. al. *Swords from Plowshares: The Military Potential of Civilian Nuclear Energy.* With a Foreword by Fred Charles Iklé. Chicago: University of Chicago Press, 1979.
Wykes, Alan. *The Biography of General Dwight D. Eisenhower.* New York: Bison Books, 1982.
York, Herbert. *Making Weapons, Talking Peace: A Physicist's Odyssey from Hiroshima to Geneva.* New York: Basic Books, Inc., Publishers, 1987.

Theses and Dissertations

Damms, Richard Vernon. "Scientists and Statesmen: President Eisenhower's Science Advisers and National Security Policy, 1953-1961." Ph.D. diss., The Ohio State University, 1993.
Davis, Zachary Shands. "Eisenhower's Worldview and Nuclear Strategy." Ph.D. diss., University of Virginia, 1989.
Duchin, Brian Roger. "The New Look: President Eisenhower and the Political Economy of National Security." Ph.D. diss., University of Texas at Austin, 1987.
Jackson, Michael Gordon. "Thinking About Armageddon: Eisenhower and the Use of Atomic Weapons, 1945-1969." Ph.D. diss., Brandeis University, 1991.
Pickering, Newman Bruce. "Passage through Armageddon: Nuclear Weapons and American Foreign Policy, 1948-1954." Ph.D. diss., University of California, Berkeley, 1998.
Rosenberg, David Alan. "Toward Armageddon: The Foundation of United States Nuclear Strategy, 1945-1961." Ph.D. diss., University of Chicago, 1983.
Smith, Martha Jane. "The Nuclear Testing Policies of the Eisenhower Administration, 1953-1960." Ph.D. diss., University of Toronto, 2001.
Taylor, Matthew D. "Toward a Nuclear Strategy: Eisenhower and the Challenge of Soviet Power, 1952-1966." Ph.D. diss., Rice University, 1992.
Wang, Zuoyue. "American Science and the Cold War: The Rise of the United States President's Science Advisory Committee." Ph.D. diss., University of California, Santa Barbara, 1994.

Unpublished Sources

Holl, Jack. "Eisenhower's Nuclear Diplomacy: From Atoms for Peace to the Test Ban Moratorium" [1990]. TMs (photocopy).
________. "Ike and the Bomb: The Foundation of Eisenhower's Nuclear Diplomacy, 1945-1952" [1999]. TMs (photocopy).
________. "Dwight D. Eisenhower: Exegetical President in the Nuclear Age" [2002] (?). TMs (photocopy).

________. "Dwight D. Eisenhower: Civil Religion and the Cold War" [2005]. TMs (photocopy).

Holl, Jack and Roger Anders. "Civil Defense and the Hydrogen Bomb" [1982]. TMs (photocopy).

Holl, Jack and Terrence Fehner. "The Nuclear Diplomacy of Eisenhower and Kennedy" [1984]. TMs (photocopy).

Index

Related titles published by Helion & Company

Learning from Foreign Wars. Russian Military Thinking 1859-73
Helion Studies in Military History No 1
Gudrun Persson
208 pages Paperback
ISBN 978-1-906033-61-3

A Military Government in Exile. The Polish Government-in-Exile 1939-45, a Study of Discontent
Helion Studies in Military History No 2
Evan McGilvray
204 pages Paperback
ISBN 978-1-906033-58-3

Forthcoming titles

Black Tuesday over Namsi. B29s vs MiGs – The Forgotten Air Battle of the Korean War, 23 October 1951
Lt Col USAF (Ret) Earl J McGill ISBN 978-1-907677-21-2

Remembering the Dragon Lady. The U-2 Spy Plane: Memoirs of the Men who made the Legend
Brig Gen (Ret) Gerald E McIlmoyle & Linda Rios Bromley ISBN 978-1-907677-20-5

Cataclysm. The War on the Eastern Front 1941-45
Keith Cumins ISBN 978-1-907677-23-6

War in the East. A Military History of the Russo-Turkish War 1877-78
Quintin Barry ISBN 978-1-907677-11-3

HELION & COMPANY
26 Willow Road, Solihull, West Midlands B91 1UE, England
Telephone 0121 705 3393 Fax 0121 711 4075
Website: http://www.helion.co.uk